D1452163

The Penguin

# HISTORICAL ATLAS of the BIBLE LANDS

Caroline Hull & Andrew Jotischky

**PENGUIN BOOKS**

Published by the Penguin Group
Penguin Books Ltd, 80 Strand, London WC2R 0RL, England
Penguin Group (USA) Inc., 375 Hudson Street, New York, New York 10014, USA
Penguin Group (Canada), 90 Eglinton Avenue East, Suite 700, Toronto, Ontario, Canada M4P 2Y3
  (a division of Pearson Penguin Canada Inc.)
Penguin Ireland, 25 St Stephen's Green, Dublin 2, Ireland
  (a division of Penguin Books Ltd)
Penguin Group (Australia), 250 Camberwell Road, Camberwell, Victoria 3124, Australia
  (a division of Pearson Australia Group Pty Ltd)
Penguin Books India Pvt Ltd, 11 Community Centre, Panchsheel Park, New Delhi – 110 017, India
Penguin Group (NZ), 67 Apollo Drive, Rosedale, North Shore 0632, New Zealand
  (a division of Pearson New Zealand Ltd)
Penguin Books (South Africa) (Pty) Ltd, 24 Sturdee Avenue, Rosebank 2196, South Africa

Penguin Books Ltd, Registered Offices: 80 Strand, London WC2R 0RL, England

www.penguin.com

First published 2009
1

Copyright © Penguin Books, 2009
All rights reserved

Made and printed in Singapore

ISBN-13: 978-0-141-02687-9
ISBN-10: 0-141-02687-1

Produced for Penguin Books by Haywood & Hall

# Preface

Writing an historical atlas is a challenge, at times frustrating, but always in the end rewarding. Viewing history primarily through its impact upon a given geographical area, and treating its topography and demography as major agencies of change, forces us to recognize new patterns, new histories; a once familiar context suddenly can yield unexpected perspectives. An historical atlas about the Bible lands is complicated both by the extraordinary length of time that must be covered to do the job properly, but also by the role of this region in the development of three of the world's most important religions – Judaism, Christianity and Islam. To approach this task in a scholarly manner, avoiding the obvious biases and strong feelings that the history (both ancient and more contemporary) of the Bible lands evokes, is perhaps impossible. At the same time, however, a balanced judgement is called for if a useful, informative introduction to the region is to be achieved. No one – scholar or student, believer or atheist, liberal or conservative – can approach this topic without a raft of inbuilt prejudices, sometimes so subtle and deeply submerged as to be almost indefinable. We would be foolish to claim exclusion from these, although we have aimed at historical impartiality in charting the rise and fall of the world's most important early empires, exploring many of humankind's most critical cultural, intellectual and technological advances and placing into historical context the impact of some of the most influential and charismatic religious leaders that the world has ever known. If biases do appear, they are unintentional.

This atlas will, we hope, present the reader with a brief, accessible overview of the long and complex history of the Bible lands. Confines of space, format and deadlines have meant that a number of topics has been dealt with rather more cursorily than we would have liked, with some touched upon in only the briefest manner, but we have attempted to convey the historical narrative, with its countless twists of plot, in a clear and informative way. Armed with a firm grounding in the complex history of this divided region, the reader will, we hope, go on to learn about particular aspects in greater depth, but still with a good understanding of the broader contexts from which so many of the region's controversies arise. We would very much like to thank Simon Hall and John Haywood for their initial impetus and calm oversight of this project, as well as Fiona Plowman and Darren Bennett for their patience and understanding during a lengthy and complicated editing process.

Caroline Hull and Andrew Jotischky

October 2008

# Contents

# Text and Archaeology

Hand-painted page from the Gutenberg Bible. This was a version of the early 5th-century Latin Vulgate translation of the Bible in Latin. It was printed by Johannes Gutenberg in Mainz, Germany in the 15th century using his moveable type system.

Most of what we know about the history and historical geography of the Bible lands comes from two distinctive sources – the material evidence of archaeology and textual evidence. Both sources, however, present problems for our understanding of the region's history. Archaeology provides answers on a large scale, is not always susceptible to clear deduction and is most reliable when the conclusions drawn from one site can be compared with others. Similarly, textual evidence, whether in the form of coherent written works such as the Bible, or fragments of papyri, or inscriptions on clay tablets, poses problems of interpretation. Fragmentary inscriptions or documentary records obviously lack a complete context in which what is being recorded can be understood. Even complete works, however, are difficult to interpret. Much of the Bible was not written to provide an objective documentary record of historical events, and even the parts we know as historical works were not all written at the time of the events they describe, and therefore represent a later generation's view of what happened and why. Like all historical narratives, they must be subject to interpretation and analysis. Moreover, the material and textual evidence does not always correspond. Which has greater authority? Opinions as to the historical veracity of the Bible are widespread, and authoritative answers about the dating of particular texts are scarce.

## Interest in the Bible Lands

A further problem for understanding the history of the Bible lands is that, unlike the neighbouring great civilizations of Mesopotamia and Egypt, they did not present such obvious targets for enquiry. Or rather, archaeological discoveries were led by particular interests in uncovering the history of the Bible itself. This is not only a problem for the archaeology of the Bible lands. It was natural for historians and archaeologists, particularly those working in periods of great discovery, to be drawn to the 'peaks' of civilization in a given area – hence the careless destruction of later layers of settlements by those early archaeologists in search of, for example, Homer's Troy or Roman towns, or the relative lack of interest in evidence of earlier – or later – settlement on the sites of such ruins. From almost the earliest days of society's scholarly interest in its past, the discovery of archaeological evidence in support of (or disputing) the Bible, and therefore relevant to three of the world's most influential religions, has overshadowed all other areas of historical interest in this region. Much work has been done over the last 100 years or so to rectify this situation, but our general knowledge about the native Levantine cultures in the period from 10,000 BC up to, arguably, the final years of the 2nd millennium BC is still in its infancy.

As most of our knowledge of the earliest periods of settlement in the Fertile Crescent comes from archaeology, it is important to understand how archaeology itself has developed as a practice in relation to the region. Biblical archaeology has its roots in the 19th-century rediscovery of the ruins of Egypt and Mesopotamia. It received a stimulus, however, from the development of critical textual scholarship of the Bible at the same time, and many of the pioneers in biblical archaeology were also scriptural scholars. In retrospect, it is easy to see how this coloured their approach to archaeology. The sites chosen for excavation in Palestine were largely 'biblical' sites, whose importance lay in associations known from the Bible. This meant, inevitably, that archaeologists thought they knew what they would find, or what they hoped to find, before the excavations began. Moreover, Christian churches and other organizations were often targeted for financial support. This contrasts with the approach taken by archaeologists in Mesopotamia, for example, who had no such narrative sources guiding them or ideological framework for their discoveries. The first field surveys of Palestine were undertaken in the mid-19th century by the American Congregationalist minister Edward Robinson, who founded the discipline of biblical geography. The London-based Palestine Exploration Fund, founded in 1865, undertook the Survey of Western Palestine in 1881–4. In 1890 Sir Flinders Petrie conducted the first scientific dig in Palestine, at Tell el-Hesi, establishing the principles of stratigraphic excavation (uncovering layer by layer to reveal consecutive bands of settlement) and ceramic typography. In this way, he proved continuous occupation of the site from c. 1700 to 450 BC.

## The Bible's Influence

Biblical archaeology grew under the British Mandate in the 1920s, largely through US and British efforts. William Albright pioneered a new terminology based on divisions of time into Early (c. 3000–1900 BC), Middle (1900–1540 BC) and Late Bronze Ages (1540–1120 BC), and Iron Age (1120–586 BC). His concern was to cement biblical narratives, which he believed to be historical events, in a physical reality. This approach, followed by his pupil George Wright, made archaeology the servant of biblical history and ultimately (Protestant) theology. Further refinements to Albright's methods, however, were made by Kathleen Kenyon, the director of the British School of Archaeology in Jerusalem (founded 1919), and the excavator of Jericho and Jerusalem. Kenyon devised a new stratigraphic method, giving archaeologists greater control over deducing what might lie within unexcavated material.

From 1948 onwards a new school of Israeli archeology emerged. Not surprisingly, the Israelis saw the discovery of material culture as a means of establishing a new national identity, generally based on social and cultural rather than political principles. Uncovering evidence for Jewish occupation of sites became the imperative driving resources for archaeology. However, the leader of the school, Yigael Yadin, was an intensely political figure who had been Chief of Defence Staff in 1949. When he excavated Hazor in the 1950s he sought to prove the biblical narrative of a complete unified conquest of Canaan by the Israelites in c. 1200 BC. Archaeology in modern Israel continues to be dominated by US and Israeli resources. Since the 1960s prominent sites such as Caesarea, Gezer, Masada, Sepphoris and Ashkelon have been excavated. Trends within the science itself have had a profound effect on the approaches of archaeologists. Specialization in forensic sciences, such as ceramic and bone analysis, have brought about a more anthropological approach to the problems of human habitation, with a focus on cultures rather than histories.

Nevertheless, political, national and cultural biases will always be inseparable from the rediscovery of the past, and because archaeology demands huge resources, the sources of finance, whether private or public, will be in a position to determine the nature – although not the results – of excavations. The problem confronted by those engaged in biblical archaeology is unique. The discoveries made by the excavators of ancient Sumerian, Hittite or Egyptian sites have a largely academic interest for the general public. Discoveries made in Israel or Palestine today, however, can resonate throughout the Western world, to challenge, confirm or comfort millions whose cultural, national or religious identities are still bound up with this small, endlessly fascinating region.

# Timeline 3500 BC–AD 350

| PALESTINE / ISRAEL | MIDDLE EAST AND NORTH AFRICA | RELIGION AND CULTURE |
|---|---|---|
| | *c.* **3500 BC** Origins of the Sumerian civilization in southern Mesopotamia. | *c.* **3500 BC** Development of the earliest pictographic writing system, in Sumeria. |
| | *c.* **3000 BC** First unified Egyptian kingdom founded by King Narmer | |
| *c.* **2600 BC** Egyptians engage in trading activity in the Levant. | *c.* **2550 BC** The Great Pyramid of Giza is built. | *c.* **2350 BC** The earliest known law code is issued, by King Urukagina of Lagash, Sumeria. |
| *c.* **2000–1800 BC** Abraham and his family migrate from Ur into Canaan. | | *c.* **2000 BC** Sumerian Epic of Gilgamesh written. |
| | **1792–1750 BC** Babylon dominates Mesopotamia under its king Hammurabi. | |
| | **1640–1532 BC** Northern Egypt is ruled by the Hyksos, a people of Semitic origin. | |
| *c.* **1500–1300 BC** Egypt rules the Levantine region. | **1532–1070 BC** Egyptian power reaches its zenith during the New Kingdom period. | *c.* **1500 BC** Alphabetic writing systems in use in the Levant. |
| *c.* **1446 BC** Hebrews enter Canaan according to the 'Early Exodus' theory. | | *c.* **1400 BC** Biblical Book of Genesis written. |
| *c.* **1250 BC** Hebrews enter Canaan according to the 'Late Exodus' theory. | | |
| *c.* **1200 BC** The Philistines, one of the Sea Peoples, settle around Gaza. | *c.* **1200 BC** Migratory Sea Peoples raid throughout the eastern Mediterranean. | |
| *c.* **1000 BC** David becomes king of a united Israel. | | *c.* **1050 BC** Biblical Book of Judges is composed. |
| **962 BC** Death of King David; his son Solomon gains the throne. | | **958 BC** Solomon completes the First Temple in Jerusalem. |
| **922 BC** Death of King Solomon; his realm is divided into the kingdoms of Israel and Judah. | **934–627 BC** Assyria is the dominant power of the Middle East. | |
| **721 BC** Israel is conquered by Assyria. | | |
| **587–586 BC** Judah is conquered by Babylon: Jews are deported to Babylonia, beginning the Diaspora. | **605–562 BC** Babylon under Nebuchadnezzar II is the dominant power of the Middle East. | **586 BC** Solomon's Temple is destroyed by the Babylonians. |
| | **538 BC** Cyrus of Persia conquers the Babylonian empire and allows Jews to rerturn home, ending the Babylonian Captivity. | **550 BC** Biblical Book of Joshua, describing the conquest of Canaan by the Hebrews, is written. |
| | | *c.* **450 BC** The Torah (the first five books of the Old Testament) grows in importance as Jewish scripture. |
| **333 BC** Alexander the Great absorbs Palestine into his empire. | **334–326 BC** Alexander the Great conquers the Persian empire. | |
| | **323 BC** Alexander the Great dies in Babylon: his empire is divided between his generals. | |
| | **264–241 BC** Rome becomes a great power after defeating Carthage in the First Punic War. | *c.* **250 BC** The Torah is translated into Greek by 70 scholars (hence the title 'Septuagint'). |
| **168 BC** Judas Maccabeus leads a rebellion against the Greek Seleucid dynasty. | | |
| **142 BC** Israel under Simon Maccabeus becomes independent of the Seleucids. | | |
| **63 BC** Pompey establishes Roman rule over Palestine. | **67–63 BC** Pompey establishes Roman dominance of the eastern Mediterranean. | |
| **37 BC** Herod the Great crowned king of Judea by the Roman Mark Antony. | **30 BC** Egypt becomes part of the Roman empire after the death of Cleopatra VII. | |
| | | **20 BC** Herod rebuilds the Temple in Jerusalem. |
| *c.* **6 BC** Birth of Jesus at Bethlehem. | | |
| *c.* **AD 30** Jesus is crucified in Jerusalem. | | |
| **66–70** The Zealots rebel against Roman rule. | | **AD 66–7** St Paul is beheaded in Rome on the orders of the emperor Nero. |
| | | **70** Destruction of the Second Temple by the Romans. |
| | | *c.* **95** St John's Revelations probably written around this time. |
| **132–5** Simon Bar Kokhba's failed Jewish rebellion: the Romans expel most Jews from Palestine. | | *c.* **210** Codification of Jewish oral law (the Mishnah) under the patronage of the rabbi Judah the Prince. |
| | | **312–13** Roman emperor Constantine legalizes Christian worship. |
| | | **325** Council of Nicea attempts to establish unified doctrine and practice through the Christian communion. |

# AD 351–2008

## PALESTINE / ISRAEL

**638** The Islamic Arabs capture Jerusalem.

**1099** The First Crusade conquers the Holy Land and establishes the Kingdom of Jerusalem.
**1187** Saladin recaptures Jerusalem.

**1291** The Crusaders are expelled from the Holy Land.

**1516** Palestine becomes part of the Ottoman Turkish empire.

**1799** Napoleon briefly occupies Jaffa, Safed and Tiberias.
**1860** Foundation of Mishkenot Sha'ananim marks the beginning of the Jewish resettlement of Palestine.

**1909** Tel Aviv, the first Jewish modern city, is founded.
**1917** The Balfour Declaration proposes the creation of a Jewish homeland in Palestine.
**1917** British general Allenby captures Jerusalem.
**1922** Palestine becomes a League of Nations Mandate territory under British control.

**1946** Irgun bombs the King David Hotel in Jerusalem.
**1948** (14 May) The independent state of Israel is proclaimed.
**1948–9** The First Arab-Israeli War (Israeli War of Independence).
**1964** Palestinian Liberation Organization (PLO) is founded.
**1967** The Six-Day War: Israel occupies the West Bank, Gaza Strip, Sinai, the Golan Heights and East Jerusalem.
**1973** Yom Kippur War.
**1978** Camp David Accords lead to Egyptian-Israeli peace treaty (1979).
**1982–5** Israeli occupation of southern Lebanon.

**1987–93** First Palestinian intifada (uprising) against Israeli occupation.
**1993** The Oslo Accords: Israel recognizes Palestinian right to self government.
**1994** Gaza Strip and Jericho returned to the Palestinians for self government.

**2000–6** Second Palestinian intifada against Israeli occupation.

## MIDDLE EAST AND NORTH AFRICA

**395** Roman empire divided: eastern half ruled from Constantinople, while the western half remains in the control of Rome.

**634–98** Islamic Arabs conquer the Middle East and North Africa.

**763** Baghdad becomes the capital of the Arab Caliphate under the Abbasid dynasty.

**969** Cairo is founded.
**1055** Baghdad captured by the Seljuk Turks.
**1071** Byzantine forces defeated by Seljuk Turks at the battle of Manzikert.
**1171** Saladin (d. 1193) becomes ruler of Egypt.

**1258** Abbasid Caliphate overthrown when Mongols capture Baghdad.

**1453** Sultan Mehmet II takes Constantinople and adds Byzantine territories to the Ottoman empire.
**1516–1918** Most of the Middle East is under Ottoman control.

**1869** Suez Canal is completed.

**1882–1924** British occupation of Egypt.

**1914–18** Ottoman empire fights and is defeated in the First World War as an ally of Germany.
**1916** Sykes-Picot Agreement by the British and the French to divide control of the Middle East.

**1923** Republic of Turkey is established.

**1939–45** Defence of the Suez Canal and Middle Eastern oil fields is a major priority for Britain during the Second World War.

**1956** Suez crisis: failed Anglo-French invasion of Egypt.

**1979** Islamic Revolution in Iran brings fundamentalist Shiite cleric Ayatollah Khomeini to power.

**1990** Iraq occupies oil-rich Kuwait.
**1991** First Persian Gulf War. US-led alliance liberates Kuwait.

**2003** Second Persian Gulf War. US-led coalition topples Saddam Hussein and occupies Iraq.

## RELIGION AND CULTURE

**380** Christianity becomes the official religion of the Roman empire.
**382–407** St Jerome translates the Bible into Latin (the Vulgate Bible).
**400** The Jerusalem Talmud is first written down around this time.

**622** The Hijra, Muhammad's migration from Mecca to Medina, marks the beginning of the Muslim calendar.
**c. 650** The Quran, the sacred text of Islam, is written down for the first time.
**691** Dome of the Rock built on the site of the First and Second Temples in Jerusalem.

**1054** Schisms between the Roman and Orthodox churches.

**1564** Jewish law code (Shulhan Arukh) is published.

**1863** Frenchman Louis de Saulcy digs at Jerusalem; this is the earliest archaeological expedition in the Holy Land.
**1881–4** Thousands of Jews are killed in Russian pogroms.
**1897** First Zionist Conference held in Basle, Switzerland.
**1898** World Zionist Council is founded.

**1933** Persecution of German Jews begun by Adolf Hitler's Nazi government.
**1939–45** The Holocaust: six million Jews are murdered by the Nazis during the Second World War.
**1947** The first of the Dead Sea Scrolls is found in a cave near the Dead Sea.

**1952–58** Kathleen Kenyon excavates at Jericho.

**2000** During a visit to Israel, Pope John Paul II apologizes to the Jewish people for past anti-Semitic actions by Christians.

# Part I: Early History
## The Bible Lands Before the Bible

The Jordan River runs from the Syrian-Lebanese border through northern Israel into the Sea of Galilee and then southwards into the Dead Sea. It provides vital water supplies to the surrounding arid lands. Mentioned frequently in the Bible, it is the scene of several miracles, as well as the baptism of Jesus by John the Baptist.

*Our understanding of the early history of the Bible lands can never be complete. For the towering ancient cultures bordering on this region, however, we have more or less continuous cultural timelines stretching from the first settlements through Sumerian, Babylonian and Assyrian dominance in Mesopotamia and through the Early Dynastic Period into the Old, Middle and New Kingdoms in Egypt.*

That the area comprising all of modern Israel, Lebanon and the Palestinian territories, as well as parts of Egypt, Syria and Jordan, is often referred to as the 'Bible lands' is testimony to the fact that our familiarity with the earliest history of this region begins only with the age of the prophet Abraham, despite recent archaeological finds predating the early 2nd millennium BC. Given the importance of Mesopotamia and Egypt for many of the first developments in human society, it is not surprising that the fertile corridor stretching along the eastern shore of the Mediterranean Sea should have been home to pioneering settlements similar to those found across Mesopotamia and the Nile valley.

The environment of the region has altered greatly since the earliest settlements. The combination of a dry climate, reliable fresh water supplies and alluvial soil attracted peoples from surrounding areas to the Jordan River valley, which, reaching a low point at 198 metres (650 ft) below sea level, thickened with silt as it wound north. Even as late as the 12th century AD, monasteries in the Jordan valley cultivated gardens with a variety of crops; latterly the region has been celebrated for its orange groves. Westwards from the rift of the Jordan valley, the land was heavily forested. Over centuries, erosion and over-grazing has turned the forest, of which only a few patches remain, into herby scrubland, unsuitable for large-scale cultivation. In the biblical period, the coastline from north Lebanon almost as far south as Jaffa had a parallel belt of forest running just a few miles inland, with alluvial soils washed down from the highlands. Ancient sources attest to the fertility of the Syro-Palestinian shoreline, which was capable of sustaining varied crops – barley, wheat, fruit trees, olives, vineyards – as well as herds of cattle and goats. Of these, olives, which survived the erosion of the soil best, ensured long-term prosperity because of their versatility, providing fuel as well as fat from their oil, without the need for fertile soil.

## The Topography of the Bible Lands

While the fertility of the land made it attractive for agricultural settlement, the topography of the region made it prone to political upheaval. There is no clear separation of boundaries in Syria and the Bible lands. Instead, cultivation and settlement take place within a series of funnelled lowlands between two major limestone ridges running parallel to the coast; one from Mount Amanus in the north to the plateau of Judea, and continuing into the Sinai; the other to the east, from the Anti-Lebanon range to the highlands of the Transjordan. These ridges are also cut with passes, making the lowlands easily accessible to traders, pastoral nomads – and invaders. The topography thus allows for small semi-independent units of settlement rather than for a unified nation or culture such as that developed to the east in Mesopotamia or to the southwest in Egypt.

If this feature of the topography made it inevitable that the region would form a crossroads between greater powers and civilizations, the presence of the Mediterranean to the west cemented it as a link in trading networks. It has been said that the Mediterranean acted as the nursery for human navigation of the seas. Although there are dangers close to the shores – from sandbanks and strong currents – the Mediterranean is tideless and largely free of shoals. More importantly, there are plenty of landmarks for sailors in the eastern Mediterranean. From Cyprus, for example, one can see the Cilician coast of Asia Minor and Syria – and the visibility is generally good. The currents flow from south to north along the eastern shore, making it possible for a small sailing ship to reach the port of Byblos from Egypt in four days. This not only facilitated coastal trade but encouraged sailors to become more daring in exploring coastlines to the west, thus bringing the more distant islands of Crete and the Aegean, and the Greek peninsula, into the economic orbit of the Syro-Palestinian region.

## Evidence of First Humans

Datable fossils prove the presence in the Levant of anatomically modern humans by around 90,000 BC. Skeletal remains from Qafzeh (in modern Israel) are in fact the earliest examples of 'modern' human remains to be found outside of sub-Saharan Africa, now generally recognized as the cradle of human evolution. In a migration lasting many generations, bands of hunters and gatherers from sub-Saharan Africa followed the Nile valley north to Egypt and crossed the Suez isthmus into the Levant, which was already populated by Neanderthals. The two human species co-existed in the region for many thousands of years before the Neanderthals became extinct. According to this 'Out of Africa' model, these early human inhabitants of the Levant continued to spread further inland and in time spread throughout Asia and into Europe, reaching the furthest parts of these continents by just after 15,000 BC.

By 9000 BC the transition from a nomadic way of life based on hunting, fishing and gathering wild foods to a settled farming way of life was under way in the 'Fertile Crescent'. The Fertile Crescent stretches in an arc from Israel north along the Mediterranean coast, then swings east through the foothills of the Taurus and Zagros Mountains to the Mesopotamian plain in Iraq. The area had light but reliable rainfall, good soils and was unusually rich in plants and animals suitable for domestication, such as sheep, goats, cattle and pigs, cereals such as wheat and barley, and peas and other vegetables. These wild resources were so abundant that some hunter-gatherers in the region, such as the Natufian people of Israel and Lebanon, were able to settle permanently in small villages. It was probably an increasing population that forced hunter-gatherers, like the Natufians, to begin experimenting with the cultivation of cereals and the penning of livestock as a way of increasing their food supply.

The transition from 'proto-farming' to complete dependence on farming took place gradually over thousands of years. By 8000 BC selective breeding of wild wheat and barley had produced fully domesticated strains that had larger grains and were easier to harvest than their wild precursors. A similar process produced domesticated breeds of goats (*c.* 7000 BC), sheep (*c.* 6700 BC), pigs (*c.* 6500 BC) and cattle (*c.* 6000 BC) that were easier to manage than wild breeds. Once agriculture was adopted, rising populations made intensification of farming inevitable in order to sustain more people. Crucial to this was the development of basic irrigation in northern Mesopotamia around 5500 BC. Simple canals allowed rain and floodwater from the Tigris and the Euphrates to be channelled to those areas with poor natural water supplies. This ultimately ensured the viability of sedentary agricultural settlements in southern Mesopotamia (by *c.* 5500 BC), which had fertile alluvial soils but little rainfall.

Terracotta plaque of a Canaanite fertility goddess, possibly Astarte. She is holding lotus blossoms in her hands. As farming communities became established and crop yields became more important so did the need for deities relating to the natural world.

## Effects of Farming

The adoption of farming had important social consequences. Farming can support much denser populations than hunting and gathering, so people were able to live in larger communities, first villages and, later, towns and cities. Farming created harder conditions of work (hunter-gatherers generally spent only a few hours a day acquiring food), so reducing the chances for leisure and mobility. Farming also stimulated the growth of new technology, such as ploughs, wheeled vehicles and pottery.

It also, crucially, provided opportunities for mechanisms of control and thus for social stratification. Farming – making food grow rather than collecting it – creates power over the environment. It also fosters the development of cultic power, creating new conditions for articulating the relationship between humans and nature. Furthermore, the harvesting of farmed food also provides opportunities for social cohesion through ceremony and feasting. Early farmers were often able to produce more food than they actually needed to feed themselves and their families. These surpluses were stored and became the earliest form of wealth, which could be traded for other goods or used to acquire power and influence over other people. From this developed social hierarchy and culture within the community.

Despite the abundant fertility of the Nile River valley, permanent agricultural settlement in Egypt lagged behind that in the Fertile Crescent, perhaps by as much as a millennium. Once farming took hold, in the years following 6000 BC, the relatively dependable and largely effortless yields quickly assured Egypt a reputation as a land of agricultural plenty. The cyclic flooding of the Nile each summer and the mild winters meant that crops planted in the autumn could be harvested in the spring, thus avoiding the flooding while at the same time allowing rising levels of water and subsequent silt deposits to replenish the soil. The borders of any settlement in the region were further determined by the vast expanses of desert to either side of the narrow verdant strip nourished by the

The Standard of Ur, dating from the 3rd century BC, was excavated from the Royal Cemetery at the ancient Sumerian city of Ur (modern Iraq). This panel, known as 'peace', shows a banquet scene where animals, fish and other goods (possibly the spoils of war) are paraded before seated figures. The Sumerians established the first known civilization in the world in southern Mesopotamia.

Nile, and it is no surprise that the unification of Egyptian settlement in the years around 3000 BC followed the contours of this mighty river.

The establishment of the necessary tools for successful continuous communal living was quickly followed by a succession of identifiable cultures in both Mesopotamia and Egypt. Each of these cultures can be distinguished by the appearance of settlements within a given geographical region, as well as through similar levels of technological advances, belief and ritual patterns and pottery fragments. Mesopotamian proto-history has been divided by archaeologists into six periods, from *c.* 5800 to *c.* 3000 BC. This early Mesopotamian civilization is generally known as Sumerian, although this term applies to the culture rather than to an ethnic or racial grouping. The Ubaid period, from the mid-5th to mid-4th millennium, was characterized by small village settlements spread across the fertile water meadows between the Euphrates and Tigris. From about 3500 BC, in the Uruk period, however, climatic changes meant that the Euphrates carried less water and was therefore less able to irrigate the land.

As the whole region was more fertile than it later became, the pattern of scattered small settlements gave way to urbanism and the concentration of power by elites. The surviving material culture is prominent in temple architecture, pottery and distinctive decorative cylinder seals. It is also at this time that writing, in the form of pictograms, began to evolve. Both Sumer and Akkad, further to the north, were divided into city-states, each comprising a chief centre that dominated surrounding settlements and farms. The largest of those so far excavated, Lagash, spread over 1800 square metres (19,375 sq ft) and may have housed 30–35,000 people. At least fourteen such sites are known from the Early Dynastic Period. The Early Dynastic Period ended in *c.* 2316 BC with the conquest of Sumer by the Akkadians from north Mesopotamia. From this period, the two regions of Mesopotamia were united in the Akkadian empire, first ruled by Sargon I. Civil war and political anarchy followed the end of his dynasty, however, culminating in revolt against Akkadian domination by Uruk and other Sumerian cities. This brought about the brief but culturally impressive Neo-Sumerian revival at the end of the 3rd millennium BC. It is from this period that much of the surviving material culture and architecture, notably the ziggurats, derive. The collapse of Sumeria marked the end of the Sumerians as a politically dominant people and the region once again became a mosaic of smaller units. The most prominent of the successor states to Sumeria was Babylon, under its king, the law-giver Hammurabi, in the first half of the 18th century BC.

## Egypt and its Kingdoms

The situation in Egypt was similar, although perhaps less disjointed than that within the Mesopotamian plains in that there appears to have been more of a sense of continuity between one 'era' and the next. Narmer, king of Upper (southern) Egypt, was the first to rule over both Upper and Lower (northern) Egypt, and his reign (r. c. 3000 BC) marks the beginning of the consolidation of ancient Egyptian culture as we know it. During the Early Dynastic Period, which lasted until the middle of the 3rd millenium BC, hieroglyphic script developed, effective centralized administration was established and the cult of divine kingship became the norm. The first literature appeared, probably in the form of poems to or concerning the gods. Medical remedies were also recorded, and the earliest investigations into mathematical science date from around 2000 BC. The artistic conventions that make Egyptian art immediately recognizable were codified, and Egyptian artists began to work frequently in stone and on a more monumental scale.

Early royal tomb structures, or 'step' pyramids, also appear towards the close of this period. Urbanism, always a major feature of Egyptian culture, became widespread in Egypt during this time; the city of Memphis functioned as a power base both for the Early Dynastic rulers and their followers from the era known as the Old Kingdom. The Old Kingdom (2575–2134 BC) was the age of the Great Pyramids, and the first century or so of this period saw a booming economy, increasing military might and strong, centralized government. Division of power and a period of famine subsequently brought an end to the Old Kingdom and left Egypt once again divided into Upper and Lower Kingdoms.

A terracotta female figurine from Ma'mariya dating from the predynastic period. During this period Egypt developed from a collection of farming communities to one of the earliest urban civilizations.

Both Mesopotamian and Egyptian cultures were organized around public religious worship in purpose-built temples. Both were polytheistic, associating divinities with aspects of the natural world. Complex hierarchies and relationships between them evolved, and a body of myths emerged to explain how the intervention of gods in the natural world had brought about the patterns of human history. Because they evolved in response to the needs of basically conservative agricultural societies, these religious systems outlived changes in dynasty.

## The Flood Myth

The earliest religious myth known to us from the Near East is the Sumerian Epic of Gilgamesh, which seeks to establish a link between gods and humans through the character of the semi-divine king Gilgamesh. Like many creation myths deriving from it, such as that known to us from the Old Testament, the Epic of Gilgamesh posits the idea of a flood covering the whole world, as a way of separating the age of gods from that of human society. When the myth was first discovered on a series of tablets in cuneiform script in the 1870s, the initial assumption was that the similarities between this and the biblical epic of Noah lent historical validity to the Old Testament narrative. Since then, many other written versions have been discovered, dating from at least 1700 BC. The archaeological evidence for a flood is at best uncertain. Although Leonard Woolley, the excavator of Ur in the 1920s, believed that he had found evidence for a flood of 7.6 metres (25 ft) in depth from stratigraphic layers of water-laid silt, other cities in Sumer have not offered similar evidence. The flood may serve, therefore, as a literary device designed to create a clear break between a putative 'age of creation' and subsequent human history. Some scholars have suggested that the flood was in fact a series of torrential rains at some time in the prehistoric past, the memory of which was passed down across the generations in oral tradition and eventually represented in writing.

## Canaan

Like a hinge between the sophisticated cultures of Mesopotamia and Egypt in the period up to the start of the 2nd millennium was Canaan. Its importance lay in its coastline and in the potential for mediation of goods offered by ports such as Byblos. That the Egyptians used Byblos to import timber from Lebanon as early as 2700 BC is confirmed by surviving inscriptions. Other goods, such as silver from the Taurus mountains, gold from Nubia, copper from Cyprus, pottery from Crete and dye from the Syrian coast also flowed through Byblos. During the 25th century BC, at the end of the 5th dynasty, the Egyptian pharaohs sought to control ports in order to protect trade, and there is evidence of Egyptian military and commercial influence in Byblos and other maritime centres. Details of one military campaign, including the slaves brought back to Egypt, survive in the report of the Egyptian commander to the pharoah.

By the early 2nd millennium, this seems to have become a periodic occurrence, and from 1971 to 1928 BC we have a detailed account of the Egyptian presence in Canaan in the memoir of Sinuhe, who fled there from the court of Pharaoh Sesostris I. He went to Byblos and then to southern Syria, where he was favourably treated by the local Amorite ruler. The account of Sinuhe's eventual return from exile to Egypt exposes the cultural gap between Syro-Palestine and Egypt at the turn of the millennium: from a pastoral tent-bound life as a nomadic chief, he returned to palaces and temples, clothes of linen and a leisurely court life. The description of Sinuhe's career in Syria, as a patriarchal leader whose wealth was counted in herds and flocks, corresponds closely to the impression given in the Book of Genesis of Abraham. Suddenly, we are in the world of the Old Testament.

The flood tablet recounts part of the Epic of Gilgamesh. Like Noah in the Bible, the legendary Uruk leader Gilgamesh had been forewarned of a great flood sent by the gods to destroy civilization. Flood myths exist in various cultures – this one is believed to have been copied from the Akkadian Atrahasis Epic.

# From Hunter-Gatherers to Farmers

*About 100,000 years ago* homo sapiens *arrived in western Asia from Africa. There is evidence of a continuing Neanderthal presence, but by 40,000 BC the more advanced newcomers occupied the Middle East and southern Anatolia. Slowly they adapted to their new habitat, with its mild climate, fertile river valleys and abundant wildlife.*

*"Hunter-gatherers live at the margins of the farmer's world; farmers live at the margins of the hunter-gatherer's world. Each way of life is the centre of its own universe. "*

Hugh Brody,
*The Other Side of Eden* (2001)

Several early hunter-gather cultures existed in the Levant, but by 10,000 BC there were a number of semi-permanent settlements. The earliest of these were probably created by the Natufian peoples, who lived along the Mediterranean coast. The Natufians may have formed active communities prior to experimenting with sedentary agriculture and attempting to domesticate animals. The domestication of farm animals and more advanced agricultural techniques were firmly established throughout the Middle East and Anatolia by c. 8500 BC, earlier than similar developments elsewhere. However, the precise order of these developments is still being debated.

The earliest, most basic methods of irrigation, crucial for successful cultivation both in the desert hinterlands and in the frequently flooded river valleys, were in place by the beginning of the 6th millennium BC, as were the use of kilns for firing clay pottery and metallurgical techniques such as smelting and casting.

## Between the Tigris and the Euphrates

By 6000 BC Mesopotamia (literally meaning 'the land between the rivers', in this case the Tigris and Euphrates) and the Levant – the narrow fertile strip between the Mediterranean coast and the unyielding western boundary of the Arabian Desert – were home to a growing number of distinct cultures. Chief among these were the Hassunian/Halafian culture in northern Mesopotamia and the Samarrans to the south. By 5000 BC the Ubaidian culture, with its proto-urban settlements, was dominant in the region, although the precise relationship between this and the earlier Mesopotamian cultures remains unclear. The Uruk civilization developed from these earlier cultures; it flourished throughout the 4th millennium BC and produced what were probably the world's first cities.

Jericho, founded over 11,000 years ago, is perhaps the best known settlement of the pre-pottery Neolithic era. Like so many of the earliest settlements in this region, it is located in a fertile river valley, in this instance that of the River Jordan. This makes it impossible for us to verify the precise role that agriculture and animal domestication may

Excavations of caves at Mount Carmel in northern Israel uncovered early human remains, including the skeleton of a Neanderthal woman at el-Tabun. The tools, bones and human burials found there in the 1930s have unlocked an important part of the story of human evolution – the transition from hunter-gatherers to sedentary agricultural societies.
The area also has religious significance as the prophet Elijah is believed to have lived there.

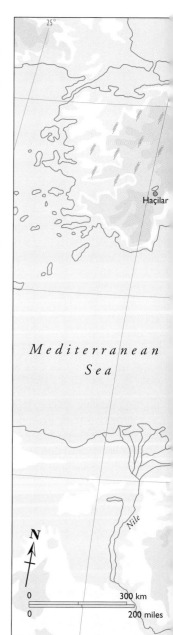

have played in Jericho's origin. The period of Ubaid dominance saw the foundation of numerous settlements that have yielded evidence of agrarian activities, as well as advanced technological craftwork – and even of established trading networks.

Perhaps the earliest true city was Uruk, which was founded around 3500 BC. Uruk and neighbouring settlements such as Eridu and Ur quickly developed into the autonomous, but loosely affiliated city-states known collectively as ancient Sumer. It is in this region, with the emergence of larger settlements exerting influence throughout the surrounding region, that we begin to witness the first codification of organized religious beliefs, government, legal systems and the beginnings of written communication.

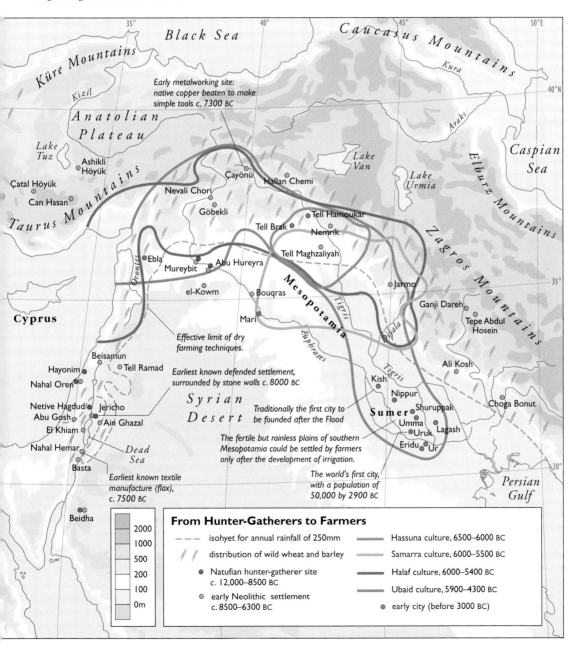

Early metalworking site: native copper beaten to make simple tools c. 7300 BC

Effective limit of dry farming techniques.

Earliest known defended settlement, surrounded by stone walls c. 8000 BC

Traditionally the first city to be founded after the Flood

The fertile but rainless plains of southern Mesopotamia could be settled by farmers only after the development of irrigation.

Earliest known textile manufacture (flax), c. 7500 BC

The world's first city, with a population of 50,000 by 2900 BC

**From Hunter-Gatherers to Farmers**

- - - -   isohyet for annual rainfall of 250mm

    distribution of wild wheat and barley

● Natufian hunter-gatherer site c. 12,000–8500 BC

● early Neolithic settlement c. 8500–6300 BC

▬▬▬ Hassuna culture, 6500–6000 BC

▬▬▬ Samarra culture, 6000–5500 BC

▬▬▬ Halaf culture, 6000–5400 BC

▬▬▬ Ubaid culture, 5900–4300 BC

● early city (before 3000 BC)

Elevation scale: 2000 / 1000 / 500 / 200 / 100 / 0m

# The First Empires of the Middle East

> *"If any one open his ditches to water his crop, but is careless, and the water flood the field of his neighbour, he shall pay his neighbour corn for his loss. "*
>
> Law Code of Hammurabi (r. 1792–1750 BC)

**The various cultures based in Mesopotamia, the Sumerians foremost among them, developed rapidly in the millennium following the founding of the earliest cities around 3500 BC. Urban settlements, often with up to 10,000 inhabitants, sprang up throughout the region, each centred on a temple site and possessing its own cultic practices, social hierarchies and trading networks.**

Advances in cultivation and animal husbandry techniques enabled cities to cope with greater populations, which in turn led to diversification of crafts and other goods. This growth in trade and commerce brought about an increasing need for written records and it is within this period that the earliest Mesopotamian scripts appear.

In such a rapidly expanding and complex environment it is no surprise that regional affiliations formed. The Sumerian city-states quickly established their dominance over southeast Mesopotamia, with looser groupings such as the Elam culture based in the city of Susa and the Ninevites controlling the north. External pressure from the Elamites, among others, led to the formation of a military alliance between the Sumerian city-states, eventually resulting in a

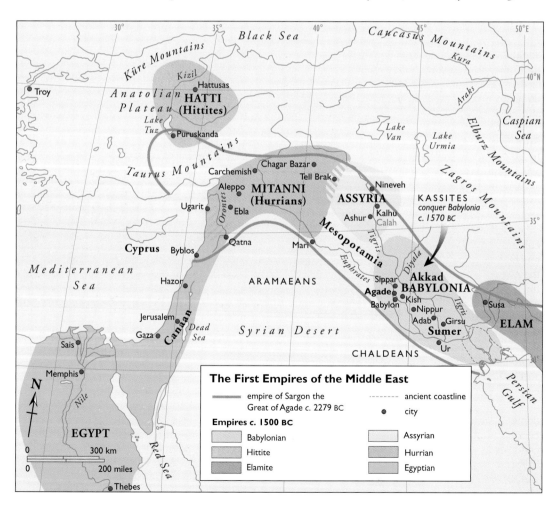

**The First Empires of the Middle East**

— empire of Sargon the Great of Agade *c.* 2279 BC

- - - - - ancient coastline

• city

**Empires *c.* 1500 BC**

Babylonian

Hittite

Elamite

Assyrian

Hurrian

Egyptian

Assyrian alabaster relief from the Khorsabad palace of king Sargon II shows timber being transported by boat. Egypt and Mesopotamia imported cedar wood from Lebanon for use in construction and furniture. Cedar wood was prized for its beauty and fragrance.

'kingdom,' with complete dynastic inheritance and early legal codes. Known as the Early Dynastic Period, this arrangement was precarious at best, characterized by increasing infighting as the rival Sumerian cities sought to attain dominance. The cities of Uruk, Ur and Kish emerged as the main rivals, although by 2400 BC the city of Lagash had assumed control.

## Sumeria the Dominant Culture

In 2350 BC Sumeria was united with neighbouring Akkad under King Lugalzagezi. His brief rule, lasting only sixteen years, set the scene for the amalgamation of much of the Middle East region into a union of kingdoms overseen by a single ruler. In fact, the Akkadian Sargon (r. 2334-2279 BC) is remembered as the founder of the world's first empire.

Sargon's lengthy and centralized rule assured the dominance of Sumerian culture, and the various empires that emerged in the following centuries owe much to the pioneering advances of the Sumerian city-states. The collapse of the Akkadian empire just after 2200 BC caused a power vacuum during which the city-state once again emerged as the norm throughout the region. In 2111 BC Ur-Nammu, ruler of the Sumerian city of Ur, founded the Third Dynasty of Ur and by his death in 2095 BC had built an empire stretching from the eastern shores of the Persian Gulf north to include the kingdom of Assyria in modern Iraq. Pressure on the Sumerian heartland from surrounding peoples brought Sumerian domination to an end with the sacking of Ur in 2004 BC.

Sculpted bronze head of an Akkadian king, possibly Sargon I, who conquered Mesopotamia from the Persian Gulf to the Levantine coastal region.

The Assyrian and Babylonian empires emerged in the 19th century BC. Both empires were founded by the Amorites from southern Mesopotamia. Amorite domination began with the taking of Assyria by Shamshi-Adad in 1813 BC. His dominance was quickly overtaken by the Amorite Hammurabi whose empire centred at Babylon eventually controlled most of Mesopotamia and whose law code is still studied today. Threatened at times by, among others, the Hittites in Anatolia and the Hurrian kingdom of Mitanni, these two great empires, in various incarnations, vied for regional domination for the next 1200 years.

# The Canaanites

*We know relatively little about the Canaanite people or the precise location of their territory; archaeologists specializing in the Levant prior to the arrival of the Hebrews (c. 1250 BC) are just beginning to disentangle the complicated cultural overlap of the area.*

The term 'Canaan' has been used at various times to designate simply the narrow strip of the Mediterranean coast now found in Lebanon, Syria and Turkey; the area traditionally known as Palestine; and, at its greatest extent, an area that includes Israel/Palestine, Lebanon, Jordan and western Syria. Any true understanding of Canaanite culture is further hampered by our limited understanding of exactly how the Canaanites themselves referred to their region: was 'Canaan' a distinct kingdom, or a loose grouping of interrelated peoples over which the Canaanites exerted some sort of dominant cultural influence? The name 'Canaan', itself equally obscure, may derive from the word for a special red dye similar to that for which the later Phoenicians (inhabitants of the same area) were well known. What can be said is that the lands bordering the westernmost coast of the Mediterranean Sea played host to some of the earliest settlements in western Asia, and that already by the formulation of the Book of Genesis (probably before 1400 BC), 'Canaan' was identified with the 'Promised Land' by adherents of the Jewish faith.

Tell Beth-She'an (background) with ruins of Hellenistic/Roman Scythopolis in the foreground. Tells – artificial hills – are created by the build-up of debris from mud-brick buildings being knocked down and repeatedly rebuilt over the centuries. Tell Beth-She'an consists of the remains of a Canaanite city.

Although earlier semi-permanent settlements have been discovered in the region, Jericho, founded *c.* 9000 BC, is among the earliest Middle Eastern settlements to exhibit an advanced communal culture complete with defensive walls. Over the next 5000 years, villages with increasingly complex layouts appeared regularly on the landscape; they evolved similarly to the settlements in Mesopotamia, though here there appears to be little sense of a unifying culture at this early period. Indeed, much of Canaan's early history indicates that this fertile corridor was so often a subject of contention between much stronger powers that it would hardly have had time to develop its own distinct culture. From the early 4th millennium BC, Canaan was repeatedly subjected to different overlords, all of whose cultures influenced local societies to varying degrees.

### The Emergence of the Israelites

Various Semitic tribes, including the Amorites, were among the first to arrive. From their heartland in the southern extremity of Mesopotamia, the Amorites infiltrated the rest of Mesopotamia around 2000 BC, and before long had supplied dynastic rulers to both the Assyrian and the Babylonian empires, as well as having extended their culture over the Canaanites. Over the following centuries, the area suffered invasions from the Hittites, Hyksos and Hurrians from the north and the Egyptians from the south. From around 1250 BC, a new culture dominated: that of the Hebrews, or Israelites.

*"Canaan is thy land and its kings are thy servants."*

El-Amarna letter 8.25

The primacy of biblical archaeology in the land of Canaan has inevitably meant that we know less about pre-Israelite remains in the region. Major Canaanite settlements included Jerusalem, Gezer, Megiddo and Lachish. Over the last century, however, archaeologists have begun to relate physical remains to information about the Canaanites in ancient texts; the history of this, the formative culture of the Levant, is slowly emerging.

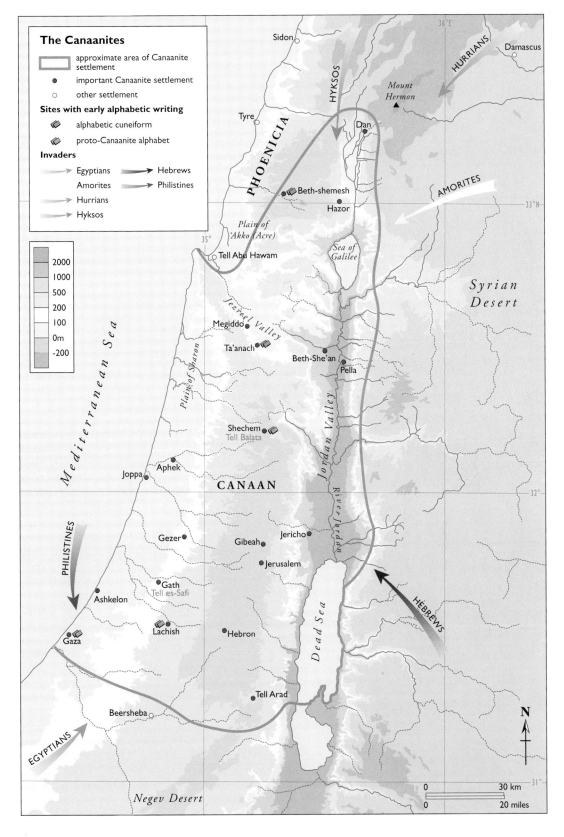

**The Canaanites**

- ▭ approximate area of Canaanite settlement
- ● important Canaanite settlement
- ○ other settlement

**Sites with early alphabetic writing**
- alphabetic cuneiform
- proto-Canaanite alphabet

**Invaders**
- → Egyptians
- → Amorites
- → Hurrians
- → Hyksos
- → Hebrews
- → Philistines

2000
1000
500
200
100
0m
-200

Sidon

Damascus

HYKSOS

HURRIANS

Mount Hermon

Tyre

PHOENICIA

Dan

AMORITES

Beth-shemesh

Hazor

Plain of 'Akko (Acre)

33°N

36°E

Syrian Desert

Tell Abu Hawam

Sea of Galilee

Mediterranean Sea

35°

Jezreel Valley

Megiddo

Ta'anach

Beth-She'an

Pella

Plain of Sharon

Shechem
Tell Balata

Jordan Valley

Joppa

Aphek

CANAAN

32°

Gezer

Gibeah

Jericho

Jerusalem

River Jordan

PHILISTINES

Gath
Tell es-Safi

Ashkelon

Lachish

Hebron

Gaza

Dead Sea

HEBREWS

Tell Arad

Beersheba

EGYPTIANS

N

31°

Negev Desert

0          30 km
0          20 miles

# The Alphabet

*"Because the messenger, whose mouth was tired, was not able to repeat it, the lord of Kulaba patted some clay and wrote the message as if on a tablet."*

1.8.2.3 in The Electronic Text Corpus of Sumerian Literature (ETCSL)

Bust of the Egyptian pharaoh Osorkon I found at Byblos. It is inscribed in Phoenician. Many other scripts including Arabic, Hebrew and Greek are descended from Phoenician.

***Early forms of writing were in use in southern Mesopotamia by 3000 BC, just as the first Sumerian cities were appearing. However, it was not until the middle of the 2nd millennium BC that scripts based on true alphabetic systems began to be developed.***

Although their precise origins remain obscure, the first alphabets – writing systems based on a set of identifiable signs representing specific sounds – are intimately associated with the Levantine region of western Asia. Until recently, the earliest known alphabet was the Proto-Sinaitic alphabet, examples of which have been found at Canaanite sites and on the Sinai Peninsula. This alphabet appears to have evolved from Egyptian hieratic script, a highly simplified version of the hieroglyphic system, and probably dates from around 1500 BC.

Many scholars have credited the Semites with developing the theory behind the use of an alphabet, despite the reliance of this very early example on an earlier Egyptian script. Recently, however, this theory has been called into question by the discovery of inscriptions in an earlier apparently alphabetic writing system (in use by 1800 BC) at Wadi el-Hol, an Egyptian settlement on the banks of the Nile. The influence on the earliest alphabets of cuneiform, developed by the Sumerians late in the 4th millennium BC, has also been argued, but its precise impact remains unclear.

## North Semitic Prototype

Regardless of the role played by the Egyptians and the Sumerians in the development of the earliest alphabets, it must be recognized that the Semitic settlers of the Levant were primarily responsible for the widespread promulgation of alphabetic systems of writing. The North Semitic alphabet – the first fully developed alphabetic system – was a consonantal alphabet of more than twenty distinct sounds and symbols, and has been found in inscriptions from Syria written just after 1100 BC. The North Semitic alphabet is the prototype of many of the various alphabets in use today; from it derive the Aramaic and Phoenician alphabets from which the Hebrew, Arabic, Greek, Latin, Indian, and even the Thai alphabets descend. Inscriptions from the Phoenician city of Byblos (modern Jubayl) are among the earliest to display a systematic and highly advanced use of a true alphabetic writing system.

Alongside, and perhaps influenced by, the North Semitic alphabet, the South Semitic or Sabean (as in the biblical 'Sheba') alphabet was developed within the relatively isolated cultures of the Arabian Peninsula. The South Semitic alphabet provides the prototypes for modern Ethiopic alphabets.

A third alphabetic system - named after a collection of inscriptions found in the ancient city of Ugarit (in modern Syria) - is based on cuneiform systems and appears to have developed largely without the influence of the dominant North Semitic alphabet. The Ugaritic alphabet was in use throughout the third quarter of the 2nd millennium BC. Inscriptions using this alphabet have been discovered elsewhere in the Levant region, suggesting the possibility that this system possessed a considerably broad sphere of influence at one time.

With a single exception, all of the alphabets mentioned so far are consonantal alphabets or 'abjads'. The Ugaritic alphabet, however,

Phoenician inscription from the sarcophagus of Eshmunazar, king of Sidon, dating to the 5th century BC. Modern study of the history and archaeology of the Phoenician city-states began with the discovery of the sarcophagus in 1855.

differs in that it possessed three proto-vowel symbols. It is the Greeks who are credited with the addition of the fully independent vowel symbol. This important development occurred around the middle of the 8th century BC, and has been adopted by all later related alphabets.

The development of the alphabetic system of writing. The North Semitic alphabet, which evolved in the late 2nd millennium BC, was the ultimate source for later writing systems used from South Asia to Western Europe.

| 1500 BC | 1000 BC | 500 BC | AD 1 | AD 500 | AD 1000 |
|---|---|---|---|---|---|
| | | | | South East Asian Scripts | |
| | | | | Tibetan | |
| | | Brahmi | | Modern Indian Scripts | |
| | Aramaic | | | Syriac | |
| Ugaritic | | | Nabatean | Kufic (Arabic) | |
| | | | Sabean | | |
| | | | | Ethiopic | |
| | | Hebrew | | | |
| Proto-Sinaitic | North Semitic | Phoenician | | | |
| | | Greek | | | |
| | | | | | Cyrillic |
| | Etruscan | | | | |
| | | | Runic | | |
| | | Latin (Roman) | | | |

# Egypt and the Middle East

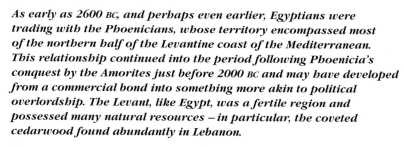

**As early as 2600 BC, and perhaps even earlier, Egyptians were trading with the Phoenicians, whose territory encompassed most of the northern half of the Levantine coast of the Mediterranean. This relationship continued into the period following Phoenicia's conquest by the Amorites just before 2000 BC and may have developed from a commercial bond into something more akin to political overlordship. The Levant, like Egypt, was a fertile region and possessed many natural resources – in particular, the coveted cedarwood found abundantly in Lebanon.**

By 2040 BC Egypt was emerging from a period of political division and turmoil. With the Upper and Lower Kingdoms reunified and a new capital city based at Thebes, Egypt was now ready to strengthen its position as a dominant regional power. It was during the Middle and New Kingdoms (2040–1070 BC) that Egypt developed its strongest links with the Levant. By 1800 BC the Egyptians had conquered Lower Nubia to the south and essentially annexed much of the Levant, forcing local overlords to pledge allegiance to Egyptian officials.

### The Hyksos

This situation was overturned around 1640 BC, when the Hyksos, a Semitic people, seized control of Lower Egypt, which they ruled from their capital at Avaris (modern Tell al-Dab'a). The precise origins of the Hyksos are difficult to determine, though both literary and archaeological sources attest to their strong connections with the Levantine cultures of Western Asia. Their power base appears to have stretched across Lower Egypt to the area around Memphis, and no doubt their control of the Nile Delta served further to threaten the much weakened kingdom of Upper Egypt. The reign of the Hyksos saw some military and technological advances, but little change in the dominant Egyptian culture. Hyksos domination was finally brought to an end by the Pharaoh Ahmose in 1532 BC. Ahmose's victory marks the beginning of the New Kingdom and his reunification of Egypt would last for over four centuries.

The stele at Beth-She'an commemorates the victory of Pharaoh Setos I over the Canaanite rebels at the Egyptian stronghold in northern Palestine.

### Egypt's Relationship with the Levant

The rulers of the New Kingdom were committed to extending their control in the Levant, both to exploit its natural resources and to provide Egypt with a buffer against the powerful Syrian and Mesopotamian kingdoms to the north. Nonetheless, the New Kingdom struggled to maintain effective control over the region. The pharaohs increasingly faced uprisings from the indigenous peoples, as well as organized military campaigns by the Hittites and the Hurrians to the north. Around 1500 BC Tutmosis I finally installed fortified garrisons to maintain control.

The discovery of a large cache of documents at el-Amarna in Egypt means that much is known about the relationship between Egypt and the various kingdoms and principalities of Mesopotamia and the Levant during the New Kingdom. These documents were part of the state archive of Amenhotep III of Egypt (r. 1390–1353 BC) and they tell of frequent diplomatic visits and gift exchanges between Egypt and, among others, the Babylonians, Assyrians, Hittites and the Hurrian kings of Mittani.

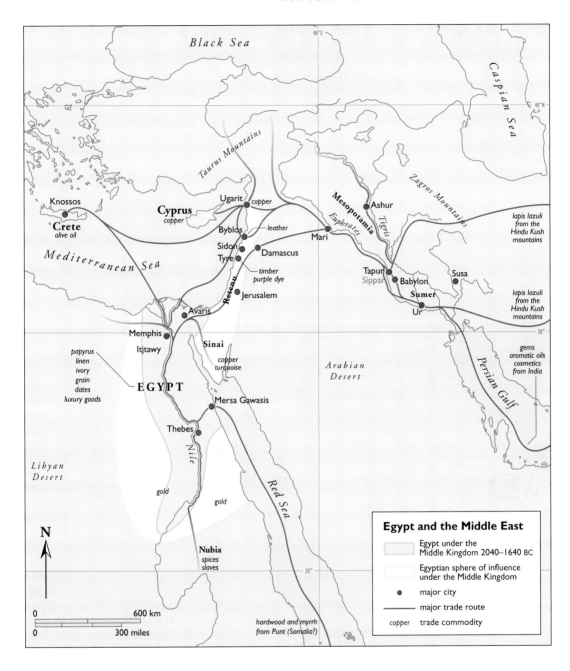

**Egypt and the Middle East**

Egypt under the Middle Kingdom 2040–1640 BC

Egyptian sphere of influence under the Middle Kingdom

● major city

— major trade route

*copper* trade commodity

The Egyptians referred to the Levant region as 'Retenu'. They divided it into three distinct territories: Amurru in the north, the central region of Upi, and Canaan, which included Palestine and the Sinai Peninsula. Each territory was overseen by its own Egyptian vizier (a civil administrator with vice-regal powers). Despite an Egyptian presence lasting the better part of two millennia, Retenu never became an effective Egyptian power base. Egyptian culture, so dominant and cohesive within the Egyptian heartland, seems to have made little impact on the indigenous peoples of the Levant; even the Amarna letters are written in Babylonian cuneiform, indicating the strong influence of Mesopotamian culture throughout the area.

# Part II: The Old Testament

*The period covered by the Old Testament cuts across the divisions of time used by archaeologists and historians to describe the broad shifts in history across the Mediterranean region. The covenant between Abraham and Yahweh, among the earliest biblical events, falls within the Middle Bronze Age, but the growth of Abraham's people into a political nation actually took place in the Iron Age.*

Although archaeological and anthropological conclusions can never be precise, they are based on a different kind of evidence from that presented in the Old Testament – material rather than textual. The lack of consensus between the evidence of archaeology and the information presented in the Bible is heightened by the patchy nature of both types of evidence. Neither source can present a complete picture and both sources are open to misinterpretation. It is therefore desirable to substantiate one or both kinds of information with an externally validated set of events as provided in other sources of evidence, such as Assyrian clay stele tablets or Egyptian papyri. Unfortunately, this is only possible rarely. Mostly experts have to rely on estimates, deductions and the skills of interpretation.

Located in the Old City of Jerusalem, the Western Wall is a 57 metre (187 ft) exposed section of ancient wall on the western side of the Temple Mount. The wall, which dates to around 19 BC, is set aside for prayer and pilgrimage, and is revered by Jews as the last surviving part of the Temple.

The period covered between Abraham and the Maccabees is of great importance. This is the era in which the Jewish people emerged as a distinct cultural and religious group: the age of the conquest and settlement of the land and the creation of the kingdoms of Judah and Israel, followed by the devastation of Jerusalem and the captivity in Bablyon, and the recovery under the Persians and Seleucids. In other words, it is this period that saw the formation of the principles on which the Judeo-Christian tradition, and Western history in general, are based.

## Biblical Israel in a Wider Context

Understanding the historical context of the Old Testament narratives provides us with an essential building block in comprehending how the Near East evolved in a wider sense. The events of the Old Testament relate to a people whose significance in the larger scale of historical events in the region was small. The tiny kingdoms of Israel had little impact on the rhythms of imperial power wielded in turn by the Egyptians, Assyrians, Persians and Seleucids. Nevertheless, they provide insight into how communities emerged, the relationship between religious, cultural and political identities, and the effects of social structures on economic developments. Above all, they shed light on how a marginal people perceived itself, forged an identity and a destiny based on the self-conscious articulation of its place in the world.

The overall picture presented in the Old Testament is of the emergence, tribulations and rise to dominance of Israel, followed by political and social disaster in the Babylonian War of 587–586 BC, and the gradual return to security through rediscovery of religious identity. The initial formation of the religious identity, particularly the rigid monotheistic characteristic of Judaism, and the idea of a special relationship between Yahweh and the people of Abraham, took place in the context of Egyptian political dominance of the whole eastern Mediterranean region towards the beginning of the 2nd millennium BC.

Stone relief showing the Assyrian siege of the strategic city of Lachish in 701 BC. Remarkably detailed, this section shows Judean captives after the fall of the city being marched through a rocky landscape before being exiled to Assyria as slaves. The captives are treated well in comparison to the Assyrian officers being tortured and executed because of their betrayal of the king Sennacherib. The Assyrian invasion of Judah is also described in the Bible books of Kings and Chronicles.

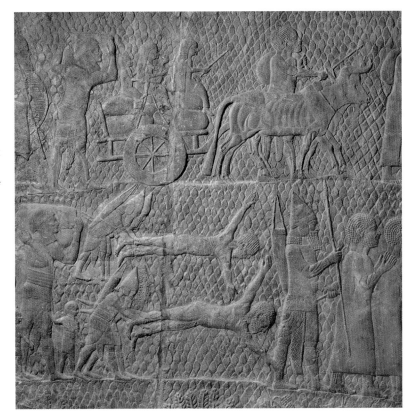

Egyptian stele inscriptions indicate military activity in Palestine in the later XIIth Dynasty, but it cannot be said that the region came under direct Egyptian rule. Indeed, Syro-Palestinian influences seem to have been just as strong in Egypt in the first half of the 2nd millennium, and the Hyksos dynasty was probably of Canaanite origin. Politically and culturally, the influence of the Amorite rulers of Upper Mesopotamia, based around Mari, was probably stronger than the Egyptian in the 18th century BC. They were succeeded from the 1790s BC by the dynasty established by Hammurabi in Babylon. The political fluidity of the region, in balance between competing orbits, enabled strong clan leaders with economic power underwritten by successful pastoral management to establish themselves in the relatively unsettled lands in the Canaanite hinterland. The main urban centres of Palestine in this period, such as Tell Kabri, Meggido and Tell Akko, were either on the coast or in nearby valleys, but by c. 1750 BC towns such as Hazor and Shechem, appeared further inland. These settlements, judging from pottery finds, also seem to reflect an influence from towns to the north, along the Lebanese and Syrian coasts.

### Palestine During the Hyksos Period

During the rule of the Hyksos Dynasty in Egypt (XVth Dynasty, c. 1630 to 1539-23 BC), which according to some scholars is the period in which the first Hebrew settlement in Egypt occurred, the landscape of Palestine became increasingly urban. Dan, Hazor, Megiddo, Jericho and other sites were protected with walls and ramparts, and Hazor, the largest town, covered almost 200 acres. Excavations at Gezer have exposed a monumental gate complex and citadel. The Late Bronze Age period between c. 1550 and 1200 BC, however, saw the rise of Egyptian power in the region, and the extension of its authority to Syria. Palestine now came under the orbit of the New Kingdom of Egypt, but it was also the scene of conflict between Egypt and the Hittites, who contested their power in Syria. Consequently, there is more information about conditions in Palestine, notably from the el-Amarna letters. It is clear that Canaanite culture survived in coastal towns such as Ugarit. In fact, ports flourished as places of interaction between economic forces, not only Egyptian and Hittite, but, to the west, that of the Mycenaean cities of Greece and Crete.

The tomb of Cyrus the Great, the founder of the Persian empire, in Pasargadae, Iran. After overthrowing the Babylonians, the new Persian ruler Cyrus gave many of the captive Jews permission to return to their native land. He also decreed the restoration of worship at Jerusalem, thus beginning a crucial era for the Jews and their re-integration into a national and religious group.

The end of this period in *c.* 1200 BC occurred in obscure, but destructive circumstances. The XIXth Dynasty in Egypt ended at about the same time as the Hittite and Mycenaean civilizations. Although ceramic finds indicate some continuity of occupation in Palestine, the urban culture of the Late Bronze Age disappeared. The traditional view of biblical archaeologists was that the Israelites were able to take advantage of the dramatic fall in pre-existing cultures in the region to conquer the land of Canaan. There is no doubt that the beginning of the period saw some kind of demographic and economic collapse throughout the eastern Mediterranean, which is sometimes referred to as a 'dark age'.

## The Rise of Israel and Judah

Historians and archaeologists are no longer confident in assigning causes, let alone a single cause, to a series of shifts that took several generations to play themselves out and had varying effects in different regions. The picture of invasion by the 'Sea Peoples', whoever they might have been, is too simplistic a cause to explain by itself the disruption to international trade, the disappearance of major settlements in Palestine and Syria and population displacements such as that described in the Old Testament. The notion of a sudden and dramatic collapse has been abandoned in the face of evidence of a more protracted series of changes. Within Palestine itself, for example, Hazor seems to have been destroyed in the mid-13th century BC, whereas Lachish was still functioning almost a hundred years later. Together with archaeological evidence pointing to the survival of indigenous identities in Palestinian settlements, this indicates that the idea of a single conquest by invading Israelites must be dropped.

The revival of Late Bronze Age Palestine came from the development of a thriving rural economy, as has been made clear by recent archaeological surveys. During this period, although the pace of development varied in different settlements, one feature was the revival of villages and towns linked in networks of economic exchange. These communities, however, do not seem to have been part of any wider homogenous political or religious identity. There is evidence of overlapping and competing religious cults, some of them indigenous, others Philistine or Egyptian. It is in this context that we must see the spread of the Israelites throughout Canaan. Another significant context is general demographic pressure from rising populations following recovery after *c.*1200 BC, which led to the creation of new urban sites. Samaria and Jerusalem, both upland settlements, came to form the nuclei of small states; traditionally, in biblical history, under the kingship of Saul, David and Solomon in the 10th century BC. The number of small settlements or towns increased across the period: for the 9th century, for example, 86 small sites have been identified in Judah, compared to 122 in the 8th century. The general archaeological evidence in both Judah and Samaria corresponds roughly to the impression given in the Old Testament of increased prosperity and political power wielded by the 'united monarchy' founded by David in the 10th century BC and continuing for some centuries thereafter, until the Assyrian and Babylonian invasions.

### Archaeological Debate

Recently, however, the coherence of the biblical narrative has been questioned by archaeologists. Monumental building, particularly gate complexes at Hazor, Megiddo and Gezer, were once taken as confirmation of the centralization of Israel by Davidic kingship. It is now less certain that these structures were linked by any overall plan or provide evidence for state structures, and some archaeologists doubt whether Jerusalem can be seen as the capital of a kingdom before the 8th century BC. Such doubts remind us that the Old Testament, even where providing verifiable historical evidence, was not in any sense a contemporary record of events. Both the dating of the different sections, and the method of composition, are still subjects of debate. The traditional view is that David's court provided a focus for the creation of the historical as well as much of the poetical content of the Old Testament, but this may rely too much on a circular logic without external evidence of the achievements of his reign.

The archaeological evidence also suggests that the expanding population did not adhere strictly to the monotheism of the Hebrews. The Old Testament narrative presents a picture of military conquest by David and Solomon as a result of which the two main areas of Hebrew settlement, Israel and Judah, were brought together in a unified kingship which imposed itself and its ideology on neighbouring hostile peoples such as the Philistines and Canaanites. This was followed by a period of moral laxity resulting in weakened political authority. It may be more realistic, however, to see the 'united kingdom' period as an attempt to establish Hebrew supremacy over the whole region, one consequence of which was the absorption of indigenous communities with their own religious traditions into the new polity.

### The Babylonian Exile

In any case, the increased prosperity of the region by the 8th century BC made it attractive to Assyria and, in the 6th century, the successor state of Babylonia. To some extent, the political decline of Samarian-based Israel signalled by its conquest at the hands of Sargon II of Assyria in 721 BC – although it had been an Assyrian vassal since the 9th century – enabled Judah, and especially Jerusalem, to expand its influence at the expense of Israel. By the early 6th century, however, it too fell prey to the conquest by Nebuchadnezzar II (597 BC.)

The Bablyonian exile lasted only 50 years or so, until the conquest of Babylon by Cyrus the Great and its absorption in a new Persian empire. Its significance in the development of the historical identity of Israel, however, is critical. The historical fact of the exile itself is supported by Babylonian evidence for the presence of Jews in Mesopotamia, particularly around Nippur. How many such exiles there were, however, and the conditions under which they were taken to Assyria and held there, are more uncertain. The Old

A full-page medieval illumination showing Joseph being sold by his brothers into slavery. The story is told in the Book of Genesis. There are parallels between Joseph's exile in Egypt, his father Jacob's sojourn in Mesopotamia (when he hides from the wrath of Esau) and the Jewish Babylonian captivity.

Testament gives contradictory accounts of the numbers deported to Assyria. The version in 2 Kings, which suggests that the whole of Judean society, save for peasants, was deported, is undermined by the evidence of Jeremiah, which gives precise numbers totalling 4,600. Even if, as some have suggested, these numbers are taken as heads of households only, the total would probably still only reach around 20,000. The total population can only be estimated, but the tribute paid to the Assyrians in c. 701 BC suggests that such a figure would represent about 10 per cent. The ideological slant given to the account of the exile is based on the assumption of a contract between a national deity and a distinct people, the breach of which incurred the penalty of enslavement. But the notion of the total destruction of Judah, as implied in the biblical narrative, squares neither with the archaeological evidence nor with historical logic. The evidence for destruction relates more closely, in fact, to Israel at the end of the 8th century BC than Judah in the 6th. Jerusalem, as the centre of Judean power, bore the brunt of the Babylonian assault, but the archaeological evidence suggests that territories to the north continued to function during the Exile.

The Babylonian Exile dispersed Israelites from the southern shores of the Caspian Sea to Nubia, but the heaviest concentrations were in southern Mesopotamia and Egypt. Probably most of the exiles lived as tenant farmers, which was economically productive for the empire. Although the Jewish people were not forbidden to worship in their traditional manner, which would have been contrary to the polytheistic norms of ancient society, it was inevitable that a degree of syncretism developed through interaction between Jews and the indigenous peoples. At Jerusalem itself worship had been characterized by the presence of the Temple, built by Solomon in the 10th century BC. Without this focal point, Jewish religious life lay open to outside influences again. In fact, there is evidence that even before the Exile, non-Jewish cults such as that of Asharah had begun to return to Judah. But the experience of exile marks a watershed in the development of Jewish identity. If biblical scholars are right to attribute the overall shape and structure of the Old Testament as we know it to the post-exilic period, then it was after the return from Exile that the idea of a people's relationship to their God relying on a written contract came to maturity.

### The Post-Exile Period

The restoration of Jewish worship to Jerusalem did not mean the return of independent kingship to Judah, which constituted a province of the new Persian empire. The Temple was rebuilt, perhaps in c. 520 BC, and became the focus for leadership on the part of a Judeo-Babylonian elite, epitomized by the High Priesthood. The Exile, indeed, confirmed the polarization of Jewish political and religious society between the former northern kingdom, which had suffered more catastrophically in the 720s at the hands of Assyria, and Judah. Samarians, indeed, opposed the rebuilding of the Temple and the increasing tendency for religious authority to be associated with it.

The historical sources for the post-exilic period up to the Maccabean Revolt are patchy. The major powers were the Persian empire and, after Darius' defeat at the hands of Alexander in 331 BC, the Greek Seleucid/Ptolemaic successor empires. Neither was interested in the Jews, or saw Palestine as strategically important, and there is little evidence for the period of consolidation from the 5th to the 2nd century BC. Hebrew sources, chiefly the minor prophets and Chronicles, indicate an attempt by a narrow sect within Judaism, represented by Nehemiah, to centre an ideological community in Jerusalem. This could not, however, prevent the gradual and quiet Hellenization of Palestine accomplished through the settlement of Greek speakers in the region in the Ptolemaic/Seleucid era. New cities were built on the Greek model, into which the concept of citizenship was introduced, and which featured indispensable mediators of Greek social ideals such as the gymnasium. The coast, Samaria and Galilee were particularly affected by new settlement; Judah less so. On the whole the Jews welcomed and co-operated with Seleucid rule from 200 BC, which began by viewing Palestine as simply a source of tax revenues, best left in peace.

### The Maccabean Revolt

From the reign of Antiochus IV, however, (175–64 BC), external Seleucid politics created conditions for internal divisions within Jewish society that resulted in the Maccabean Revolt and a brief period of independent statehood once

again in Palestine. Antiochus, in order to raise funds for an invasion of Ptolemaic Egypt, interfered in the succession to the High Priesthood in Jerusalem for a bribe in favour of Jason, a Hellenized Jew. On his return from campaigning in Egypt in 169 BC, he looted the Temple in Jerusalem of its treasure to pay for his military expenditure. The compliance of Jason indicates that a Hellenistic wing within Judah supported sweeping reforms of Jewish society. A list of citizens was drawn up and a gymnasium planned for Jerusalem.

The Maccabean Revolt, led by Mattathias and his sons, particularly Judas Maccabeus, in 168 BC, arose initially from the internal contest for the office of High Priest, and thus from the opposition of factions for and against Hellenization. But the revolt drew strength from Antiochus' insensitivity to Jewish identity. His attempt to eradicate Jewish worship in Jerusalem altogether is virtually unprecedented in the polytheistic ancient world. The outlawing of circumcision, the destruction of copies of the law scrolls and the erection of a pagan altar in the Temple were subsequently characterized as 'the abomination of desolation'. Although this lasted only until Antiochus' death in 164 BC, the revolt had gathered

Illumination of a *menorah*, from the Jewish Cervera Bible. The seven-branched candelabrum was used in the Temple in Jerusalem and has been a key symbol of Jewish identity and faith for around 3,000 years. It is said to symbolize the burning bush as seen by Moses in the Book of Exodus.

momentum and now aspired to national independence. By 140 BC Simon Maccabeus had established autonomy in Jerusalem, and the first quarter of the 1st century BC saw a Jewish king, Alexander Janneus (103–76 BC) rule over more territory than any predecessor. A series of civil wars within the Hasmonean dynasty, however, after Alexander's death, weakened Jewish autonomy. The new power in the eastern Mediterranean, after the defeat inflicted on Mithridates of Pontus in 69 BC, was Rome, and it was to the Roman legate in the East, Pompey, that both sides in the Jewish civil war appealed. Pompey's entry into Jerusalem in 63 BC effectively marked the end of Jewish independent statehood, for although he permitted the continuation of Temple worship and confirmed the status of the Hasmonean family, it was as a client kingship of Rome. Under the *pax romana* Palestine would adopt once again its customary position as a peaceful, prosperous but obscure province in an empire whose centre of gravity lay elsewhere.

# The Wanderings of Abraham

*The story of Abraham, the first Old Testament patriarch, is told in the Book of Genesis (chapters 11–25). Abraham – 'the Father of many nations' – was a son of Terah, a descendant of Noah's son Shem. Terah fled his native city of Ur in southern Mesopotamia and settled with his extended family at Haran (modern Harran, Turkey).*

> *"Yahweh said to Abram, 'Leave your country, your family and your father's house, for the land I will show you.'"*
>
> Genesis 12.1

Following Terah's death, Abraham, believing that God desired him to settle in Canaan and that his new home and his descendants would be specially blessed, headed south with his family, living for a while in the largely unsettled Negev region. Famine eventually drove Abraham and his clan into Egypt where they thrived until they were expelled following an attempt by the Egyptian pharaoh to claim the beautiful Sarah (originally Sarai), Abraham's wife, for his harem. Abraham returned to Canaan and settled in Mamre, now believed to be just northwest of Hebron.

Assured once again by God that Canaan would be the home of his favoured progeny, the elderly and still childless Abraham achieved fatherhood by bearing a son, Ishmael, by Hagar, Sarah's handmaid. This was an acceptable practice among barren couples at the time. After undergoing circumcision as part of his covenant with God, Abraham (at age 100) and his wife finally produced a legitimate son in Isaac, whose life was spared despite God's demand that Abraham offer his young son as a sacrifice. After long and eventful lives, Abraham and Sarah were buried in a family burial chamber in the cave of Machpelah.

## Evidence for the Life of Abraham

Terah's migration and Abraham's subsequent travels are generally agreed to have taken place in the early 2nd millennium BC. The period between *c.* 2000 and *c.* 1800 BC for Abraham and his immediate descendants is supported both by historical references found within the Genesis text and more recent archaeological discoveries, such as the vast collection of contemporary documents unearthed in the royal complex at Mari on the Euphrates in central Mesopotamia. Many sites from Abraham's life are marked with shrines that were erected later, but the intervening time and the unavoidable blending of history with local tradition often make it difficult to determine whether such monuments identify the correct sites.

Abraham's motives for moving south from Haran can also be questioned; as it is likely that Abraham's people were semi-nomadic, it is impossible to know whether their frequent relocations represent a conscious attempt to move further south through the Canaanite territories, or in fact merely the need for fresh pastureland. Archaeological finds in the locations cited in the biblical texts, such as Shechem, Hebron and Beersheba, certainly indicate prosperous settlements before 2000 BC and thus support the specifics of Abraham's journey, although Chapter 14 of Genesis, which outlines Abraham's rescue of his nephew Lot, his campaigns against regional kings and his meeting with Melchizedek is much less verifiable. Scholars also note that Abraham's monotheistic devotion to his God may spring from the pre-eminence of one god (such as Nanna or Sin for the Sumerians, or El for the Canaanites) in several of the polytheistic cultures of his day.

Abraham and Isaac from the Hispano-Moresque Haggadah, a medieval Castilian work. A *haggadah* (literally meaning telling or narration) is a collection of illustrated Jewish prayers and readings that were written to accompany the ritual meal of Passover.

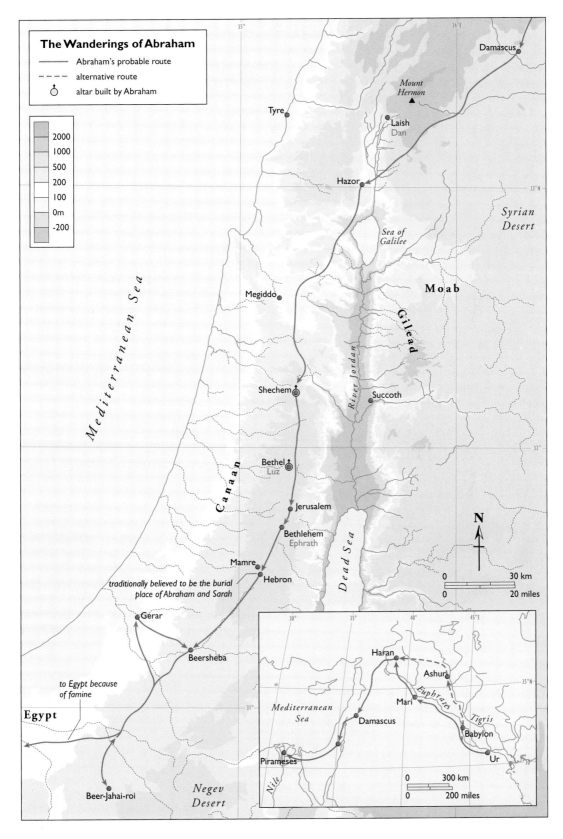

## The Wanderings of Abraham

— Abraham's probable route

- - - alternative route

⚲ altar built by Abraham

2000
1000
500
200
100
0m
-200

Damascus

*Mount Hermon* ▲

Tyre

Laish
Dan

Hazor

*Syrian Desert*

*Sea of Galilee*

Megiddo

**Moab**

**Gilead**

Shechem

Succoth

*River Jordan*

*Mediterranean Sea*

**C a n a a n**

Bethel ⚲
Luz

Jerusalem

Bethlehem
Ephrath

Mamre

*traditionally believed to be the burial place of Abraham and Sarah*

Hebron

*Dead Sea*

Gerar

Beersheba

*to Egypt because of famine*

**Egypt**

N

0 — 30 km
0 — 20 miles

Beer-Jahai-roi

*Negev Desert*

Haran

Ashur

Mari

*Euphrates*

Damascus

*Tigris*

Babylon

*Mediterranean Sea*

Pirameses

Ur

*Nile*

0 — 300 km
0 — 200 miles

35

# The Land of Canaan

*Abraham's son Isaac had twins, Esau and Jacob. The younger son, Jacob, was the chosen one, and his twelve sons – Reuben, Simeon, Levi, Judah, Issachar, Zebulon, Benjamin, Joseph, Dan, Naphtali, Gad and Asher – would go on to found the twelve tribes of Israel.*

*"Stay in the land I shall tell you of. Remain for the present here in this land, and I will be with you and bless you. "*

Genesis 26.2–3

Isaac lived much of his life in Canaan in the area settled by his father. He spent some time in Gerar in neighbouring Philistine territory, before settling in Beer-sheba, the largest settlement in the Negev. Having received Isaac's blessing (and thus usurping Esau's birthright), Jacob fled north to Haran in order to escape his brother's wrath. Tradition holds that Bethel, just north of Jerusalem, was named by Jacob following a dream in which God appeared to him as he slept there. God promised to keep Jacob safe and to bring him and his family back into Canaan. After fourteen years in Haran (during which time he married his cousins, Leah and Rachel), Jacob and his family returned to Canaan. A second dream, involving a wrestling match with an angel, resulted in Jacob adopting the new name of Israel, meaning 'He who fights with God.' Jacob named the site of this dream Penuel ('face of God') and, having made his peace with his brother Esau there, Jacob and his family settled in Bethel.

### The Story of Joseph

Joseph was Jacob's favourite son and, thus, the least popular among the twelve brothers. Sold by his brothers as a slave, Joseph was taken to Egypt where he eventually achieved the position of chief minister in the pharaoh's household. When his brothers, desperate to buy grain, arrived in Egypt during a famine, Joseph secured permission for his family, including the elderly Jacob, to settle in Goshen, probably in the eastern Nile Delta. Jacob died in Egypt, but was buried back in Canaan in the cave of Machpelah alongside Abraham, Sarah, Isaac and his first wife, Leah. Joseph was buried at Shechem on land previously purchased by Jacob.

Abraham's Mosque in the West Bank city of Hebron. Also known as the cave of Machpelah, it is thought to be the burial site of the biblical couples Adam and Eve, Abraham and Sarah, Isaac and Rebekah, and Jacob and Leah. The site is holy to Jews, Muslims and Christians.

Scholarly debate over whether to date Joseph's employment in Egypt to the 19th century BC (XIIth Dynasty) or to the years around 1600 BC, during the period of Hyksos domination, continues to rage. Arguments concerning Syro-Palestinian influence in Egypt during both periods can be mounted fairly easily given the tantalizing, but incomplete, documentary and visual evidence. Regardless of the precise centuries during which Jacob, Joseph and their families wandered throughout Canaan and north-eastern Egypt, several interesting observations about the region in the first half of the 2nd millennium BC can be made.

First the numerous locations described in the biblical accounts of the patri-archal movements indicate a fairly urban, settled lifestyle for the region as a whole. While there are open unsettled areas, many thriving settlements are mentioned whose existence has been proved through archaeology. Despite this, a centralized regional government or rudimentary power structure seems to be lacking. Squabbling and open warfare between cities and lesser commu-nities were rife. The frequent resettlement of Canaanites in the eastern Nile Delta in the years after 2000 BC may well be an indirect result of the unsettled political situation throughout Syro-Palestine. Finally, and somewhat paradoxi-cally, it should be noted that the relative success of the Egyptian dynasty of the

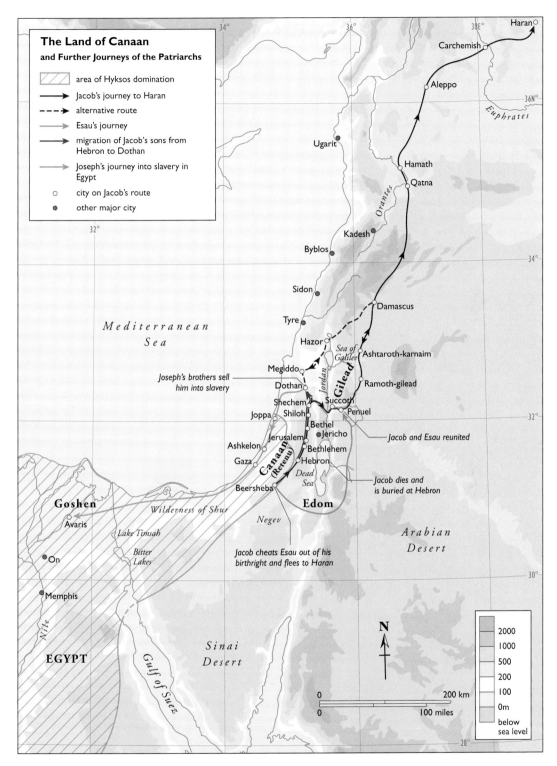

**The Land of Canaan**

**and Further Journeys of the Patriarchs**

- area of Hyksos domination
- Jacob's journey to Haran
- alternative route
- Esau's journey
- migration of Jacob's sons from Hebron to Dothan
- Joseph's journey into slavery in Egypt
- ○ city on Jacob's route
- ● other major city

Joseph's brothers sell him into slavery

Jacob and Esau reunited

Jacob dies and is buried at Hebron

Jacob cheats Esau out of his birthright and flees to Haran

Hyksos (who were almost certainly of Canaanite origin) strongly indicates the relatively advanced nature of Canaanite culture even despite the lack of centralized regional powers.

# Conjectured Routes of the Exodus

*Scholarly debate surrounds every aspect of the Exodus story. The Bible tells of the Israelites (descendants of Jacob), mercilessly enslaved by Egyptian rulers, fleeing Egypt under the leadership of Moses, an Israelite brought up at the pharaoh's court.*

*" Then all the sons of Israel grumbled against Moses and Aaron, and the whole community said, 'Would that we had died in the land of Egypt, or at least that we had died in this wilderness!' "*

Exodus 16.2–3

Moses led the Israelites from the eastern Nile Delta across the Sinai Peninsula back into Canaan, the narrow strip of fertile land between the Mediterranean Sea and the Arabian Desert. Numerous episodes from the story – among them the first Passover and the delivery of the Ten Commandments to Moses on Mount Sinai – are not only familiar to most of us, but crucial to later developments within the Judeo-Christian tradition. The conclusions of theologians, archaeologists and biblical historians vary on everything from the factual likelihood of the story itself to the size of the fleeing population. The two areas of greatest contention involve the date and the route of the Exodus.

## Dating the Exodus

The Early Exodus and Late Exodus theories are the two most popular hypotheses about the date. The Bible does not specifically name the pharaohs involved during the Israelites' time in Egypt. Scholars generally feel that its 'internal' chronology is verifiable only as far back as the reign of Solomon. Egyptian chronologies, however, extend further. If the Exodus occurred 480 years before the building of Solomon's Temple in *c.* 958 BC (1 Kings 6:1), a date of 1438 BC presents itself. This date is problematic for several reasons, including the contradiction between it and other dated events within the biblical chronology, the absence of any corroborative evidence within the documents for the reign of Thutmose III, the contemporary Egyptian pharaoh, and the lack of conclusive archaeological evidence of the Israelite conquest of Canaan which the Bible tells us took place 40 years after the Exodus from Egypt.

The Late Exodus theory, based on archaeological evidence, advocates a date of *c.* 1250 BC. There is virtually no evidence of conquest or of Hebrew culture in Canaan during the 14th and 15th centuries BC., but there is some evidence of social upheaval from the years around 1200 BC, roughly 40 or 50 years after the proposed date of *c.* 1250 BC. The Bible states that Ramesses II, the Egyptian pharaoh at this time, forced Hebrew slaves to build the cities of Pithom and Ra'amses (both in the eastern Nile Delta) during this period. Egyptian documents record only that Ramesses enslaved two separate peoples and that he enlarged Ra'amses. Coincidentally the Merneptah (or Israel) Stele from the reign of Ramesses' son contains the earliest surviving reference to the tribe of Israel living within Canaan. The inscription dates from just before 1200 BC and describes the Israelites as ruined and 'without seed'.

The Bible lists around 40 stops along the Exodus route. Most of those linked with the first part of the journey (as opposed to the later 40 years of wandering) remain unidentified. As the fleeing Israelites probably avoided the royal highways between Egypt and Canaan, two main routes present themselves: the northern route heads east to Kadesh-barnea; the southern route turns south into the Sinai Peninsula and then north to Kadesh-barnea. From here both routes move into Canaan, around the Dead Sea and through the kingdoms of Edom and Moab to Mount Nebo, where Moses is said to have died. In either case, a crossing of the

The church on the summit of Jebel Musa in Sinai. This is the most widely accepted site for the biblical Mount Sinai.

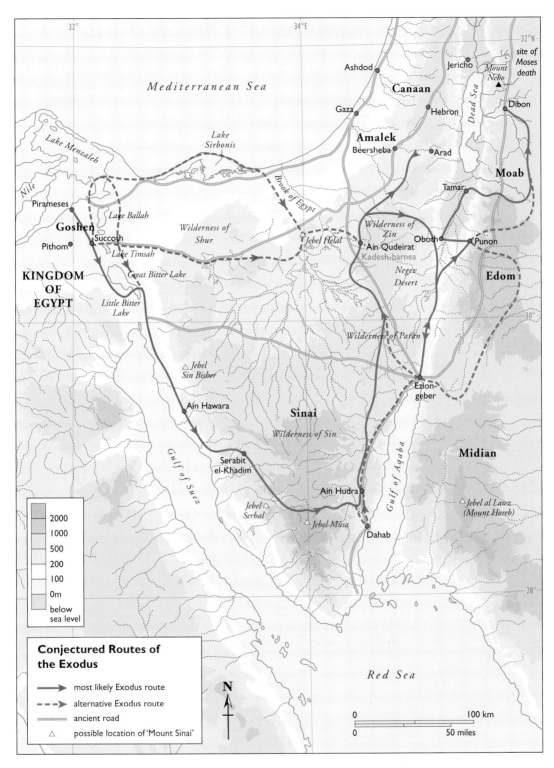

Red Sea is unlikely; it may be that this story arose because of a mistranslation of the Hebrew 'sea of reeds' – which was probably a reference to the reedy marshes in the Nile Delta.

# The Hebrew Conquests

*After 40 years of wandering through neighbouring territory, the Bible tells us, the Israelites, led by Moses' successor Joshua, conquered Canaan. As with the Exodus, the Bible itself is the primary evidence for the conquest and, yet again, there is little correlation between the biblical narrative and the archaeological evidence.*

An illuminated manuscript from the 12th century showing the battle of Jericho. According to the biblical account, when the people heard the sound of the trumpets, the walls of the city fell down, giving the Israelites their first victory in the conquest of Canaan.

> *"When they heard the sound of the trumpet, the people raised a mighty war cry and the wall collapsed then and there."*
>
> Joshua 6.20

While the Book of Exodus is typically viewed as part of the earliest literary 'unit' of the Bible, the Book of Joshua is understood to open a new segment of the scriptural texts. It was written *c.* 550 BC during the Babylonian Captivity when the Israelites were exiled from their homeland in Canaan, a fact which may go some way towards explaining the author's over-enthusiastic descriptions of the might and glory of Israel and of Joshua's military prowess. The reality appears rather less dramatic and altogether less organized, with the Israelites gradually coming to dominate the region as the indigenous rulers subjected themselves over time to the overlordship of the Hebrews. The biblical chronology places Joshua's conquest of Canaan 40 years after the Exodus, for which there is no firmly agreed date. Archaeological evidence points to a period from *c.* 1200 BC to the reign of King David (*c.* 1000–*c.* 962 BC).

## The Narrative of Joshua

The Book of Joshua describes a tightly structured military campaign which results in which the Israelite onslaught is effectively unstoppable. Crossing the River Jordan, Joshua and his troops watched the walls of the city of Jericho collapse, after which they destroyed the entire city and offered its contents to God. Next the inhabitants of Ai, near Bethel, were slaughtered and their city burned to the ground. In turn, the Gibeonites were enslaved and the Amorites defeated at Gibeon, and their strongholds at Makkedah, Libnah, Lachish, Eglon, Hebron and Debir systematically sacked and plundered. After the subjugation of Goshen, Gaza and south Canaan, Joshua turned his attention to the north, which the Israelites soon dominated after resounding victories at Merom Brook and Hazor. The final chapters of Joshua's story recount the specific territories and kings conquered under Moses and Joshua and set out the division of Canaan between the twelve tribes of Israel.

From this narrative, one would expect to find many examples of sites showing signs of armed conflict and devastation during the same time span, but the archaeological evidence does not entirely bear this out. Excavations of Jericho have yielded inconclusive evidence, although it appears that the ancient city may have sustained some damage in the late 14th century BC, with little evidence of resettlement before the Iron Age (*c.* 1200 BC). The el-Amarna letters, Egyptian documents dating from the early 14th century BC, mention the fall of Jericho and attacks across Canaan from the east by the 'Hapiru' (possibly Hebrews), thus serving as an important factor in any Early Exodus/Conquest dating theories. Ai and Hebron appear to have been uninhabited during the period under discussion, and Gibeon, while occupied, gives no indication of sustained military damage. Lachish, a flourishing city *c.* 1200 BC, was in fact unwalled and so its conquest (for which there is archaeological evidence) could have been achieved with relative ease. Cities such as Eglon and Debir have not been conclusively identified. In any case, there is little evidence of organized Israelite rule over Canaan before the end of the 1st millennium BC.

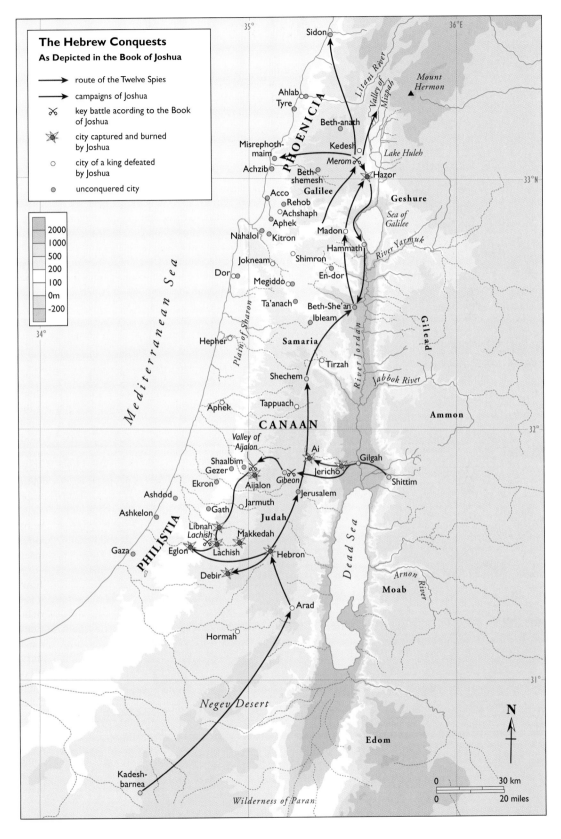

**The Hebrew Conquests**

**As Depicted in the Book of Joshua**

→ route of the Twelve Spies

→ campaigns of Joshua

✄ key battle according to the Book of Joshua

✳ city captured and burned by Joshua

○ city of a king defeated by Joshua

● unconquered city

2000
1000
500
200
100
0m
-200

*Mediterranean Sea*

Sidon

*Litani River*

*Valley of Mizpah*

▲ *Mount Hermon*

Ahlab
Tyre

Beth-anath

PHOENICIA

Misrephoth-maim
Kedesh

Achzib
Merom
Hazor

Beth-shemesh

Acco
Rehob
Achshaph
Aphek

Galilee
*Lake Huleh*

Geshure

Nahalol
Kitron

Madon
Hammath
*Sea of Galilee*

Jokneam
Shimron

Dor
Megiddo
En-dor

*River Yarmuk*

Ta'anach
Beth-She'an
Ibleam

Hepher

*Plain of Sharon*

Samaria

*River Jordan*

Gilead

Tirzah

Shechem

*Jabbok River*

Aphek
Tappuach

CANAAN

Ammon

*Valley of Aijalon*

Ai
Gilgah

Shaalbim
Gezer

Gibeon
Jericho

Shittim

Ekron
Aijalon

Jerusalem

Ashdod

Gath
Jarmuth

Judah

Ashkelon

Libnah
*Lachish*
Makkedah

Hebron

Gaza
Eglon
Lachish

PHILISTIA

*Dead Sea*

Debir

*Arnon River*

Arad

Moab

Hormah

31°

*Negev Desert*

**N**

Edom

Kadesh-barnea

0          30 km

0          20 miles

*Wilderness of Paran*

35°          36°E

33°N

34°

32°

# Jericho

*Long known as the biblical city whose 'walls came tumbling down' as Joshua and his troops surrounded it, Jericho is now recognized as probably the earliest 'town' in the world, with archaeological evidence of permanent settlement on the site by c. 9000 BC.*

> "*Now Jericho had been carefully barricaded against the Israelites; no one came in, and no one went out.*"
>
> Joshua 6.1

A reliable fresh water spring (still in existence today) made the Jericho area attractive to those looking to settle in a region otherwise too dry and inhospitable to sustain year-round habitation. Jericho's long history is complex – with several gaps of hundreds of years – but it is now believed to have developed over three neighbouring sites that represent three distinct cultural periods in its history. The earliest settlement, located about 2 km (1.2 miles) from the modern city, was inhabited from prehistory into the Old Testament period, with Jericho II, lavishly constructed by King Herod, dating from the Roman period and located about 1 km (0.6 miles) south of the original site. Jericho III, out of

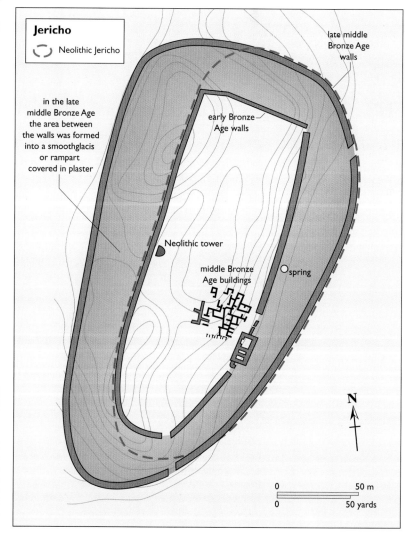

Jericho

Neolithic Jericho

late middle Bronze Age walls

in the late middle Bronze Age the area between the walls was formed into a smoothglacis or rampart covered in plaster

early Bronze Age walls

Neolithic tower

middle Bronze Age buildings

spring

N

0        50 m
0        50 yards

One of the Jericho skulls discovered by Kathleen Kenyon. Seven similar plaster skulls, with cowrie shells in the eyes, were uncovered at the site and are believed to be part of an ancestor cult.

Excavations at Jericho during the 1950s. The ancient round tower was attached to the original city walls at Jericho. The structure, thought to have been a watchtower, is believed to date to *c.* 7000 BC.

which grew the modern city, was refounded following the conquest of the region by the Crusaders in the years around 1100 AD.

By 8000 BC Jericho exhibits archaeological evidence of permanent residence by inhabitants living together as a community, subsisting by means of agriculture and animal husbandry, and displaying rudimentary signs of a recognizable 'culture' including large-scale stone building, ritualistic burial and primitive art forms. A second wave of inhabitants arrived around 7000 BC and occupied the site for the next millennium. Between 6000 and 5000 BC Jericho was unoccupied, and when a new occupation did begin, evidence suggests that on this occasion – despite their production and use of basic clay pottery – the culture of Jericho's residents was in fact less advanced than that of their predecessors. Occupation over the succeeding millennia was sparse and not continuous.

In the years up to 3000 BC, the final inhabitants of Jericho I arrived. Over the next thousand years the city was occupied by several of the various ethnic groups wandering throughout the region, among them the Amorites and the Canaanites. It was the Canaanites whose general culture and occupational patterns were adopted by the Israelites as they came to dominate the region in the centuries before 1000 BC.

## Unearthing the Archaeology

Numerous archaeological expeditions have explored Tell es-Sultan, the site believed to be Old Testament Jericho, and most set out to find the Jericho destroyed by Joshua. The earliest was conducted in 1868 by Charles Warren, a British engineer, with work by other British and German archaeologists following in turn. The team led by Dame Kathleen Kenyon from 1952–8 is probably the best known, and Kenyon's conclusion that Jericho was largely unoccupied in the late 2nd millennium BC – and therefore unable to be 'destroyed' – has long been accepted by most scholars.

More recently, however, the archaeologist Bryant Wood has reassessed Kenyon's work at Jericho and suggested that there is indeed evidence of occupation and violent destruction that is datable to *c.* 1400 BC – the proposed date of Joshua's conquest if one follows the Early Exodus theory. Wood's hypothesis supports work done by John Garstang in the 1930s. Historians and archaeologists continue to seek conclusive proof of the veracity of the biblical account.

# Beersheba

*Beersheba is now one of Israel's largest cities and serves as the administrative and cultural centre of the Negev. Fortified almost from its inception, Beersheba clearly served as a barrier between the towns and cities of the fertile, settled northern regions and the nomadic tribes of the southern deserts.*

*"Abraham planted a tamarisk at Beersheba and there he invoked Jahweh, the everlasting God."*

Genesis 21.33

Rock-hewn subterranean dwellings dating from *c*. 6000 BC are the earliest indication of human habitation in Beersheba. Discovered in Nahal Beersheba within the modern city, these dwellings suggest that the area was occupied seasonally by nomadic peoples. Ancient Beersheba, located several kilometres from the modern city, appears to have been settled only from the 4th millennium BC. It was abandoned by *c*. 3000 BC, although its frequent appearance in the Old Testament, beginning with the story of Abraham, suggests that it probably re-emerged as a settlement during the 2nd millennium BC. Beersheba was initially part of the lands of the tribe of Simeon, but soon became absorbed by the kingdom of Judah.

### Biblical Settlement

Almost nothing survives of the Beersheba inhabited by Abraham, Isaac and their descendants, nor of the new city rebuilt by King David early in the 10th century BC (which was probably destroyed during an Egyptian invasion just before 900 BC). Most of the impressive remains visible today - largely excavated between 1969 and 1976 by a team from Tel Aviv University - date from the reign of the Hebrew king Hezekiah (*c*. 715–*c*. 686 BC), although the layout and foundations of the city date from several centuries earlier. Frequent occupation and destruction by numerous invading peoples - among them the Egyptians, Assyrians and Persians - while underscoring the strategic importance of Beersheba, have left a complex archaeological legacy.

Beersheba's reliable water supply must have made it attractive to settlers. According to the Bible, Abraham and Isaac engaged in frequent disputes with their enemies over local water rights. The ancient well existed just outside the

Aerial view of the archaeological site of Tell Sheva, a few kilometres northeast of the modern city of Beersheba. Early inhabitants of Beersheba lived in caves and raised cattle. Abraham and Isaac arrived there at the beginning of the 3rd century BC.

main gates into the city and, by the 8th century BC, water was channelled from there and from numerous collecting points throughout the city by means of an impressive conduit system. The surviving double fortified walls date from the 9th century BC, although they were rebuilt on earlier foundations. Notable remains include the grand Governor's Palace, numerous storage rooms and private houses from the age of Hezekiah as well as from later periods.

Beersheba's pivotal role in Israel's history did not end with the close of the Old Testament period. The city was an important Byzantine border fortress in the middle of the 1st millennium AD, and served in turn as an Arab border fortress during the 7th and 8th centuries AD before being largely abandoned. It fell to the Turks in the 16th century AD, although they were unable to

A Bedouin market at Beersheba. The historic town continues to function as a trading centre for the nomadic tribes of the southern desert region.

exercise firm control in the area. In 1917 Beersheba was the first city in Palestine to be captured by the British, and it served as the headquarters for British rule in the region. During the Arab-Israeli struggle to gain control of Israel in 1947–8, Beersheba was controlled by Egyptian forces and served as their command post throughout their invasion of Israel. Beersheba was recaptured by the Israeli army in October of 1948 and was resettled by Israelis after 1949.

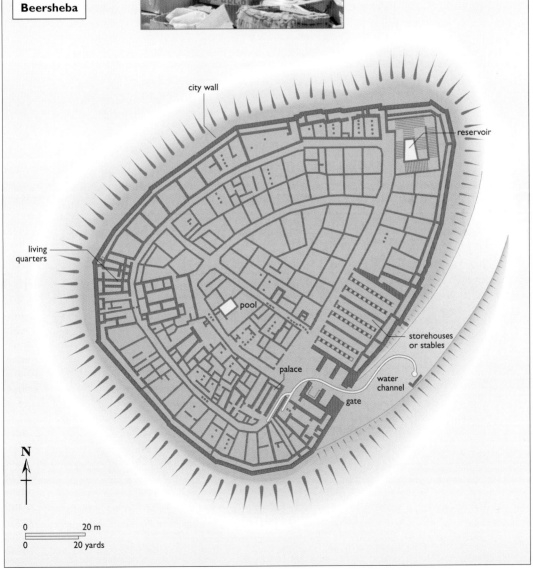

## Beersheba

city wall

reservoir

living quarters

pool

storehouses or stables

palace

water channel

gate

N

| 0 | 20 m |
| 0 | 20 yards |

# The Sea Peoples and the Philistines

*The Egyptians coined the name 'Sea Peoples' for the loose confederation of diverse peoples who wreaked havoc along the shores of the eastern Mediterranean during the final centuries of the 2nd millennium BC. These people, with their military prowess on land and sea, destroyed numerous cities throughout the region, twice threatened the Egyptian heartlands and crushed the Hittite empire.*

*" ... scenes on the funerary temple show the sea peoples in boats and also moving on land in oxcarts with women, children, and their possessions. They were dragged in, enclosed, and prostrated on the beach, killed and made into heaps from tail to head. Their ships and their goods were as if fallen into the water. "*

Inscription from the tomb of Ramesses III on the defeat of the Sea Peoples

Despite their military accomplishment, little is known about the tribes that made up the Sea Peoples. Information about them survives mainly in Egyptian texts and images, although texts unearthed at Byblos, Tyre and other ancient Middle Eastern sites also provide important corroborative evidence. The names of the individual tribes are unfamiliar to most of us, and their identification and precise origins remain tentative. Despite their countless victories – many of which resulted in the collapse of local and regional political power structures – the Sea Peoples offered no monumental power structure of their own. They replaced kingdoms and empires with much smaller culturally distinct territories. Perhaps the best known and among the longest lasting of these was Philistia, the kingdom of the Philistines. This tribe – typically referred to as the 'Peleset' – were based along the narrow strip of coastline between Canaan and the Mediterranean Sea. The term 'Palestine' comes from the word Philistine.

## Migration to the Mediterranean

It is generally agreed that crop failure and famine drove large numbers of displaced people from central and eastern Europe southwards into Asia Minor, the Mediterranean islands, the northern coast of Africa and the eastern shores of the Mediterranean Sea. This mass migration began in earnest in the late 13th century BC, and accounts of the destruction of cities all over the region continue until *c.* 1150 BC and beyond.

Cities and towns throughout the Mediterranean islands were among the first to feel the effects of these peoples. The earliest detailed descriptions of them, however, come from Egyptian sources, which initially mention the various tribes both separately and as a collective threat, and subsequently outline large-scale military campaigns against them during the reigns of Merneptah (1236-23 BC) and Ramesses III (*c.* 1198-66).

Although the Egyptians, through careful strategy and a degree of luck, were able to repulse the Sea Peoples active around the Nile Delta, their neighbours to the north were less fortunate. The Hittite empire in Anatolia and northeastern Syria – already threatened by weak leadership and internal warfare – was crushed by the onslaught of various tribes (among them the Lukka and the

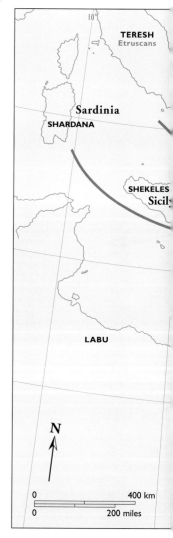

Denyen), only to be occupied soon after by the Phrygians from Thrace who would control central Anatolia by 800 BC. City-states and kingdoms along the eastern coast of the Mediterranean also suffered from the actions of the Sea Peoples; the ancient cities of Ugarit, Aleppo and Hazor were among those destroyed.

The Philistine kingdom consisted of five largely independent city-states: Gaza, Ashkelon, Ashdod, Gath and Ekron. The Philistines set their sights on southern Canaan at much the same time as the Israelites, who planned to enter Canaan from the east. The Philistines had numerous advantages, including their ability to manufacture iron weapons and their dominance and control of the coastal trading ports. The Israelites held the central hills of southern Canaan, while the Philistines controlled the coast. Armed conflict between the two expansonist powers to secure dominance of the region was inevitable.

A Theban relief sculpture shows scenes from a naval battle between the Philistines, who are wearing feather hats, and the Egyptians.

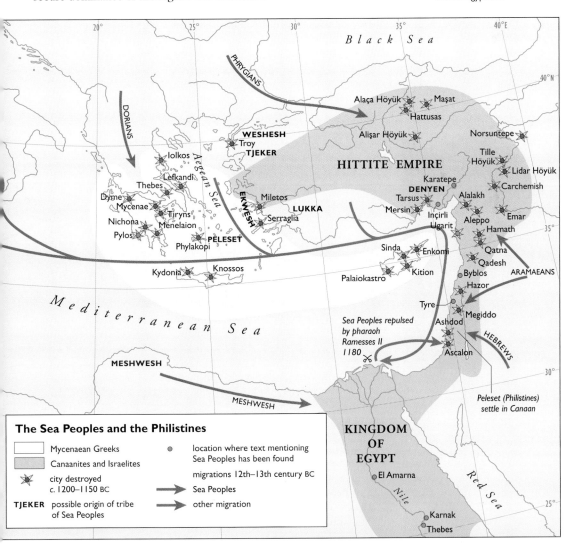

## The Sea Peoples and the Philistines

- ☐ Mycenaean Greeks
- ▨ Canaanites and Israelites
- ✹ city destroyed c. 1200–1150 BC
- **TJEKER** possible origin of tribe of Sea Peoples
- ● location where text mentioning Sea Peoples has been found
- migrations 12th–13th century BC
- → Sea Peoples
- → other migration

# Tribal Divisions in the Age of the Judges

*The final centuries of the 2nd millennium BC were a time of great political and cultural upheaval in Canaan. The Philistines had firm control of their territory along the southern coast, and their attempts to expand into the southern half of Canaan threatened the plans of the Israelites to rule over their 'Promised Land'.*

*" And Samson said, 'With the jawbone of an ass I have thrashed them; with the jawbone of an ass I have struck down a thousand men.' "*

Judges 15.16

Other surrounding kingdoms, such as Moab, Edom, Ammon and Aram, effectively boxed in the Israelites, at times posing military threats and certainly offering little support against the indomitable Philistine armies. Canaanite strongholds remained throughout the region, and even as Israelite control over the territory strengthened, the Canaanite culture – however broadly defined – appears to have been favoured by the new arrivals.

### Judges as Role Models

The Book of Judges was probably written around the mid-11th century BC, just as the tribal kingdoms of Israel consolidated their power and unified in a monarchy under King David. The book tells of 300 years of rule within the various 'kingdoms' by judges, mostly men who were expected to lead by moral and religious example. If the 300-year span is taken literally, it is difficult to make the numbers fit unless one opts for the Early Exodus date of 15th century BC. Proponents of the Late Exodus date (*c.* 1250 BC) prefer to see the period of the Judges as lasting only a little more than a century and consider the various judges' terms as overlapping, which is not implausible as they are each linked with different areas. Much of the text focuses on the military defeats and other misfortunes of the Israelites as they turn their backs on their own traditions and adopt Canaanite cultural and religious practices. The unnamed author views success as possible only once the Israelites have returned to their Hebrew God and his commandments.

### From Saul to King David

Constant pressure from the Philistines, the Canaanites and other neighbouring peoples served to unite the various tribes of Israel in their struggle against their common enemies. A series of defeats at the hands of the Philistines resulted in the capture by the Philistines of the Ark of the Covenant, long sacred to the Israelites, at the battle of Ebenezer (modern Izbet Sartah) around 1050 BC. The Ark was apparently returned to the Israelites after several months of plagues and other disasters that followed its journey throughout Philistia.

Shortly after this episode, the Israelites forced the judge Samuel to select and anoint a single king to lead the tribes of Israel. Accounts differ as to the details of the story, but Saul, a tall, young man from the tribe of Benjamin, was chosen and he appears to have enjoyed some initial success against the Amalekites (to the south) and the mighty Philistines. Saul and his sons were killed at the battle of Jezreel while attempting to defend an important trade route against the Philistines. The young David – well known as the small boy who felled the Philistine warrior Goliath with a single shot from his sling – emerged as Saul's successor and under his rule Saul's fledgling kingdom was united and Israel's hold over central Canaan – from the Negev to the northern city of Dan – assured.

Tell Dan, which lies close to the border with Lebanon, is identified with the tribe of Dan and was the northernmost city in the Kingdom of Israel. A fragment of a stele found there includes letters thought to refer to the House of David, making it the earliest reference to David, though this is disputed.

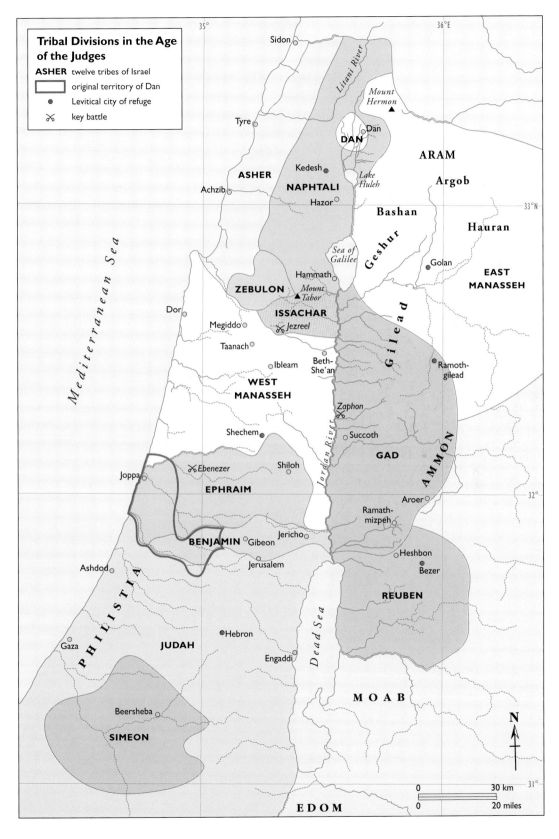

**Tribal Divisions in the Age of the Judges**

ASHER  twelve tribes of Israel

⬜  original territory of Dan

●  Levitical city of refuge

✂  key battle

Sidon

Litani River

Tyre

Achzib

ASHER

Kedesh

NAPHTALI

Hazor

Lake Huleh

Mount Hermon

Dan

DAN

ARAM

Argob

Bashan

Hauran

Sea of Galilee

Geshur

Golan

EAST MANASSEH

Hammath

ZEBULON

Mount Tabor

ISSACHAR

Jezreel

Gilead

Dor

Megiddo

Taanach

Ibleam

Beth-She'an

Ramoth-gilead

WEST MANASSEH

Zaphon

Shechem

Succoth

GAD

AMMON

Joppa

Ebenezer

Shiloh

EPHRAIM

Jordan River

Aroer

BENJAMIN

Gibeon

Jericho

Ramath-mizpeh

Ashdod

Jerusalem

Heshbon

Bezer

REUBEN

PHILISTIA

Hebron

JUDAH

Gaza

Engaddi

Dead Sea

MOAB

Beersheba

SIMEON

Mediterranean Sea

EDOM

N

0        30 km

0        20 miles

35°   36°E

33°N

32°

31°

49

# The Kingdom of Saul

*Saul's kingdom encompassed much of the territory divided between the twelve tribes of Israel as described in the second half of the Book of Joshua. The Israelites ruled almost all of the central hills of Canaan, from Beersheba in the south to the northern city of Dan.*

The David Spring is one of four springs that feed into Engaddi, an oasis lying on the eastern edge of the Judean Desert and the western shore of the Dead Sea. The oasis is famed for its vineyards and, according to biblical tradition, is where the future king David hid from Saul.

There is some dispute, however, as to Israel's sovereignty over the area assigned to the tribe of Manasseh in the desert to the east of the River Jordan. Jerusalem, the area around Beth-she'an and a strip of land running from Mount Gilboa to the Mediterranean coast remained in Canaanite hands. Crucially, Saul controlled none of the area's Mediterranean coastline, which was commanded by the Philistines in the south and the Phoenicians in the north. Lack of access to the sea prevented the Israelites from developing the lucrative trading connections so highly prized by empires and kingdoms situated along the Mediterranean coasts.

Saul ruled from his home town of Gibeah (modern Tell al-Ful) in the lands of the Benjaminites, just north of Jerusalem. Previously, according to the Bible, Gibeah had been the scene of the devastating defeat of the Benjaminites by the united forces of the other tribes of Israel. This attack followed the killing of a Levite's concubine by the Benjaminite citizens of Gibeah. Archaeological finds on the site indicate occupation during the first half of the 2nd millennium BC, with new fortifications added around 1200 BC, the time of the Israelite 'conquest' of Canaan. A citadel was erected sometime just before 1000 BC and this presumably was Saul's official seat; excavations show that this complex was destroyed soon after its completion, but rebuilt along the same lines almost immediately. This may have occurred as a result of Saul's death and the victorious Philistines gaining temporary control. Gibeah was destroyed around 70 AD during the First Jewish Revolt against Roman rule over Judea.

### Evidence for Saul's Reign

The Bible is the only surviving documentary source for Saul's life and specific details about his kingdom. Archaeological evidence, particularly from the Benjaminite territory just north of Jerusalem, strongly suggests heavy settlement during the years running up to 1000 BC, but it has yet to provide conclusive evidence of Saul's reign over the Israelites. Gibeah, for example, appears to have been expanded and refortified in the late 11th century BC, but other locations mentioned in biblical accounts of Saul's exploits have yet to be identified conclusively, such as Jabesh-Gilead (probably modern Tell Abu al-Kharaz), and so it becomes difficult to reconstruct the history of the Israelites under Saul independently. Recent excavations at Beth-she'an - at which the bodies of Saul and his sons were hung following their deaths defending Mount Gilboa from the Philistines - unearthed no evidence of long-term Philistine occupation of this site during the 11th century BC, casting some doubt on the biblical account of events following Saul's death. Remains at sites such as Aphek in Philistia show increasing Israelite presence during the 11th and 10th centuries BC and perhaps support the notion that, despite frequent and at times large-scale skirmishes with the Philistines and other neighbouring peoples, the Israelites at least in part (and perhaps primarily) established dominance in the region through cultural and social assimilation and not simply through the military campaigns of warrior kings, such as the biblical Saul and David.

*" Saul had the trumpet sounded throughout the country, and the whole of Israel heard the news: Saul has smashed the Philistine ptllar... "*

I Samuel 13.3–4

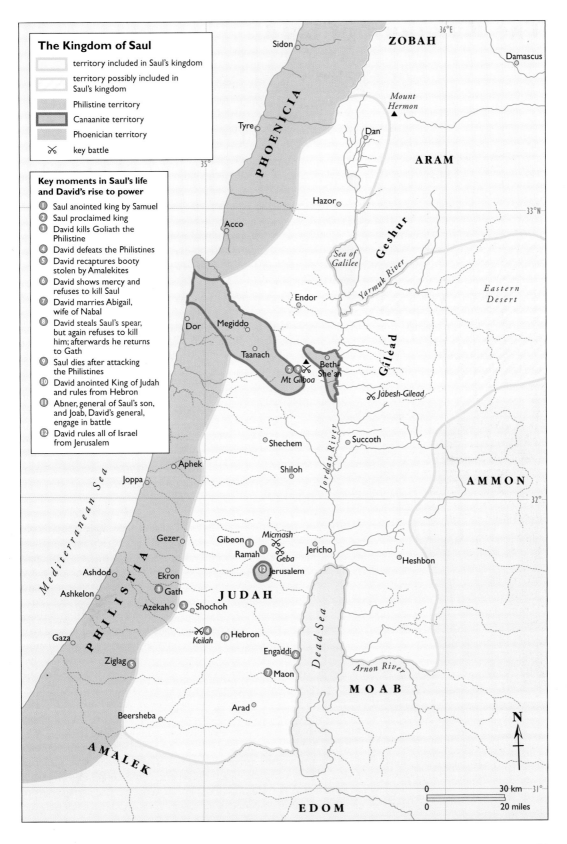

## The Kingdom of Saul

- territory included in Saul's kingdom
- territory possibly included in Saul's kingdom
- Philistine territory
- Canaanite territory
- Phoenician territory
- ✂ key battle

**Key moments in Saul's life and David's rise to power**

1. Saul anointed king by Samuel
2. Saul proclaimed king
3. David kills Goliath the Philistine
4. David defeats the Philistines
5. David recaptures booty stolen by Amalekites
6. David shows mercy and refuses to kill Saul
7. David marries Abigail, wife of Nabal
8. David steals Saul's spear, but again refuses to kill him; afterwards he returns to Gath
9. Saul dies after attacking the Philistines
10. David anointed King of Judah and rules from Hebron
11. Abner, general of Saul's son, and Joab, David's general, engage in battle
12. David rules all of Israel from Jerusalem

# The Kingdom of David

*"And David danced whirling around before Yahweh with all his might, wearing a linen loincloth around him. Thus David and the House of Israel brought up the Ark of Yahweh with acclaim and the sound of the horn."*

2 Samuel 6.14–15

***David, the youngest son of Jesse, came from Bethlehem in Judah. He was anointed as Saul's successor by the judge Samuel when he was still a young man. Over time the mentally unstable Saul (and his sons) grew jealous of David, forcing him to spend much of his time in hiding, often across the border in the lands controlled by the Philistines.***

On Saul's death David was crowned king of his native Judah and, following the death of Saul's sole surviving son, the remaining tribes of Israel also recognized David as their ruler. Initially David ruled from Hebron in Judah, but after several years he moved his capital to Jerusalem, which he captured from the Jebusites. Jerusalem soon became a political power base and, after David's relocation of the sacred Ark of the Covenant to his new capital city, a cultic centre for all of the tribes of Israel. David's move to Jerusalem is dated to *c.* 1000 BC; he ruled over Israel and many neighbouring territories until his death in *c.* 962.

## The House of David

David's story and the lines of succession that he founded appear in the biblical books of Samuel, Kings and Chronicles, the first two probably written within two centuries of David's death, while Chronicles was a later redaction of the two earlier versions. For Jews, Christians and Muslims, David personifies ideal kingship, and his name occurs in the Bible more often than any other except Jesus. For historians, the biblical narrative of David's life and his descendants represents the earliest conscious historiographical text written in the Western world.

Most scholars accept that the historical chronology presented in the Bible is more or less accurate from the reign of David, although examples of external documentary evidence are few, and these far from conclusive. The most generally accepted reference to the 'House of David' as the royal lineage of the rulers of Israel occurs in the Tell Dan Stele found in northern Israel in the early 1990s. Probably erected by an Aramean king of Damascus to commemorate his victory over the Israelites, the stele dates to the 9th century BC and includes a phrase that can be read as the 'House of David'; elsewhere the inscription mentions Israel as a nation. The stele's incomplete state means that these references are inconclusive, and there are those who argue strongly for alternative readings. Other possible references to David in the centuries immediately following his life are at least as unreliable as that on the Tell Dan Stele.

The biblical account of David's activities is extremely detailed, but so far has not been confirmed by independent archaeological evidence. The Bible states that David conquered Jerusalem and pushed far into Philistia, bringing the Philistines into vassalage and thereby gaining control of almost the whole Mediterranean coast from Egypt as far north as the Phoenician city of Tyre. The biblical account suggests that David and his army were victorious over all the kingdoms bordering Israel, among them Moab, Aram, Ammon and Edom, but in fact archaeologists continue to search for firm evidence of any aspect of King David's reign.

Sculpture of Moses, King David (centre) and a prophet. David, shown here as an older man, was a popular subject in medieval and Renaissance art.

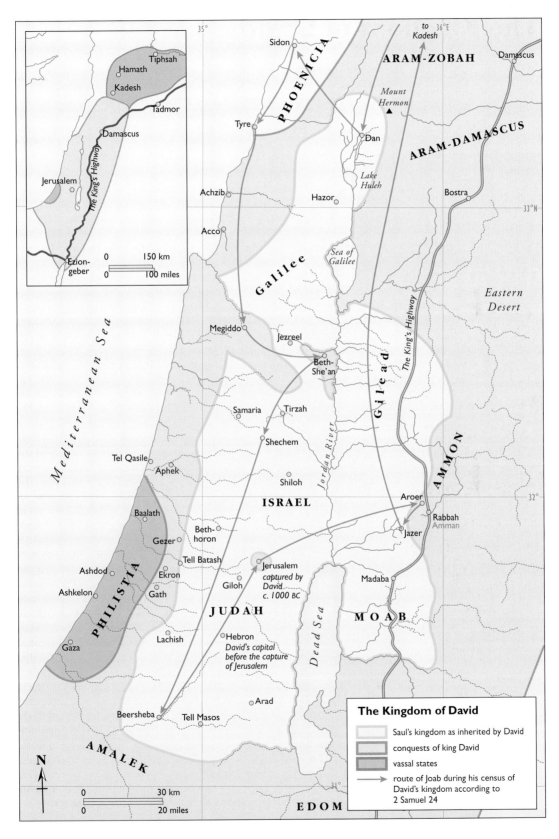

Inset map labels:
Tiphsah
Hamath
Kadesh
Tadmor
Damascus
Jerusalem
Ezion-geber
The King's Highway
0 — 150 km
0 — 100 miles

Main map labels:
Sidon
PHOENICIA
to Kadesh
ARAM-ZOBAH
Damascus
Mount Hermon
ARAM-DAMASCUS
Tyre
Dan
Achzib
Lake Huleh
Hazor
Bostra
Acco
Sea of Galilee
Galilee
Eastern Desert
Megiddo
Jezreel
Beth-She'an
Samaria
Tirzah
Gilead
The King's Highway
Mediterranean Sea
Shechem
Jordan River
Tel Qasile
Aphek
Shiloh
AMMON
ISRAEL
Aroer
Baalath
Rabbah
Amman
Beth-horon
Jazer
Gezer
Tell Batash
Ashdod
Ekron
Giloh
Jerusalem
captured by David
c. 1000 BC
Madaba
Ashkelon
Gath
PHILISTIA
JUDAH
Dead Sea
MOAB
Gaza
Lachish
Hebron
David's capital before the capture of Jerusalem
Arad
Beersheba
Tell Masos
AMALEK
N
0 — 30 km
0 — 20 miles
EDOM

**The Kingdom of David**

Saul's kingdom as inherited by David
conquests of king David
vassal states
route of Joab during his census of David's kingdom according to 2 Samuel 24

53

# The Kingdom of Solomon

*By David's death in c. 962 BC, Israel was a united nation, with its neighbours subdued or befriended, and with a firm grip on the crucial trading nexus between Egypt, Mesopotamia and Anatolia. David's final years as king were plagued by family infighting and courtly intrigues concerning his successor.*

An Ethiopian painting showing a meeting between Solomon and the Queen of Sheba. Ethiopian Christians believe that Sheba was an Ethiopian queen (Makeda or Saba) who returned from a visit to Solomon's court in Jerusalem bearing his son who became the first king of Ethiopia, Menelik I. The biblical account of Sheba's visit to Solomon is in I Kings 10.1–10.

Solomon, David's son by the beautiful Bathsheba, was eventually chosen as king, and the Bible tells us that Solomon became the wisest and most successful of Israel's rulers. Solomon ruthlessly quelled potential rebellions among neighbouring peoples and built on his father's friendship with the seafaring Phoenicians to expand Israel's trading capabilities. He kept a large standing army, courted kingdoms wealthy in exportable luxuries and ensured that Israel maintained a technological advantage by mastering the techniques of mining and metal refining. He is also famed for his building campaigns. Solomon divided Israel into twelve tax districts – each to support his household for one month every year. His avoidance of the traditional tribal boundaries helped foster 'national' unity and attested to his political as well as financial acumen. To cement tribal and regional unity, Solomon reputedly took 700 wives and 300 concubines, among them the daughter of an Egyptian pharaoh (his powerful neighbour to the south) and perhaps even the Queen of Sheba, a wealthy kingdom in Arabia.

### The Evidence for Solomon's Reign

As with David's reign, contemporary documentary and archaeological sources independent of the Bible have yielded little evidence of the wealth and fame of such a great ruler. Much work has still to be done, of course, but many of the excavated remains once attributed to Solomon's great building operations have been scientifically shown to post-date Solomon's reign by as much as two centuries; the remains at Gezer and Megiddo are among these.

Surviving contemporary documents and inscriptions are also eerily silent. The most relevant is perhaps a fragmentary inscription describing the occupation of Megiddo by the Egyptian ruler Shoshenq I (the biblical Shishak). This inscription does not mention Solomon by name, but it does offer external proof that this pharaoh did raze the Israelite city as the Bible states. However, it has been interpreted by some as proof of the veracity of the whole of Solomon's story. Solomon's mines, praised for the high quality of their products, have long been placed in the Timna valley in the Negev, but these too have been subjected to rigorous archaeological attention and shown to reflect Egyptian mining techniques and later, post-Solomonic occupational patterns.

Many scholars continue to point to the large building complexes such as that at Megiddo as proof of Solomon's activities, arguing that radio-carbon dating is not always accurate and that it is logical that subsequent rulers merely refurbished Solomon's earlier constructions. Certainly the many centuries of continuous occupation and Solomon's attention to sites that were already flourishing make the task of sifting through surviving remains challenging. Biblical references to Israel and its rulers in the second quarter of the 1st millennium BC marry so well with surviving documentary evidence from neighbouring cultures that it is tempting to extrapolate backwards and to see the stories of David and Solomon as essentially correct. Until the emergence of more conclusive evidence for these great rulers, however, it seems best to tread cautiously.

*"Solomon was seated upon the throne of David, and his sovereignty was firmly established."*

I Kings 2.12

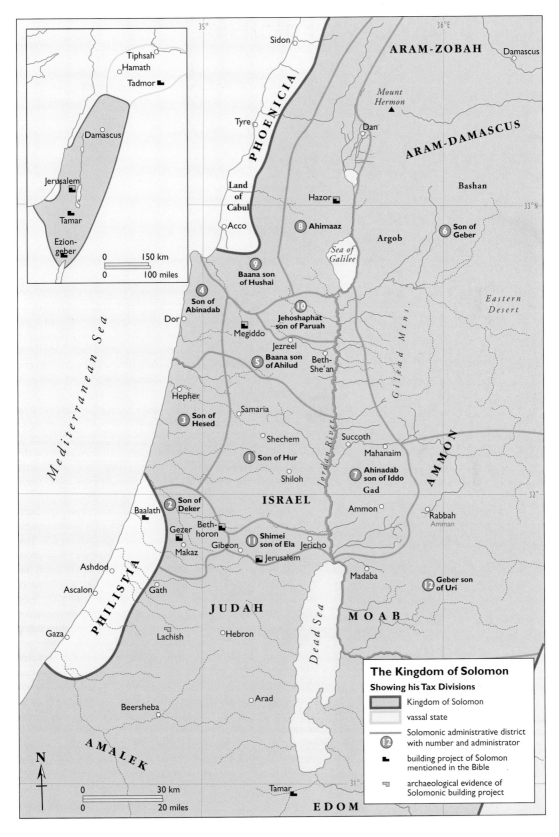

Tiphsah
Hamath
Tadmor

Damascus

Jerusalem
Tamar
Ezion-geber

0    150 km
0    100 miles

Sidon
ARAM-ZOBAH
Damascus

Mount Hermon

Tyre
PHOENICIA
Dan
ARAM-DAMASCUS

Land of Cabul
Hazor
Bashan

Acco
⑧ Ahimaaz
Sea of Galilee
Argob
⑥ Son of Geber

⑨ Baana son of Hushai
Eastern Desert

④ Son of Abinadab
⑩ Jehoshaphat son of Paruah
Dor
Megiddo
Jezreel

⑤ Baana son of Ahilud
Beth-She'an

Hepher

③ Son of Hesed
Samaria

Shechem
Succoth
Mahanaim

① Son of Hur
⑦ Ahinadab son of Iddo
Gad
AMMON

Shiloh

② Son of Deker
ISRAEL
Ammon
Rabbah
Amman

Baalath
Gezer
Beth-horon
Makaz
Gibeon
① Shimei son of Ela
Jericho
Jerusalem

Ashdod
Madaba
⑫ Geber son of Uri

Ascalon
Gath

PHILISTIA
JUDAH
MOAB

Gaza
Lachish
Hebron

Beersheba
Arad

**The Kingdom of Solomon**
**Showing his Tax Divisions**

Kingdom of Solomon
vassal state
Solomonic administrative district with number and administrator ⑫
building project of Solomon mentioned in the Bible
archaeological evidence of Solomonic building project

N

0    30 km
0    20 miles

AMALEK
Tamar
EDOM

Mediterranean Sea
Jordan River
Gilead Mtns.
Dead Sea

# Old Testament Jerusalem

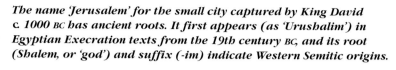

*The name 'Jerusalem' for the small city captured by King David c. 1000 BC has ancient roots. It first appears (as 'Urushalim') in Egyptian Execration texts from the 19th century BC, and its root (Shalem, or 'god') and suffix (-im) indicate Western Semitic origins.*

> *"David and his men marched on Jerusalem against the Jebusites living there. They said to David, 'You will not get in here. The blind and the lame will hold you off.'... But David captured the fortress of Zion, that is, the citadel of David."*
>
> 2 Samuel 5.6-7

Numerous archaeological finds indicate continuous settlement from *c.* 3000 BC, although the Egyptians, who held the city throughout the first half of the 2nd millennium BC, emerge as the earliest known rulers. The city was controlled by various tribes in the years before David's conquest, but by 1000 BC it was in the hands of the Jebusites, a Canaanite people who may be connected to the Hittites or the Amorites.

## The City of David

The Bible recounts that following David's establishment of Jerusalem (renamed the City of David) as both his seat of power and the centre of the cult of Yahweh, the Jewish God, Israel's new king expanded the ancient settlement, building a large palace and a special area for the Ark of the Covenant, sacred to the Israelites. Under David's successor, Solomon, building activities in Jerusalem were stepped up. With timber and engineers on loan from Hiram, the Phoenician king of Tyre, Solomon erected a new palace and a large temple to house the Ark. Solomon extended the city, rebuilding the walls to enclose the ancient city as well as the new temple precinct to the north. In the centuries following Solomon's death (*c.* 922 BC) Jerusalem was conquered by the Egyptians, the Philistines, the Assyrians, the Babylonians and the Persians, among others. Following the takeover of the region by Cyrus II of Persia, Jerusalem was once again rebuilt and the Temple restored (*c.* 515 BC).

This complex history of continuous occupation and repeated destruction and rebuilding, combined with Jerusalem's perilous setting atop a series of steep slopes, makes the site far from ideal for systematic archaeological excavation. The special significance of this site for Jews, Christians and Muslims alike has made the situation even worse, attracting the interest of excavators – amateur and professional – from the earliest days of archaeology of the Holy Land. The first excavation in Jerusalem (and the earliest in Palestine) was conducted by the Frenchman Louis de Saulcy in 1863. Although his work focused on the Tomb of the Kings in the ancient city, most excavations since have centred on the City of David and the Temple Mount. The dense occupation of the site meant that many of the earlier campaigns involved the digging of underground tunnels, a practice that has resulted in loss of data and disturbance of chronological strata.

Dame Kathleen Kenyon, the British archaeologist who excavated in Jerusalem during the 1960s, was instrumental in the establishment of modern archaeological practices there. Her work resulted in the first complete stratigraphic chronology of the ancient site. She also spent time excavating outside the city walls, and her work, although increasingly contested in the light of more recent finds and improved scientific testing, continues to serve as the basis for archaeological work in the area. Recently an Israeli archaeologist, Eilat Mazar, using

The Pool of Siloam in Jerusalem. The pool, mentioned in the Bible, acted as a cistern for the City of David. The water came from the Gihon spring in the Kidron valley.

Kenyon's earlier discoveries, has located what she believes to have been the palace constructed by King David shortly after 1000 BC. This find remains hotly contested by experts all over the world, but should she be proven correct her discovery would provide the first concrete evidence for the reigns of David and Solomon as outlined in the Bible.

Remains of the ancient fortified walls in Jerusalem. The City of David, the site of biblical Jerusalem, lies outside the present Old City walls to the southeast.

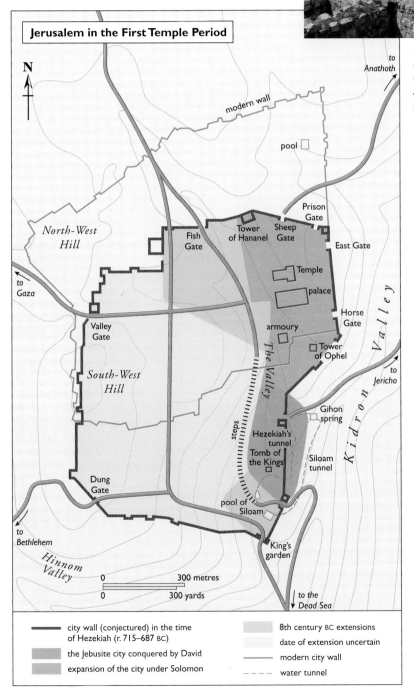

## Jerusalem in the First Temple Period

N

to Anathoth

modern wall

pool

Prison Gate

North-West Hill

Fish Gate

Tower of Hananel

Sheep Gate

East Gate

Temple

palace

to Gaza

Valley Gate

armoury

Horse Gate

South-West Hill

Tower of Ophel

The Valley

to Jericho

steps

Gihon spring

Hezekiah's tunnel

Tomb of the Kings

Siloam tunnel

Kidron Valley

Dung Gate

pool of Siloam

to Bethlehem

King's garden

Hinnom Valley

| 0 | 300 metres |
| 0 | 300 yards |

to the Dead Sea

city wall (conjectured) in the time of Hezekiah (r. 715–687 BC)

the Jebusite city conquered by David

expansion of the city under Solomon

8th century BC extensions

date of extension uncertain

modern city wall

water tunnel

# The Temple

*"In the 480th year after the Israelites came out of the land of Egypt, in the fourth year of Solomon's reign over Israel, in the month of Ziv, which is the second month, he began to build the Temple."*

I Kings 6.1

**At the command of his father, King David, King Solomon undertook to build a temple to house the Ark of the Covenant. Chapters 28 and 29 of the first Book of Chronicles outline David's plans and preparations for the building of the Temple and here it is made clear that God had chosen Solomon, and not David, as its builder.**

According to the Bible, Solomon began to build the Temple 'in the second month of his fourth year as king' (II Chronicles 3:2; I Kings 6:1), and most scholars agree that this means that the Temple was begun *c.* 958 BC. The acceptance of this dating has serious implications for the dates of earlier events in the biblical saga of the Israelites, especially the date of the Exodus, when the Israelites escaped bondage in Egypt and returned to Canaan. The Bible states that this took place 480 years before Solomon's Temple was begun (I Kings 6:1). II Chronicles also tells of the preparations for the building campaign, including Solomon's negotiations with King Hiram of Tyre for materials and craftsmen, and the actual construction and furnishing of the complex. This passage also includes a detailed description of the Temple complete with measurements.

The Temple was to be built on a flat surface on top of Mount Moriah to the north of the Jebusite city. It was to consist of a rectangular building – 27 metres long x 9 metres wide (88 x 29 ft) – with an entrance porch, antechamber and sanctuary. The latter was referred to as the Holy of Holies and would house the sacred Ark of the Covenant. The Temple sat within an inner courtyard, for use by the priests, which in turn sat within a second larger courtyard. Precious materials, notably gold and rich fabrics, were used in the lavishly decorated interior with its soaring ceilings and panelled and gilded walls. The entrance to the Temple was flanked by two bronze columns. Each stood 15.5 metres (51 ft) tall and was decorated with ornate capitals and incised patterns. A large bronze altar sat in front of the Temple and a huge bronze tub (for ritual washing by the

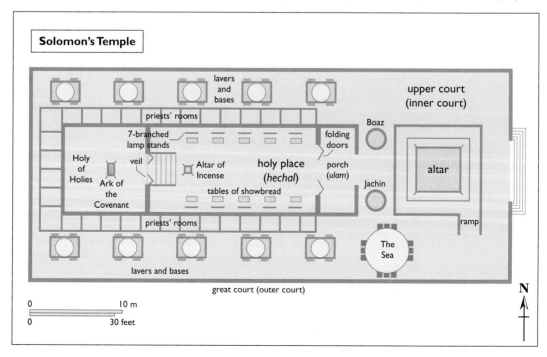

Solomon's Temple

lavers and bases

upper court (inner court)

priests' rooms

Boaz

7-branched lamp stands

folding doors

Holy of Holies

veil

Altar of Incense

holy place (hechal)

porch (ulam)

Jachin

altar

Ark of the Covenant

tables of showbread

priests' rooms

lavers and bases

The Sea

ramp

great court (outer court)

N

0    10 m
0    30 feet

priests) also occupied this space. Ten smaller basins for use during animal sacrifices lined the two long sides of the Temple. Further details of specific furnishings are also given.

Solomon's Temple was destroyed by Nebuchadnezzar II of Babylonia in c. 586 BC and was rebuilt in the late 6th century BC under the auspices of the Persian ruler Cyrus II. During this period the tablets inscribed with the Ten Commandments and contained within the Ark of the Covenant disappeared; from this time the Holy of Holies, the innermost sanctum of the Temple, remained empty. The Temple sustained much damage during the Hellenistic and imperial Roman periods and was again rebuilt under Herod the Great in the decades to either side of the birth of Jesus. It was again destroyed in 70 AD, and by the late 7th century AD the Temple Mount was in the hands of the Muslims. The Dome of the Rock, an Islamic shrine that presently occupies the site, was erected c. 690 AD by the Umayyad Caliph Abd el-Malik, although its iconic golden dome is a modern addition (the original was lead). The al-Aqsa mosque,

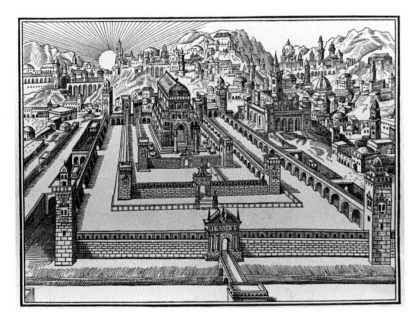

Solomon's Temple in Jerusalem from a 17th-century woodcut. Illustrations and reconstructions of the Temple have been made using the detailed descriptions in the Bible. Stone and cedar transported from Lebanon were used to build the Temple.

situated about 200 metres (656 ft) to the south of the Dome within the original Temple complex, was built between 705 and 715 AD, making it the earliest dated mosque in Palestine. The original structure of al-Aqsa, which commemorated Muhammad's legendary 'Night Journey', was destroyed in the 8th century AD by an earthquake, and a good deal of the present structure dates from the 12th century. In July 1099 the whole of the Temple Mount came under Crusader control. The Crusaders consecrated al-Aqsa and the Dome as churches, but left the architecture largely intact. Al-Aqsa initially became the palace of the Latin kings of Jerusalem, then from 1119 until 1187 the headquarters of the Knights Templar. The Dome of the Rock became an Augustinian priory. Both were revered by Latin pilgrims for their associations with the Jewish Temple.

No archaeological remains of Solomon's Temple have come to light; however, this is hardly surprising given the later history of the site and its probable location beneath the Dome of the Rock, one of the most important pilgrimage sites in the Islamic world. Jewish tradition still demands that three times per day all Jews should pray for the restoration of the Temple.

# Tyre and the Phoenicians

*The ancient land of Phoenicia occupied a narrow strip of coastline stretching from the river Eleutherus (the Orontes) in the north to Mount Carmel in the south. Today its territory is part of Israel, Lebanon and the westernmost section of Syria.*

Pendant of a Phoenician ship. The Phoenicians were seafarers renowned for their shipbuilding skills. Traders rather than warriors, they introduced the 'round boat', a ship that depended on sails rather than oars and had a much larger cargo space than the narrow galleys.

Its earliest inhabitants, whose origins are unknown, called themselves Canaanites. Phoenicia is a later term most likely derived from the Greek *phoînos* meaning blood-red, and no doubt referring to the precious purple dye for which the region was famous. Phoenicia as a whole appears to have been settled from about 3000 BC, although several specific sites were occupied long before this date, and, like Philistia, its neighbour to the south, Phoenicia was almost certainly 'invaded' by the Sea Peoples late in the 2nd millennium BC.

The native culture was urban in nature, centring on the burgeoning seaports that supported overseas trade, the mainstay of Phoenicia's economy. Major Phoenician cities included Byblos (modern Jubayl; settled by 8000 BC and the site of the earliest surviving examples of the Phoenician alphabet), Berytus (modern Beirut), Sidon and Tyre. These and other Phoenician cities were typically ruled by separate 'kings' and together they are best viewed as a loose confederation of culturally related populations rather than as a politically and militarily united kingdom. During the first half of the 1st millennium BC, the Phoenicians founded numerous colonies and trading centres throughout

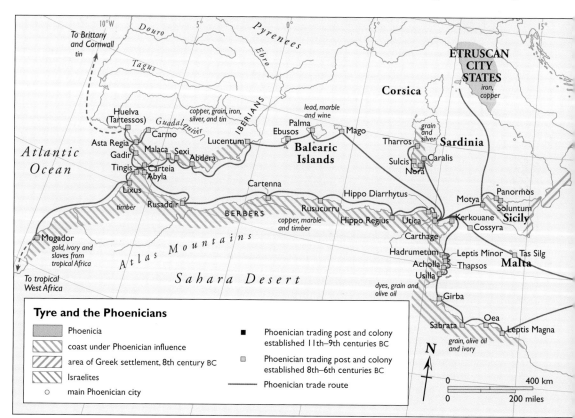

**Tyre and the Phoenicians**

- Phoenicia
- coast under Phoenician influence
- area of Greek settlement, 8th century BC
- Israelites
- ○ main Phoenician city
- ■ Phoenician trading post and colony established 11th–9th centuries BC
- ▫ Phoenician trading post and colony established 8th–6th centuries BC
- — Phoenician trade route

the Mediterranean. Founded initially as small trading bases, many of these, most notably Carthage on the coast of North Africa, developed into prosperous and politically powerful ports.

For much of its early history Phoenicia was under Egyptian control, no doubt benefiting from the lucrative trading opportunities and military protection that this afforded. Byblos was ruled by the Egyptians from just after 2000 BC, and Phoenician cities are mentioned in the el-Amarna letters (c. 1400 BC). During this time the Phoenicians became highly respected merchants and shipbuilders, and increasingly well-known for their vast naval fleets and luxury exports, in particular timber, glassware, and the 'royal' purple dye so prized by rulers everywhere. Egyptian influence in Phoenicia weakened from the 14th century BC, and, after a few centuries of relative independence, Phoenicia fell under Assyrian domination. In 538 BC the region was conquered by the Persians and in 332 BC Alexander the Great claimed it for his Macedonian empire. After brief spells of Egyptian and Seleucid domination, Phoenicia was annexed to Rome in 65 AD.

Several Phoenician cities, most notably Sidon and Tyre, retained much of their independence throughout the numerous political upheavals. Sidon was founded in the 3rd millennium BC. Excavations, presently conducted by a team from the British Museum, have yielded evidence of permanent settlement from Sidon's foundation and many finds of imported wares from Greece, Egypt and elsewhere attest to Sidon's importance as a trading centre throughout the 1st millennium BC. The city of Tyre, like Sidon, is mentioned frequently in the Bible. King Hiram of Tyre, who reigned from 969 to 936 BC, was a valued ally of the biblical kings David and Solomon, supplying materials and expert craftsmen for Solomon's Temple in Jerusalem and helping the Israelites to develop maritime trading links with other Mediterranean cultures.

*"This gateway and doors did I make in fulfilment of [my vow]. I built it in the 180th year of the Lord of Kings, and in the 143rd year of the people of Tyre, that it might be to me a memorial and for a good name beneath the feet of my lord, Baal-Shamaôm, for ever. May he bless me."*

Inscription at Um al-Amawid

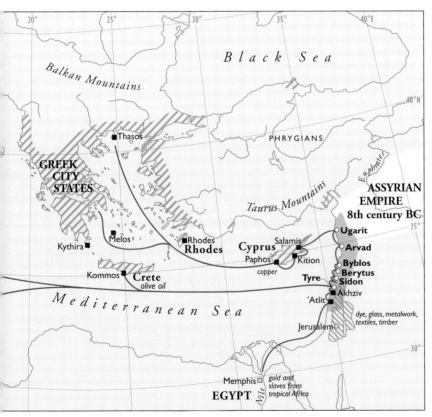

# The Divided Monarchy

*On Solomon's death in 922 BC, his son Rehoboam (r. 922–911 BC) came to the throne. Heavy tax and labour burdens enforced by Solomon had already caused social and political unrest. The new king's decision to increase these split the tribes of Judah and Benjamin in the south from the ten remaining tribes of Israel to the north.*

An Israelite fortress at Tell Arad, dating from the 8th to 7th centuries BC. The fort was built under the Divided Monarchy to guard the southern frontier of Judah.

The House of David retained control of the south, known as Judah, until it fell to the Babylonians in 586 BC, while Israel (or Ephraim) was ruled over by numerous short-lived dynasties until the region was conquered in 722 BC by the Assyrians.

The era of the Divided Monarchy has produced much archaeological evidence and many external documentary sources to support the biblical account of the history of ancient Israel and the surrounding kingdoms. This represents a radical shift from the isolated incidences of – often inconclusive – evidence generally used to substantiate events described in the earlier parts of the Bible. The Egyptians and the Babylonians are just two of the cultures from the region known for their meticulous record-keeping. They frequently mention the various rulers of Judah and Israel, along with their victories, defeats and changing allegiances, lending a credibility to the contemporary biblical accounts that few can question. The Moabite Stone, now in the Louvre in Paris, is one such document. Carved during the reign of the Moabite king Mesha in *c.* 850 BC, this commemorative stele tells of Moab's unsuccessful rebellion against Israel during the reign of King Omri. The Black Obelisk of Shalmaneser III, now in the British Museum in London, dates from only slightly later and records tributes paid to Assyria by Jehu, king of Israel (r. 842–814 BC).

### The Balance of Power

During the Divided Monarchy the balance of power between the two Israelite kingdoms and their neighbours shifted frequently. Essentially, however, the territories of Israel and Judah maintained the boundaries set by Solomon and David. Judah held Jerusalem and the lands to the south, while Israel occupied the coastal plain and the lands along the Jordan north to Mount Hermon. Jerusalem was the capital city of Judah throughout the Divided Monarchy. The Canaanite city of Shechem was the scene of the formal break between Judah and Israel, and served as the power base of the earliest kings of Israel. During the 9th century, Israel's capital was briefly relocated to Tirzah before King Omri (r. 882–871 BC) founded the city of Samaria (*c.* 880 BC), which served as Israel's capital until the kingdom fell to the Assyrians.

During the first half of the 1st millennium BC the tribes of Israel faced many enemies. Early on the Philistines were defeated and the Phoenicians befriended, but other neighbours continued to pose a danger. The first threat came from the Egyptians, with whom Jeroboam (r. 928–907 BC), eventually the first king of Israel, had sought refuge from Rehoboam after Solomon's death. Under Pharaoh Shoshenq I, Egyptian forces entered Judah and eventually headed north into Israel. Contemporary reliefs at Karnak celebrate Shoshenq's exploits in Palestine and there is evidence that Rehoboam fortified many cities in Judah to withstand the Egyptian invasion. The Egyptians sustained a presence in the region, but it was the Assyrians, with their stronghold in the Aramean city of Damascus, who posed the most serious threat to the people of Israel and Judah.

*"When all Israel heard that Jeroboam had returned, they summoned him to the assembly and made him king of all Israel; no one remained loyal to the House of David, except the tribe of Judah."*

I Kings 12.20

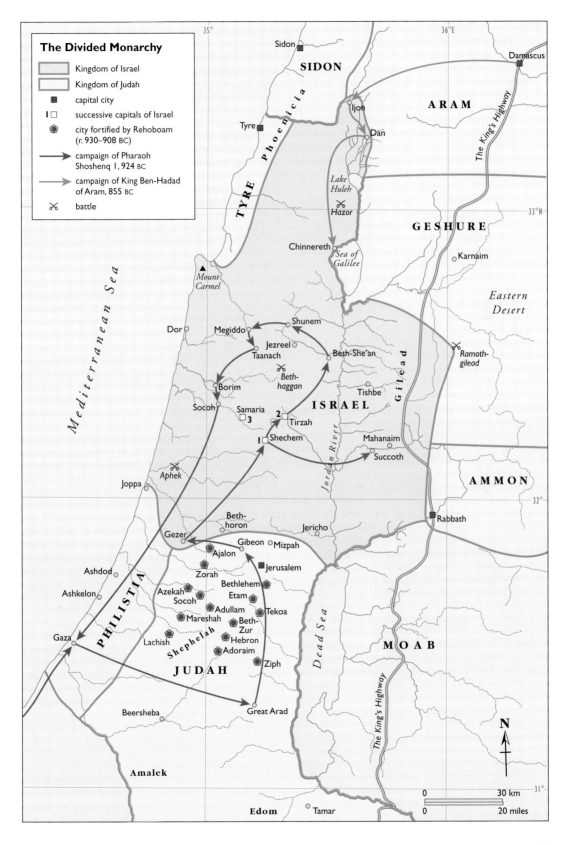

**The Divided Monarchy**

- Kingdom of Israel
- Kingdom of Judah
- ■ capital city
- I □ successive capitals of Israel
- ◉ city fortified by Rehoboam (r. 930–908 BC)
- ⟶ campaign of Pharaoh Shoshenq 1, 924 BC
- ⟶ campaign of King Ben-Hadad of Aram, 855 BC
- ✕ battle

Sidon

SIDON

Damascus

ARAM

Ijon

Tyre

Dan

TYRE

Phoenicia

The King's Highway

Lake Huleh

33°N

✕ Hazor

GESHURE

Chinnereth

Sea of Galilee

Karnaim

Eastern Desert

▲ Mount Carmel

Mediterranean Sea

Dor

Megiddo

Shunem

Jezreel

Taanach

Beth-She'an

Gilead

✕ Ramoth-gilead

Borim

✕ Beth-haggan

Tishbe

ISRAEL

Socoh

Samaria
□ 3

2 □ Tirzah

Mahanaim

Jordan River

I □ Shechem

Succoth

✕ Aphek

AMMON

Joppa

32°

Rabbath

Beth-horon

Gezer

Jericho

Gibeon

Mizpah

Ajalon

Jerusalem ■

Ashdod

Zorah

Bethlehem

Azekah

Etam

Ashkelon

Socoh

Adullam

Tekoa

Mareshah

Beth-Zur

Gaza

Lachish

Hebron

Adoraim

PHILISTIA

Shephelah

Ziph

Dead Sea

MOAB

JUDAH

Beersheba

Great Arad

The King's Highway

N

Amalek

31°

0       30 km

0       20 miles

Edom      ◉ Tamar

# Megiddo

*Megiddo was occupied before 5000 BC, and it was rebuilt up to 30 times before it was finally abandoned in the 5th or 4th century BC. Its strategic location in the Jezreel valley on the trade route between Egypt and Mesopotamia meant that it often drew the attention of regional powers. Despite several valiant attempts to withstand sieges and invasions, Megiddo was at the mercy of most of the region's political powers at some point during its long history.*

*"[Manasseh] did not drive out the inhabitants of Dor and its outlying villages, or of Ibleam and its villages, or of Megiddo and its villages; in those parts the Canaanites held their ground."*

Judges 1.27

Early in the 2nd millennium BC Megiddo emerged as a wealthy Canaanite royal city, presumably with links to Egypt and its eastern trading neighbours. The encroaching Egyptians angered the Canaanites and in 1468 BC an uprising throughout the area was put down by Egyptian forces under the Pharaoh Thutmose III. Megiddo, the last Canaanite stronghold to withstand the invading Egyptians, was occupied only after a siege lasting seven months. Inscriptions at Karnak and letters from the el-Amarna collection are among the many Egyptian documentary sources that describe Megiddo's important role as an Egyptian colonial administrative centre.

## Changing Fortunes of the City

Egyptian influence in northern Palestine declined steadily from 1200 BC, leaving Megiddo to be fought over by local peoples including the Philistines and the Israelites. The city emerged in the 10th century in the firm possession of the Israelites, and the Bible describes its inclusion in King Solomon's famous building and fortification campaign. The Egyptians took the city back in the 920s BC, but the following century saw Megiddo returned to its former glory by Omri and Ahab, kings of Israel. The Assyrians, Babylonians and Persians would control Megiddo in the years before it was finally abandoned. In September of 1918 a decisive battle for control of Megiddo was fought between the British and a smaller Turkish army attempting to halt the Allied invasion of the Ottoman empire. The British forces were under the command of General Sir Edmund Allenby (later Viscount Allenby of Megiddo). Repeating the daring tactic successfully employed nearly 3,500 years previously by the Egyptians, Allenby sent his forces through the narrow Aruna Pass, taking the Turkish force by surprise and seizing Megiddo and its environs.

## Important Archaeological Site

One of the largest archaeological sites in modern Israel, ancient Megiddo has been the focus of much scholarly attention. Excavations have recently been undertaken by an international team coordinated by Tel Aviv University. Its findings, alongside those of earlier archaeological campaigns and together with the help of modern scientific analysis, have greatly added to our understanding of Megiddo's physical remains as well as its historical importance. The main gate into the city is on the north side, although it was rebuilt several times before the latest (9th century BC) gate. Remains of numerous temples, particularly from the Canaanite period (early in the 2nd millennium BC), have been found in the eastern quadrant of the city below what appear to be later palace complexes. The huge building against the south side of the fortification wall was long thought to be a Solomonic stable complex, but recent tests have provided a

'Solomon's Stables' at Megiddo. Some scholars think that the structures above were troughs at a chariot stables; others believe that the area was a storeroom. However, most experts agree that they were built by King Ahab in the 9th century BC and not by Solomon.

revised date of the 9th century BC, during the period when Megiddo became a 'chariot city' under King Ahab of Israel. Another important recent discovery appears to be a Christian 'prayer hall' of the 3rd century AD, a unique example of an overt Christian presence in the Levant before the age of Constantine.

Megiddo continued to play an important role in the Levant into the New Testament period and beyond. Its long association with kings, refined culture, extensive trade and commerce informed the popular reputation of this ancient city for centuries after its cultural apex during the Canaanite period. Ancient oral and literary echoes of Megiddo as a site of many bitter struggles between mighty rulers of great empires must account in large measure for its appearance in the Bible's Book of Revelations (16:16) as Armageddon (literally, the mound of Megiddo), the predestined location of what Christians believe will be the final struggle between the forces of good and evil.

Canaanite stone gates at Tell Megiddo. An important city of the ancient world, Megiddo was the site of many famous battles.

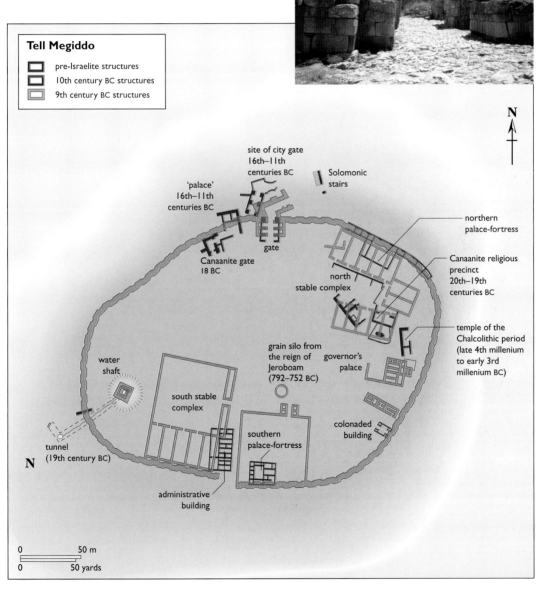

**Tell Megiddo**

- pre-Israelite structures
- 10th century BC structures
- 9th century BC structures

site of city gate 16th–11th centuries BC

Solomonic stairs

'palace' 16th–11th centuries BC

gate

Canaanite gate 18 BC

northern palace-fortress

Canaanite religious precinct 20th–19th centuries BC

north stable complex

temple of the Chalcolithic period (late 4th millenium to early 3rd millenium BC)

water shaft

grain silo from the reign of Jeroboam (792–752 BC)

governor's palace

south stable complex

colonaded building

tunnel (19th century BC)

N

southern palace-fortress

administrative building

0    50 m
0    50 yards

# The Assyrian Empire

Ruins of the great ancient city of Nineveh. It lay on the east bank of the Tigris River, near modern-day Mosul in Iraq.

*Originally a colonial outpost of the Babylonian empire, the city of Ashur, a cultic centre of the eponymous local god, was settled by c. 2500 BC. Its inhabitants, known as the Assyrians, would, by 650 BC, control all of Mesopotamia, the Levantine coastal areas and Egypt.*

Following the overpowering of the Babylonians by the Kassites early in the 2nd millennium BC, the Assyrians achieved political and military independence from their neighbours to the east. From *c.* 1400 BC the Assyrian kingdom consolidated its power within a relatively small territory alongside the banks of the middle Tigris River. However, threats from the Kassites to the southeast and the Arameans from the west prevented the infant state from expanding its original borders for the first few centuries of its existence. By the reign of King Ashurdan II (934–912 BC), however, Assyrian culture and territory had been cemented and a new age of expansionism dawned.

During the Neo-Assyrian period successive rulers were able to increase the sphere of Assyrian influence throughout the Middle East. The powerful

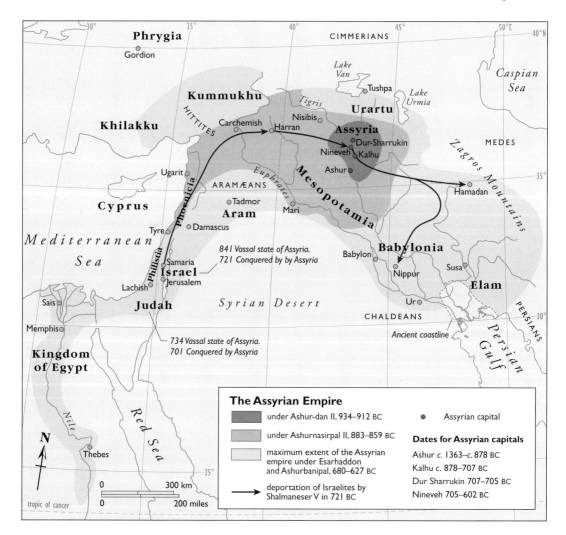

The Assyrian Empire

- under Ashur-dan II, 934–912 BC
- under Ashurnasirpal II, 883–859 BC
- maximum extent of the Assyrian empire under Esarhaddon and Ashurbanipal, 680–627 BC
- → deportation of Israelites by Shalmaneser V in 721 BC

● Assyrian capital

**Dates for Assyrian capitals**
Ashur c. 1363–c. 878 BC
Kalhu c. 878–707 BC
Dur Sharrukin 707–705 BC
Nineveh 705–602 BC

841 Vassal state of Assyria.
721 Conquered by by Assyria

734 Vassal state of Assyria.
701 Conquered by Assyria

Relief from the palace at Kalhu (modern Nimrud). Ashurnasirpal II, the last great Assyrian king, is shown seated between two attendants.

Kassite-Babylonians to the east and the desert to the south meant that initial territorial gains were most easily sought to the west, conveniently a region of smaller political units including the kingdoms and city-states of Phoenicia, Philistia and the highly factionalized tribes of Israel. Ashurnasirpal II (883–859 BC) ruled over an empire stretching from the Mediterranean to the western borders of Babylonia, maintaining a firm control on trade and commerce throughout his territories. He made his capital at Kalhu (modern Nimrud in Iran), an ancient Assyrian city on which he lavished great riches, building a vast palace and

*"I built chariots fitted to the yoke for the use of my people in excess of those which had existed before. I added territories to Assyria, and I added populations to her population. I improved the condition of the people, and I obtained for them abundance and security."*

Inscription of Tiglath Pileser I (British Museum)

garden complex. The city of Nineveh, which would become the final capital city of the Assyrians, was also rebuilt by this ruler.

Assyrian dominance of the region continued over the next two centuries. Syria was conquered gradually during the 740s and 730s BC, with Judah and Philistia becoming vassal states around the same time. The kingdom of Israel, a vassal of Assyria since the mid-9th century BC, was finally taken by Sargon II (r. 721–705 BC) in 721 BC; many of Israel's inhabitants were deported to eastern Mesopotamia and their territory was resettled by loyal Assyrian followers.

## Height of Power under Ashurbanipal

The Assyrian empire achieved its greatest extent following the conquest of Egypt in 671 BC by Esarhaddon (r. 680–669 BC). Esarhaddon's son Ashurbanipal, who reigned from 669–627 BC, is perhaps the best known Assyrian ruler. He spent much time putting down rebellions throughout his vast realm, but he was also a man of great learning and culture. His great library at Nineveh contained an enormous variety of literary, historical, religious and scientific texts and was the first such foundation in the region. After several unsuccessful rebellions, the Egyptians finally ousted their Assyrian overlords in 654 BC, although the two powers continued their commercial and trading connections. Several years later, in 648 BC, Ashurbanipal gained complete control over Babylonia, which had been left to his brother on the death of their father. Following Ashurbanipal's death Assyria rapidly weakened, its huge expanse simply too large to be controlled effectively from a single power base. By 600 BC, the empire had been dealt its final blow by a united offensive mounted by the Chaldeans from the south and the Medians (Medes) from over the Zagros Mountains to the northeast.

# Lachish

The fortified Assyrian army camp prior to the siege of Lachish. When the vassal king Hezekiah rebelled by refusing to pay tribute to the Assyrians, their leader Sennacherib responded by attacking the Judean stronghold. Proud of his victory, Sennacherib decorated the walls of his palace at Nineveh with stone reliefs showing the events leading to the capture of Lachish.

*Lachish was an important Canaanite city, and Egypt's el-Amarna letters contain frequent references to the trade relations between the city and its Egyptian overlords. It came under Israelite control during the final quarter of the 2nd millennium BC, when they dominated Canaan, and following the division of the United Monarchy on Solomon's death in 922 BC, Lachish emerged as the second most important city in Judah, eclipsed only by Jerusalem.*

*"The prophet Jeremiah repeated all these words to [Hezekiah] king of Judah ... while the army of the king of Babylon was attacking Jerusalem and the towns of Judah which still held out, namely Lachish and Azekah ... for they were fortified."*

Jeremiah 34.7

Lachish occupied a strategically important position at the head of the mountain pass on the route to Jerusalem, providing a crucial line of defence for the Judean capital city. During the revolt against Assyria led by King Hezekiah of Judah, Lachish was captured by the Assyrians under Sennacherib following a prolonged and bloody battle (701 BC). By 600 BC Lachish was once again under Judean control. It succumbed, along with the entire kingdom of Judah, to the Babylonians in 586 BC.

For many years the site of ancient Lachish was believed to be located at Tell el-Hesi, excavated in the 1890s by two pioneering British archaeologists, Sir Flinders Petrie and F. J. Bliss. One of the largest surviving mounds in Palestine, Tell el-Hesi proved rich in finds dating from c. 2500 BC and many later periods. The first site in Palestine to be excavated stratigraphically (that is, using stratigraphy and seriation to build a chronology of the site), Tell el-Hesi grew in fame when Petrie was able to apply his recently developed Egyptian chronology to the site. The numerous discoveries of imported Egyptian wares allowed the various phases of the site to be dated using an externally verifiable chronology, a new departure from the reliance on the Bible as the primary determinant of a site's historical context. Since 1929 another site, Tell ed-Duweir, has been positively identified as ancient Lachish and important findings from this site have provided much insight into the city itself and, more particularly, its role within the Kingdom of Judah.

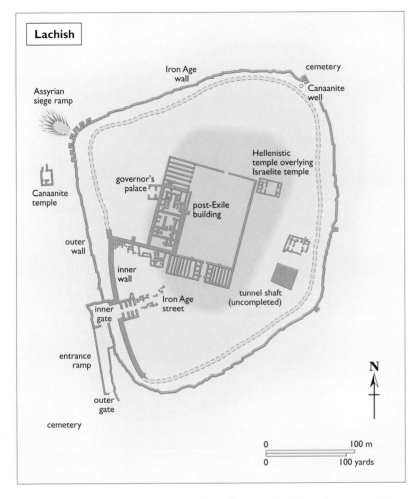

Lachish

- Iron Age wall
- cemetery
- Assyrian siege ramp
- Canaanite well
- Canaanite temple
- governor's palace
- Hellenistic temple overlying Israelite temple
- post-Exile building
- outer wall
- inner wall
- Iron Age street
- tunnel shaft (uncompleted)
- inner gate
- entrance ramp
- outer gate
- cemetery

N

0    100 m
0    100 yards

The first of the Lachish Letters. They were discovered in 1935 written on *ostraca* (pottery shards) in an ancient Hebrew script. They provide essential information about the final days of the Kingdom of Judah and they confirm the account of the prophet Jeremiah in the Bible.

Some minor, domestic structures from the period of Egyptian control have been unearthed at Tell ed-Duweir and there is nothing to suggest that during this period Lachish was fortified in any way. There is evidence that the city was destroyed by fire during the 12th century BC and shortly afterwards the city fell into Philistine hands. Some rebuilding took place around 1000 BC – perhaps during the reign of David or Solomon – but this phase of reconstruction was again destroyed, possibly by Egyptian invaders, about 100 years later. Lachish was rebuilt and strongly fortified during the Divided Monarchy; a large palace complex signifies the important role of the city within the kingdom of Judah. Following two further destructive episodes, it was once again rebuilt during the 7th century BC. An important collection of documents, known as the Lachish Letters, were discovered in a gatehouse erected at this time. The letters date from the early 6th century BC and include correspondence between military leaders during the Babylonian conquest of the region. The letters are written on pottery shards known as ostraca, frequently used for letter writing during this period. Numbering 21 in all, the letters were discovered in the 1930s by the British archaeologist J. L. Starkey.

# The Neo-Babylonian Empire

*The ancient civilization of Babylonia, located in the fertile southern region between the Tigris and Euphrates rivers, is among the most important in the early history of the Middle East. The Babylonian heartland, constantly under threat from neighbouring powers with deeply expansionist tendencies, finally achieved dominance in the region during the first half of the 2nd millennium BC.*

*" Because of my faithful reign, Marduk, the merciful one, bestowed favour upon that temple, and Shamash, the lofty judge, commanded its renovation. Me, the shepherd who fears them, they gave orders to rebuild it. "*

Prayer of Nebuchadnezzar II at dedication of temple

The Babylonian empire became known for its refined culture, literature and advanced legal and record-keeping systems. Despite dynastic upheavals, most notably by the Kassites and the Elamites, the empire essentially flourished until the 9th century BC when the mighty Assyrians conquered Babylon and its surrounding territories. Under the Assyrians Babylonia maintained an impressive degree of independence, at least until the Assyrian king Ashurbanipal was forced to raze the city of Babylon to assert his authority over his younger brother Shamash-shum-ukin in 648 BC. By 625 BC Assyrian dominance in the region had been replaced by a new Babylonian dynasty whose founder was Nabopolassar, a military leader who, with the help of the Medians to the north, finally succeeded in ousting the Assyrians from power. Babylonia's new rulers were Chaldeans, a name originating from the bordering region on the north coast of the Persian Gulf, and their territory is referred to as the Neo-Babylonian empire.

### Nebuchadnezzar

The Neo-Babylonian empire reached its fullest extent under Nabopolossar's son Nebuchadnezzar II (r. 605–562 BC). During his reign the Babylonians captured all of the major cities from the Persian Gulf to the Red Sea, eventually controlling a vast arc of territories bounded by the Taurus and Zagros mountains to the north and the Arabian Desert to the south. On his accession to the throne Nebuchadnezzar had already captured Syria, defeated Egyptian forces and reduced most of Palestine to a series of vassal states. During his reign he regularly mounted campaigns to the north and west to expand his territories as well as swiftly quelling numerous rebellions closer to home.

Nebuchadnezzar rebuilt Babylon on an unprecedented scale. The huge palace complex and Babylon's famous Hanging Gardens were constructed under his patronage. Later to become one of the Seven Wonders of the ancient world, the gardens probably sat on a series of terraced rooftops and so appeared suspended above the city. They may have been erected by Nebuchadnezzar as a gift to his wife Amytis, a Median princess. The Hanging Gardens are the only ancient wonder to possess no contemporary textual evidence of its existence. The gardens are first mentioned in a description of the deeds of Nebuchadnezzar which, though credited to the Babylonian historian Berossus (fl. 4th century

Lion from a reconstruction of the Ishtar Gate. The lion was a symbol of the goddess Ishtar. Some 120 lions like this lined the walls of the Processional Way leading out of the city and through the massive gateway that dates to Nebuchadnezzar.

BC), survives only within the works of later historians. It is perhaps telling that the Greek historian Herodotus, writing in the mid-5th century BC, tells of the magnificent walls, palaces and temples of Babylon but fails to mention the gardens. Contemporary tablets describe large gardens at nearby Nineveh, probably built just before 700 BC, and it is possible that the city rebuilt by Nebuchadnezzar and the gardens in Nineveh were conflated in later sources.

Nebuchadnezzar also resurrected many of the intellectual and scientific advances that had been associated with his Babylonian predecessors. The earliest Babylonians were

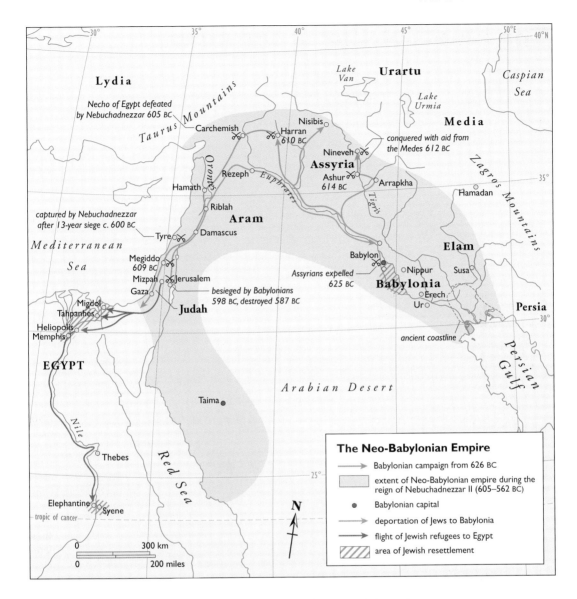

The following labels appear on the map:

**The Neo-Babylonian Empire**

- → Babylonian campaign from 626 BC
- extent of Neo-Babylonian empire during the reign of Nebuchadnezzar II (605–562 BC)
- ● Babylonian capital
- → deportation of Jews to Babylonia
- → flight of Jewish refugees to Egypt
- //// area of Jewish resettlement

Lydia

Necho of Egypt defeated by Nebuchadnezzar 605 BC

Taurus Mountains

Carchemish

Nisibis

Lake Van

Urartu

Caspian Sea

Lake Urmia

Media

conquered with aid from the Medes 612 BC

Harran 610 BC

Nineveh

Assyria

Ashur 614 BC

Arrapkha

Hamadan

Zagros Mountains

Rezeph

Euphrates

Hamath

Riblah

captured by Nebuchadnezzar after 13-year siege c. 600 BC

Aram

Tyre

Damascus

Mediterranean Sea

Megiddo 609 BC

Mizpah

Jerusalem

Gaza

besieged by Babylonians 598 BC, destroyed 587 BC

Judah

Migdol

Tahpanhes

Heliopolis

Memphis

Babylon

Assyrians expelled 625 BC

Babylonia

Nippur

Erech

Ur

Elam

Susa

Persia

ancient coastline

Persian Gulf

EGYPT

Arabian Desert

Taima

Nile

Red Sea

Thebes

Elephantine

Syene

tropic of cancer

N

0    300 km
0    200 miles

known for their advanced writing, astronomy and mathematics. It is to the Babylonian numerical system based on 60 rather than 10 that we owe the system of timekeeping in use today. The Babylonians divided the day into 24 hours, each of 60 minutes and each minute of 60 seconds. They also produced mathematical tables and astronomical charts. This work was largely abandoned under intervening rulers, but reintroduced and refined by the Neo-Babylonians.

Nebuchadnezzar took Jerusalem in 597 BC and the Judean king Jehoiachin and his household were sent to Babylon, foreshadowing the deportation of large sections of the Judean population in the next decade. Known as the Babylonian Captivity, this exile cemented the attitudes of the Jews towards their religion and their homeland. Much of the biblical text outlining the early history of the Israelites was written during this time. There is some dispute as to the number of Jews who were relocated, the extent to which many may have fled to Egypt and the exact length of the exile. The Captivity officially ended with the fall of the Neo-Babylonian empire to the Persians in 538 BC.

# Conquests of Cyrus the Great

*Cyrus the Great was the first ruler of the Persian empire. Crowned king of the Persian state of Ashan on his father's death in 559 BC, Cyrus went on to establish the largest empire that the ancient world had ever seen.*

*"In the first year of Cyrus the king, King Cyrus decreed: 'The Temple will be rebuilt as a place at which sacrifices are offered and to which offerings are brought to be burned.'"*

Ezra 6.3

The legacy of Cyrus and the succeeding members of the Achaemenid dynasty embraced aspects of civilization as disparate and far-reaching as models for centralized government, human rights issues and the first postal network. The rise of Persia effectively ended the control of Mesopotamia by those indigenous cultures that had dominated the region for the preceding millennia.

Cyrus's first conquest was of Media, the largest political and military power in the region and the overlord of his homeland of Ashan. The king of Media was then Astyages, an unpopular ruler and possibly Cyrus' grandfather. The revolt against Media led by Cyrus in 550 BC was swift and successful, and the unification of Media, Ashan and the smaller Persian kingdoms posed few problems, as all were closely related culturally and linguistically. With Media came various occupied territories, for the Medians had been expanding to the east and west for some time. For example, a coalition between the Medians and the Chaldeans had finally ended Assyrian dominance in Mesopotamia at the close of the 7th century BC. Cyrus, probably in his thirties at this time, found himself in charge of territories stretching from the Helmand River in the east into Asia Minor.

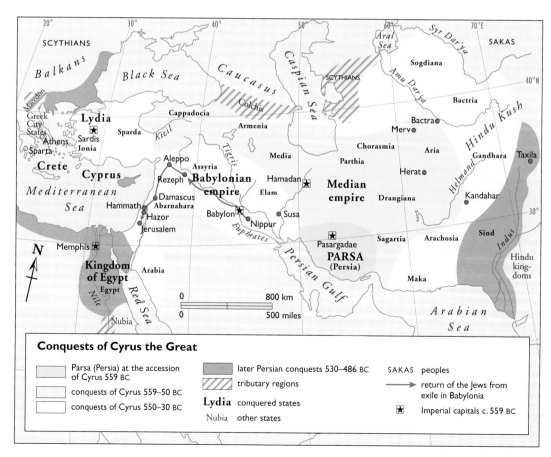

**Conquests of Cyrus the Great**

- Parsa (Persia) at the accession of Cyrus 559 BC
- conquests of Cyrus 559–50 BC
- conquests of Cyrus 550–30 BC
- later Persian conquests 530–486 BC
- tributary regions
- **Lydia** conquered states
- Nubia other states
- SAKAS peoples
- → return of the Jews from exile in Babylonia
- ★ Imperial capitals c. 559 BC

Ruins of Pasargadae, the capital city Cyrus established in the 6th century BC. It marked the location of Cyrus' first important victory over Astyages and the Medians. Today it is an important archaeological site in Iran.

Cyrus had precious little time to strengthen his new vassal states because he was forced almost immediately to defend his western borders against the Lydians, the chief power within Asia Minor. Sardis, the Lydian capital, fell to the Persians in 546 BC, and within four years Cyrus's forces had conquered all of Asia Minor, including the wealthy Greek ports along the Mediterranean and Aegean coasts. In 538-9 BC Cyrus wrested control of Mesopotamia, Syria and Palestine from Nabonidus, the last of the Chaldean emperors of Babylonia.

### Cyrus in the Bible

Biblical references to Cyrus describe him in very favourable terms, claiming that he released the Jews from their bondage in Babylonia and allowed them to return to Palestine. Although the restoration of Palestine to the Jews may simply have been a pragmatic attempt by Cyrus to create a buffer between the Persian empire and Egypt, tolerance for the religions and cultural traditions of others does seem to have been a key factor in Cyrus' success as an emperor. He remained true to his own system of beliefs, but he appears not to have forced Persian traditions on his occupied territories.

Though it is not known whether Cyrus was himself a Zoroastrian, he was certainly influenced by Zoroastrianism, the religion indigenous to the Persian heartlands. Probably formulated just after 1000 BC, the tenets of Zoroastrianism stress the existence of one uncreated god, honoured above all other 'created' deities, and the concept that earthly existence represents a constant battle between the forces of goodness and evil. With the extension of Persian political control and cultural influence throughout the Middle East, it is no surprise that the philosophic underpinnings and other traditions espoused by Zoroastrians influenced the development of other religions in the region – including Judaism and Christianity – during the period of Achaemenid domination.

Cyrus was also interested in the lands to the east of the Median empire, with their wealth of exotic spices and luxury goods and their control of ancient trade routes to the rest of Asia. The precise extent of Cyrus' conquests here is not known, although sources record that he died, late in 530 BC, fighting somewhere in modern Kazakhstan. The main sources for information about Cyrus' life and conquests are Greek. The writings of historians such as Herodotus, who died c. 430 BC, no doubt reflect contemporary Greek concerns over the encroachment of the Persians into their territories.

# The Hellenistic Kingdoms

The sanctuary of Pan at Baniyas, built in the 3rd century BC as part of the Greek city of Paneas. During excavations here archaeologists discovered thousands of animal bones from goats consumed at ritual feasts honouring Pan, the Greek god of shepherds.

*The Greeks, or the Hellenes as they called themselves, with their wealthy maritime colonies, became ever more interesting to the expansionist Persians during the reigns of those who succeeded Cyrus the Great. The Greeks had never formed a unified nation, but rather existed as a confederation of fiercely independent city-states.*

On the whole, the Greek city-states were able to pull together to repel foreign invaders, as they did with the Persians in the early 5th century BC. However, persistent in-fighting and power struggles between city-states weakened the fragile alliance sufficiently to allow the rise of the neighbouring Macedonians during the 4th century BC. Under Philip II of Macedon (r. 359–336), Macedonia achieved a prominent position within the region. Having previously adopted the language and many of the cultural traditions of the Greeks, Macedonians were able to hold favour with various Greek city-states as they jockeyed for power within Hellenic territories. An excellent strategist and diplomat, as well as a hardened warrior, Philip had already begun to plot an attack on the powerful Persian empire and expand into Asia Minor before his assassination. This followed a series of uncharacteristically rash decisions that turned much of his family and the court against him. Philip was succeeded by his son, Alexander III of Macedon (r. 336–323 BC), whose brief but extraordinarily successful military career would topple the Persian empire and make him the stuff of legends.

> *And they built a gymnasium in Jerusalem according to the manner of the Gentiles. They also submitted themselves to uncircumcision, and repudiated the holy covenant.*
>
> I Maccabees 1.15

### Alexander the Great
Educated by the Greek philosopher Aristotle and having inherited his father's military and diplomatic prowess, Alexander was crowned king of Macedonia at the age of 20. He immediately set out to subdue the neighbouring peoples, among them the Illyrians and the Thracians, and to quell several rebellions within Greece that had begun to foment in the aftermath of his father's assassination. With Macedonian dominance among the Balkan peoples and the Hellenes assured, the young Alexander wasted no time in crossing into Asia Minor to launch his campaign against the Persians. Between 334 BC and Alexander's death in Babylon in 323 BC, his formidable army of Macedonians, Greeks and other loyal mercenaries ploughed through every defence mounted by the Persians, eventually capturing the entire empire, as well as pushing further into the Indus valley and securing control over the eastern third of the North African coast. He

founded numerous cities, many of which – including Alexandria in the western Nile Delta – would increase in importance throughout the following centuries. Alexander also oversaw the spread of a new culture drawn primarily from the Greeks, which enabled, with its single language (used for business, diplomacy and record-keeping) and unified currency, direct communication across his vast dominions. This culture is termed 'Hellenistic', and its echoes still reverberate in the foundations of many Western cultures today.

On Alexander's death, which, like that of Philip, was preceded by a period of unwise personal and policy decisions, his empire rapidly disbanded, and five separate kingdoms emerged. Each was initially run by one of Alexander's generals, with Seleucos – who founded the Seleucid dynasty – gaining the largest territory, and Antigonus controlling Asia Minor, Mesopotamia and Palestine. Much of Antigonus' kingdom quickly fell to Seleucos, whose successors were great champions of Hellenistic culture. The Seleucids dominated the region well into the 2nd century BC. Greece and Macedonia were ruled by Antipater; following his death in 319 BC, his lands passed to his son Cassander, though succession disputes between Cassander and Alexander's family plagued his reign. Thrace and the Gallipoli peninsula were ceded to Lysimachus, who, with Seleucos, helped to engineer the death of Antigonus at the battle of Ipsus in 301 BC. The Egyptian dynasty, founded by the general Ptolemy, was to be the longest lasting of the five kingdoms, falling to the Romans only in 30 BC.

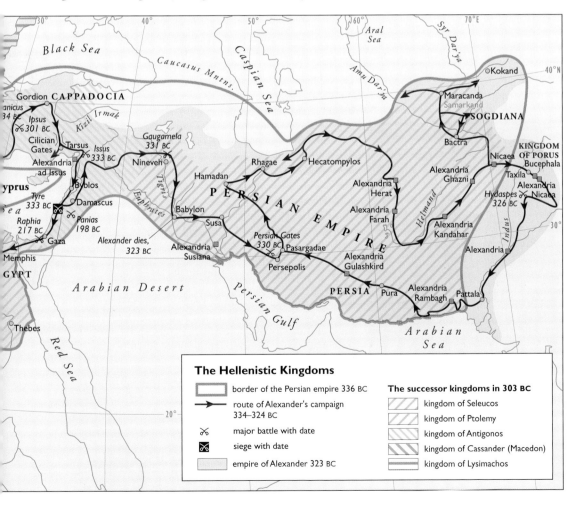

### The Hellenistic Kingdoms

- border of the Persian empire 336 BC
- → route of Alexander's campaign 334–324 BC
- ✂ major battle with date
- ☒ siege with date
- empire of Alexander 323 BC

**The successor kingdoms in 303 BC**
- kingdom of Seleucos
- kingdom of Ptolemy
- kingdom of Antigonos
- kingdom of Cassander (Macedon)
- kingdom of Lysimachos

# The Maccabean Revolt

*The 2nd century BC opened with the Seleucid empire reaching its greatest extent. By 196 BC the conquest of Thrace in the Balkan peninsula had even secured the Seleucids a foothold in Europe. The mantle of European power was passing from Greece to the Romans, who soon saw their chance to remove the Seleucid invaders from Europe and potentially to weaken their hold on western Asia by pursuing their defeated armies into Anatolia.*

*"Nevertheless many in Israel stood firm and determined in their hearts that they would not eat unclean things, and chose rather to die so that they might not be defiled with meats, thereby profaning the holy covenant, and they did die."*

I Maccabees 1.64

Over the next fifty years the Seleucids saw their empire disintegrate partly through their squandering of resources and alliances, and partly at the hands of rising powers, among them the Parthians and the Bactrians in the east and the Romans and Egyptians in the west. Although the northern and southern extremes of the Bible lands remained firmly in the hands of the Seleucids and the Ptolemies respectively, the central regions of Israel, Judah, Idumea (formerly Edom), Philistia and Phoenicia were the subject of constant territorial dispute during the century following the death of Alexander the Great. The Ptolemies officially controlled Palestine from Egypt for most of the period, but the Seleucids applied constant military and diplomatic pressure before eventually assuming control in 200 BC. The Seleucids imposed their strict rule and strongly Hellenistic culture on the region, making it very difficult for the monotheistic and culturally distinct Jews to accept the Seleucids as overlords.

## The Seeds of Revolt

Initial attempts to Hellenize the Jews met with some success, with a significant portion of the Jewish population eager to support the new Greek-inspired reforms. The Jewish High Priest, who oversaw the region for the Seleucid king Antiochus IV Epiphanes (r. 175–164 BC), was of the reforming faction by the 170s BC. Conflict between rival High Priests saw the capture of Jerusalem by the reforming High Priest Jason in 169 BC; two years later Antiochus swept into Jerusalem and forced its inhabitants to accept his rule and his cultural preferences. Judaism was outlawed and Jews were forced to sacrifice to the Greek gods and representatives of Antiochus. Outraged by the erection of a statue of Zeus at the Temple in Jerusalem, an elderly Jewish priest called Mathathias and his five sons rebelled against the Seleucids. The third son, known as Judas Maccabeus, led the revolt, including the recapturing of Jerusalem (save for the Seleucid fortress there), until he was killed by Syrian forces at the Battle of Elasa in 160 BC. In 162 BC the Seleucids had reversed their policy to stamp out Judaism in an effort to put down the rebellion, but against the odds, Judas had fought on and liberated most of Judah, now known as Judea, from Seleucid domination.

Fifteenth-century illumination from a history of the Jews showing Antiochus and his soldiers pillaging Jerusalem. Antiochus defiled the Temple by slaughtering a pig there and trying to force the men to eat the meat. This was pivotal in making the Jews rise up against Seleucid rule.

Judas' youngest brother Jonathan continued to lead the resistance until he was executed in 143 BC. In 152 BC he was elevated to the office of High Priest for Judea and Samaria, and he worked tirelessly to secure religious and political freedom for the Jewish people. His brother Simon (r. 142–134 BC) finally achieved Judean political independence in 142 BC. The Maccabeans continued to rule the kingdom of Judea, which eventually encompassed most of modern Israel, until 63 BC. The dynasty was continued by Simon's heirs and came to be known as the Hasmoneans.

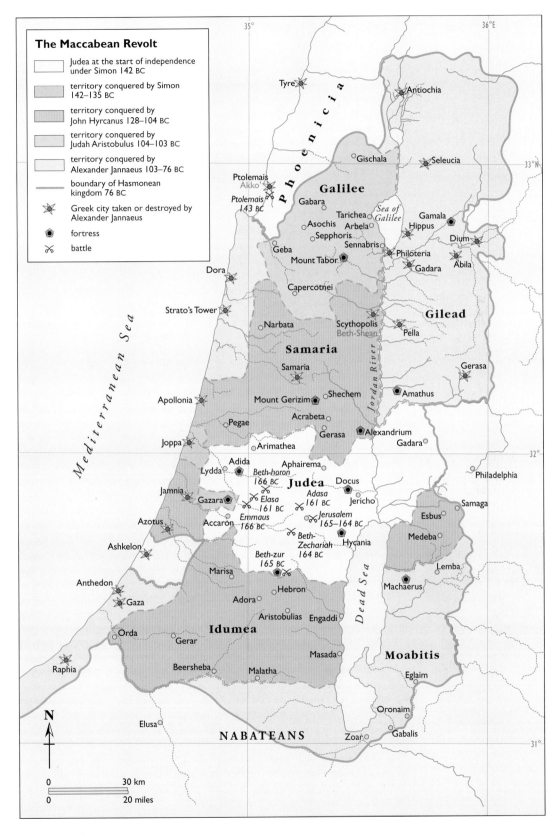

**The Maccabean Revolt**

Judea at the start of independence under Simon 142 BC

territory conquered by Simon 142–135 BC

territory conquered by John Hyrcanus 128–104 BC

territory conquered by Judah Aristobulus 104–103 BC

territory conquered by Alexander Jannaeus 103–76 BC

boundary of Hasmonean kingdom 76 BC

Greek city taken or destroyed by Alexander Jannaeus

fortress

battle

Tyre

Antiochia

*Phoenicia*

Gischala

Seleucia

Ptolemais
Akko

**Galilee**

Ptolemais *143 BC*

Gabara

Taricha

*Sea of Galilee*

Gamala

Asochis

Arbela

Hippus

Sepphoris

Dium

Geba

Sennabris

Philoteria

Mount Tabor

Gadara

Abila

Dora

Capercotnei

Strato's Tower

Narbata

Scythopolis
Beth-Shean

Pella

**Gilead**

**Samaria**

Samaria

Gerasa

Shechem

Amathus

Mount Gerizim

Apollonia

Acrabeta

Pegae

Gerasa

Alexandrium

Gadara

Joppa

Arimathea

Philadelphia

Adida

Aphairema

Lydda

*Beth-horon 166 BC*

**Judea**

Docus

Samaga

Jamnia

*Adasa 161 BC*

*Elasa 161 BC*

Jericho

Gazara

*Emmaus 166 BC*

*Jerusalem 165–164 BC*

Esbus

Accaron

Medeba

Azotus

*Beth-Zechariah 164 BC*

Hycania

Lemba

Ashkelon

*Beth-zur 165 BC*

Anthedon

Marisa

Machaerus

Gaza

Hebron

Adora

Aristobulias

Engaddi

*Dead Sea*

**Idumea**

Orda

Gerar

Masada

**Moabitis**

Raphia

Beersheba

Malatha

Eglaim

Oronaim

Elusa

**NABATEANS**

Zoar

Gabalis

*Mediterranean Sea*

*Jordan River*

**N**

0        30 km

0        20 miles

# Pompey's Eastern Settlement

*"For we lost our freedom and became subject to the Romans, and the territory which we had gained by our arms and taken from the Syrians we were compelled to give back to them, and in addition the Romans exacted from us in a short space of time more than ten thousand talents."*

Josephus,
*Antiquities XIV,*
*69-79*

**By the middle of the 2nd century BC the Romans were the undisputed rulers of the western Mediterranean, in control of the Italian peninsula, Sicily, Corsica, Sardinia, Spain, Carthage, Greece and Macedonia. Rome's official presence in Asia began in 133 BC with the creation of the province of Asia from the former kingdom of Pergamum and surrounding Greek colonies in western Anatolia. Firm Roman control of the Levant was largely the result of the efforts and strategies of one man: Gnaeus Pompeius Magnus.**

Pompey's father was Gnaeus Pompeius Strabo (*c.* 130-87 BC), a distinguished Roman general and consul. Strabo came from a wealthy family from the Roman province of Picenum, the region of Italy's Adriatic coast later known as the Marches. Although his family was socially well-connected, Strabo was not a member of the Roman senatorial elite and throughout his life supported the rights of Rome's provincial populations. He fought valiantly for Rome during the Social War (91-88 BC), a revolt staged by a number of northern Italian cities against Roman rule. Strabo's military successes and adroit political skills no doubt informed many decisions taken by his son.

## Rise to Power

Pompey initially gained recognition as a talented military leader under Sulla, who controlled the Republic in the late 80s BC. His popularity increased after military successes in Sicily, Africa and Spain, and he was first elected Consul in 71 BC. During the first half of 67 BC Pompey cleared the Mediterranean of pirates, whose stranglehold on numerous ports and sea routes prevented effective communication and trade throughout the region. Soon after, Pompey was sent to subdue the rulers of western Asia, in particular Mithridates VI of Pontus whose ambition to control Anatolia had made him an enemy of Rome. Pompey took Pontus and chased Mithridates into the Crimea, along the way making an ally of the Armenian king, Tigranes the Great. In 64 BC Pompey marched south, deposing Antiochus XIII of Syria, and in the following year he occupied Coele-Syria, Phoenicia and Judea. Pompey arrived in Judea during the middle of a civil war between two heirs to the Hasmonean throne: Hyrcanus and Aristobulus. Eventually siding with Hyrcanus, Pompey entered Jerusalem (after besieging the city for three months), took possession of the Temple and proclaimed Hyrcanus High Priest.

By 62 BC, the eastern Mediterranean had been subdued and carefully organized into a manageable collection of provinces and annexed territories. Rome's grasp on its acquisitions within the Asian interior grew firmer with the suicide of Mithridates of Pontus in 63 BC. Control of the north African coast was achieved piecemeal between the end of the second Punic war in 201 BC and the defeat of Mark Antony and the Egyptian queen Cleopatra by Octavian (later the Emperor Augustus) at the Battle of Actium in 31 BC. The Parthians continued to be a thorn in the eastern side of the Roman empire. In 53 BC the Roman Crassus, who ruled alongside Pompey and Caesar, was killed along with vast numbers of his men while attempting to defeat the Parthians at Carrhae (in modern Turkey), and by 40 BC the Parthians occupied much of southern Anatolia and the Roman province of Syria. Throughout the 1st and 2nd centuries AD the Romans and the Parthians fought over control of Mesopotamia and Armenia, and although the Parthians eventually retreated to the east, the Romans were never able to conquer them.

Sculpted marble head of Gnaeus Pompeius Magnus, known commonly as Pompey. A renowned political and military leader, he was aged about forty at the time.

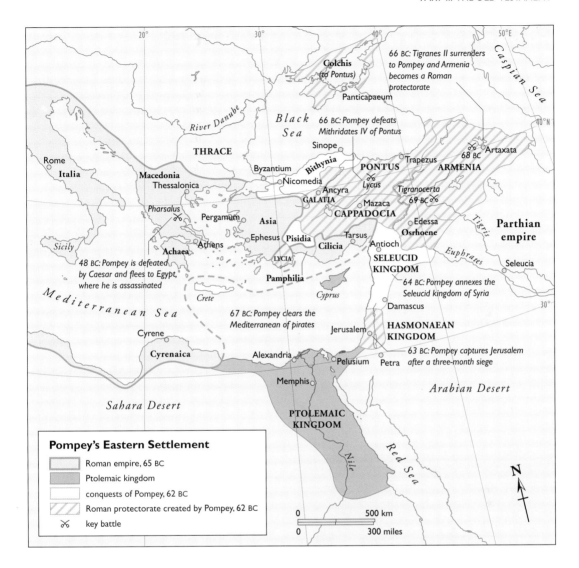

**Pompey's Eastern Settlement**

- Roman empire, 65 BC
- Ptolemaic kingdom
- conquests of Pompey, 62 BC
- Roman protectorate created by Pompey, 62 BC
- key battle

66 BC: Tigranes II surrenders to Pompey and Armenia becomes a Roman protectorate

66 BC: Pompey defeats Mithridates IV of Pontus

48 BC: Pompey is defeated by Caesar and flees to Egypt, where he is assassinated

67 BC: Pompey clears the Mediterranean of pirates

64 BC: Pompey annexes the Seleucid kingdom of Syria

63 BC: Pompey captures Jerusalem after a three-month siege

0   500 km
0   300 miles

Pompey's political career was not run with the strategic genius that he employed when planning military campaigns or reordering the bureaucratic structure of the eastern provinces. He struggled to achieve a balance of power (tipped when possible in his favour) between Crassus, Caesar and himself. At the same time he was forced to contend with a powerful faction of Roman nobles determined to prevent his political dominance. Like many statesmen of his time, he married (more than once) for political reasons, but he was often ridiculed for the deep devotion that he displayed towards his wives, in particular to his fourth wife, Julia, the only daughter of Caesar, to whom he was married between 59 BC and her death in 54 BC. Following Julia's death, the personal ties between the two co-rulers largely dissolved and Pompey spent the final years of his life attempting to outmanoeuvre Caesar and his supporters and gain control of Rome. He was murdered at Pelusium in Egypt in 48 BC, the victim of Ptolemaic sympathizers determined to appease Caesar. Pompey's military conquests in Palestine and his gifted vision for the re-organization of the eastern Mediterranean territories set the stage for the world that would very soon witness the birth of Jesus Christ and the beginnings of Christianity.

# Conquests of Herod the Great

*Herod (r. 37–4 BC) was the son of Antipater (d. 43 BC), the governor of Idumea who rose to power under the patronage of Pompey and Julius Caesar. Antipater sided with the Hasmonean John Hyrcanus II (r. 64–40 BC), High Priest of Judea, against Hyrcanus' brother Aristobulus (r. 66–63 BC) during their embittered struggle for power.*

*"He caught [Ezekias] and put him and many of the brigands to death. This welcome achievement was immensely admired by the Syrians."*

Josephus
*Jewish War,* 1, 123–6

When the Romans reinstated Hyrcanus as High Priest, Julius Caesar appointed Antipater as the secular ruler of Judea in 47 BC. Antipater immediately made his sons, Phasael and Herod, governors of Jerusalem and Galilee respectively. Antipater and his sons may have successfully gained patronage from the Romans, but they were not popular with their subjects. This was both because the family had only recently converted to Judaism (during the enforced conversion following the conquest of Idumea by John Hyrcanus I in 109 BC) and because of a reputation for strict rule. Despite formal complaints against him by his subjects, Herod maintained a high position in the eyes of the Romans, receiving the governorship of Coele-Syria in 47 BC. Antipater was poisoned in 43 BC, leaving Phasael and Herod in charge. In the face of renewed public complaints, Mark Antony awarded each of the brothers the title of 'tetrarch'.

## King of Judea

In 40 BC the Parthians invaded Palestine and installed Antigonus (40-37 BC), nephew of John Hyrcanus II, as High Priest of Judea. Herod and Phasael led a resistance movement, championing the weakened Hyrcanus. Phasael and Hyrcanus were captured by the Parthians, who maimed Hyrcanus to prevent him from holding office. Phasael took his own life, leaving Herod the sole survivor of his dynasty. Herod left Judea for Rome where, after much courting of Mark Antony, he was proclaimed king of Judea; in 37 BC Herod, with Roman military aid, recaptured Jerusalem and the Judean throne. Antigonus was immediately put to death and King Herod quickly married Mariamne, a Hasmonean princess, to legitimize his position further. By 20 BC, following more gifts of territory from his Roman patron Augustus, Herod's realm stretched from Idumea in the Negev north to Iturea, together with newly acquired lands in the northeast.

The high level aqueduct at Caesarea. Herod built a raised aqueduct in the 1st century BC to bring water to the growing city from springs at the foot of Mount Carmel 10 kilometres (6 miles) away. The Roman Emperor Hadrian later expanded the aqueduct, building a second lower channel that doubled its capacity.

Throughout his reign Herod, a practising Jew despite his Idumean ancestry, attempted both to appease his subjects and to impress his Roman patrons. He embarked on an extensive building campaign, which included the erection of numerous fortified strongholds and the refounding of ancient cities such as Jericho and Samaria (Sebaste). He also lavishly rebuilt the Temple in Jerusalem, enlarging the Temple Mount to accommodate greater numbers of worshippers. Herod's new port, Caesarea, would become the capital city of Judea in 6 AD.

Over time Herod's personality grew increasingly unstable. He had, in the habit of the time, taken numerous wives in order to secure political alliances, but he grew ever more concerned about conspiracies to overthrow him and more than once this paranoia resulted in the execution of a wife or child. The biblical account of the Massacre of the Innocents - when Jewish males under the age of two from Bethlehem were slaughtered at Herod's command - is not confirmed by any independent sources, but many scholars agree that such an act is consistent with Herod's mental state towards the end of his life. Herod died in 4 BC; he was buried in Herodium, a new town just south of Jerusalem, which he had founded and named after himself.

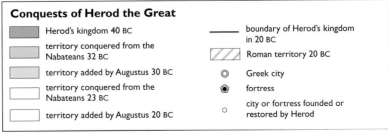

### Conquests of Herod the Great

| | |
|---|---|
| Herod's kingdom 40 BC | boundary of Herod's kingdom in 20 BC |
| territory conquered from the Nabateans 32 BC | Roman territory 20 BC |
| territory added by Augustus 30 BC | ◎ Greek city |
| territory conquered from the Nabateans 23 BC | ◉ fortress |
| territory added by Augustus 20 BC | ○ city or fortress founded or restored by Herod |

# Part III: The New Testament

*The Palestine into which Jesus was born may have seemed politically stable, but there were serious tensions beneath the surface of Roman rule. The Roman imposition of Herod as a client ruler over the Jews in 37 BC upset the unequal relationship between the Jewish religious elites in Jerusalem and the non-Jewish inhabitants of Palestine.*

Aerial view of Herod's palace at Herodium, constructed over a small pre-existing hill. Herod the Great (73–4 BC) built the fortress-palace as a refuge from Jerusalem 13 kilometres (8 miles) away. The Romans made Herod the sole ruler of Judea in 37 BC, replacing the Hasmonean dynasty. He is remembered for his massive building projects.

Nominally Jewish, Herod in fact sympathized with the non-Jewish population, who had long formed a majority of the population in Galilee and Samaria. He cultivated the image of a Hellenistic monarch: his coins bore Greek rather than Hebrew inscriptions, he built new Hellenistic towns at Sebaste in Samaria and on the coast (Caesarea), while the classical ruins of Sepphoris and Beth-She'an bear witness to impressive building campaigns in this period. Yet he also rebuilt the Jewish Temple, beginning in 20 BC, on a grandiose scale, perhaps to appease the aspirations of the priestly elite, the Sadducees.

Within Palestine, although Judaism was dominant it was not the only religion. In Judea, Jews were predominant in the population. Galilee, however, had only been systematically settled by Jews for a few generations, and there were large non-Jewish communities. Galilee's major town, Tiberias, seems to have had little or no Jewish character. The central region of Samaria, likewise, was hostile to Jews. The Samaritans practised a fledgling form of Judaism but refused to accept any scriptures beyond the first five books, subscribing to neither the Jewish prophetic tradition nor the Jewish sense of identity in the history and poetry of the rest of the scriptures.

## Division Among the Jews

Jewish society was characterized by division between two dominant groups, the Sadducees and Pharisees. The Sadducees were a wealthy nationalist elite who represented priestly authority in the Temple. Although opposed to Herod politically, they also rejected the religious methods of the Pharisees, insisting on the purity and self-sufficiency of the Jewish scriptures themselves. In contrast, the Pharisees emphasized intricate study of the law through commentary and analysis, with a view to observing it with absolute integrity. This laid them open to the criticism of the Gospel writers that they cared more for the observance of laws than for the religious impulses underlying them.

The Pharisees, far more than the Sadducees, represented the religious sentiments of the majority of Jews in Palestine, which explains why their opposition to Jesus' teachings brought about his execution by the Roman authorities. The Pharisees were not as fundamentally opposed to the Hasmonean monarchy as were the Sadducees, but they regarded kingly power in any case as inferior to sacred. The Pharisees also promoted a strong strand of social morality in Judaism, particularly works of charity towards the poor. This tendency, which later became a significant feature of early Christianity, was remarked upon by Romans. The 4th-century AD emperor Julian noted, 'No Jew ever has to beg'. The Pharisees were more politically attuned to circumstance than the Sadducees, and whereas the Sadducees regarded rebellion against political authority as unacceptable, the Pharisees not only supported the revolt against the Romans in AD 70 but were also able to guarantee the survival of Judaism after the destruction of the Temple by the Romans.

There was also an extremist and apocalyptic strand within Judiasm, characterized by the 'covenanters', or Essenes, based in communal groups at Qumran, in the desert by the Dead Sea. This group seems to have begun as a protest against the Hasmonean regime's attempts to negotiate a position for itself within the larger political spheres of power in the Roman world, which they saw as compromise with idolatry. Although it is difficult to prove exact correspondences between Essene ideals and Gospel teachings, there are similarities of outlook and approach between Essene withdrawal from the world and early Christian communal living, which was partly inspired by the conviction that the world would soon end. In fact, all three of these Jewish sects contributed some ideas to the formation of early Christianity: the sacerdotalism of the Sadducees to the Christian priesthood, the social and moral code of the Pharisees to Christian ideals of charity and fraternity, and Essene apocalypticism to Christian ideas about the kingdom to come.

Stone relief from the Arch of Titus showing Roman soldiers carrying away the Temple *menorah* after the sack of Jerusalem in AD 70. Although this second destruction of the Temple is not recorded in the Bible because it took place after it was written, it is described in detail by the Jewish historian Flavius Josephus.

Despite Herod's unpopularity with many of his own subjects, attested in Jewish sources, Palestine at the time of the Gospels was a thriving and prosperous society. Josephus vividly describes the magnificence of the Temple, in which the interior surfaces were overlaid with gold and marble. This suggests a sophisticated economy based on long-distance trade with Egypt, Arabia and Mesopotamia as well as more local markets in agricultural produce. The Jewish diaspora across the Mediterranean and to the east in Persia made Jerusalem a cosmopolitan city, attracting visitors from a wide radius. Moreover, Judaism itself encouraged the rise of a literate and well-educated middle class. As the Romans found in the 1st and 2nd centuries AD, the Jews presented a remarkably well-defined and coherent social as well as religious grouping, with the capacity to resist overwhelming force in defence of their traditions.

## Cultural Diversity in the Diaspora

Much of the strength of Judaism at the time of the New Testament came from the cultural diversity of the diaspora. The descendants of the Jews who had remained behind in Babylonia in the 6th century AD were by the 1st century AD subject to the successor to the Seleucids, the Parthian empire. As a military aristocracy, the Parthians left Hellenistic culture and even forms of government alone, and Jews seem to have served in the Parthian civil service as well as to have enjoyed freedom of worship and over internal jurisdiction. Jews in the Parthian empire seem to have maintained close links with Jerusalem, but although the Roman-Parthian hostility of the period led to Roman fears that Babylonian Jews would support the revolt against Rome in AD 66, this does not seem to have occurred. To the west, the main concentrations of Jews were to be found in the major Hellenized cities, notably Alexandria, Antioch and Cyrene, but also as far west as Rome and Carthage. As is now clear from documents such as the Cairo Genizah papyri, the diaspora communities maintained contact with Palestine, through trade and regular visits to Jerusalem. Philo, the most important intellectual among diaspora Jews, claimed Jerusalem as a 'capital' for all Jews. Something of this sense of Jerusalem as a centre for diaspora Jews comes across from the description of the preaching of the Apostles in different languages at Pentecost after the death of Jesus. Since most of the diaspora Jews spoke Greek, the majority language of the eastern Mediterranean, interpreters would normally have been needed. The financial significance of the attraction of Jerusalem was considerable, since all male Jews over the age of 20 were required to pay two drachmas for transmission to the Temple.

The messianic preaching of Jesus exposed the faultlines within Judaism, but the extension of his message beyond the Jewish people does not seem to have been in the minds of the Gospel writers. The disciples of Jesus found a place similar to that of other messianic sects, although, unlike the Essenes, they supported and participated fully in worship at the Temple. However, they understood themselves to be a separate group, and established a strict communal governance for themselves. The keynote was prophetic repentance in Jesus' name, backed up by the apparent power of his disciples to work miracles like those attributed to Jesus himself. The early Christians may have acted as a focus for existing discontent among Hellenized Jews against the Temple-based power of the Sadducees. The execution of Stephen, who spoke out against the 'man-made' Temple, in contrast to the transmission of direct revelation from God, indicates not so much that Christians caused dissension between Jewish groups as that they were caught up in existing religious conflicts. It is in this context that Saul (later Paul) came to prominence as a Hellenized diaspora Jew determined to enforce obedience to traditional pharisaic methods and traditions.

Even before Paul's conversion and the beginning of his missionary activity, however, Jesus' disciples had begun to encounter interest from non-Jews in Palestine. Philip is recorded as having made the first Gentile convert, an Ethiopian eunuch, in Gaza. Meanwhile, Peter penetrated Samaria – long hostile to Jews – and then preached in the coastal strip at Lydda and Joppa (Jaffa). The breakthrough, however, came with the conversion of the Roman centurion Cornelius at Caesarea, which seems to have been accomplished through networking among existing Christians. Peter's action in eating with the gentile Cornelius signalled an important break with the direction of the community of disciples to that point, and a new aspiration to reach beyond the different Jewish communities to the wider world.

### Early Christian Identity

It was around this time that the first stirrings of persecution by the public authorities, rather than hostility from other Jews, began. Herod Agrippa's execution of James and arrest of Peter were designed to shore up support for his client kingship from the Sadducees, his political allies. It also reveals divisions in outlook between the Sadducees, who firmly opposed the Christians, and the Pharisees, some of whose members were active supporters of the Church, at least up until the council of Jerusalem. This is hardly surprising, given that theologically the Christians had much in common with the Pharisees, not least on the matter of the resurrection of the dead. Indeed, Paul after his conversion appealed for support from the Pharisees on the understanding that Jesus' message fulfilled their own understanding of Judaism.

The distinctive identity of 'Christians' – the followers of Christ – is first recorded in Antioch, however, in c. AD 40, superseding the label of 'Nazarenes' applied to them in Palestine. Once the Christians moved geographically beyond the regions known to Jesus, they confronted people to whom the context of Jesus' preaching was unfamiliar. This raised serious questions about the meaning of the new preaching. A Hellenized Jew such as Paul had little in common with the rural poor of Galilee from whom Jesus had chosen his first followers.

Paul's identity was multi-layered. A Hebrew and Greek speaker, he wrote in Greek, and based his missions in the Hellenized cities of Asia Minor and Greece. Yet, in response to Jews who sought to challenge his authority, he insisted on his Jewish ancestry. Yet he was born a Roman citizen, a privileged position granted by the comparative prosperity of his family, and his Roman identity permitted an ease of movement and a relationship with local civic authorities that greatly facilitated his mission. His letters to diaspora communities reveal the tensions implicit in Mediterranean religious identities in the 1st century AD.

### Organization, Theology and Leadership

Events such as the Jewish revolt of AD 66–70 and the destruction of the Temple, followed by Bar Kokhba's rebellion of AD 135–6 and Hadrian's attempt to eradicate Jerusalem as a Jewish centre altogether, forced Christians to shape a new identity for their Church. Effectively, the loss of the Temple meant that there was no longer a ritual centre for Judaism. Diaspora Jews had long-established synagogues and schools across the Mediterranean In Palestine itself the Pharisees re-organized themselves at an academy at Jamnia and established a new leadership. It was now necessary for Christians to establish their own organizational framework. Moreover, after the deaths of James, Jesus' brother, at the hands of the Sadducees in AD 62 and Paul in Rome in AD 66–67, no obvious leader emerged. This lack of central authority is clear from the diversity of Christian writing from the late 1st century to the 3rd, when a systematic theology first emerged. In so far as Christianity had a centre, it was Antioch, the first seat of Peter and at the end of the 1st century AD, of his successor Ignatius, whose

writings en route to his martyrdom in AD 107–8 continue the epistolary tradition of Paul. From Antioch Christianity spread north to Edessa, where an ascetic Aramaic-based version of Jesus' teaching is evident in the Gospel of Thomas, and, in the early 3rd century, into Osrhoene. In Egypt, early Christianity took different forms: a philosophical encounter with Platonism on the one hand, and a Jewish-rooted tradition that must have had links with the Jewish centre of Alexandria on the other. By the mid-2nd century, various Christian writings were circulating in Egypt. Rome, by virtue of its centrality to the Roman world, offered a logical base for Christianity, and writings such as First Clement, purportedly by Peter's successor Pope Clement to the Corinthians, suggest an organization based on a committee of elders.

An inevitable result of the spread of the new religion was that Christians came to the attention of the Roman authorities. The first act of systematic persecution, Nero's scapegoating of Christians in Rome for the fire of AD 64, was approved by the Roman historian Suetonius, who, probably like most Romans, thought the Christians morally subversive. Roman religious tradition was pluralist and syncretistic. As long

Today custody of the Church of the Holy Sepulchre, Jerusalem, (above) is shared by the Greek Orthodox, Coptic, Armenian Apostolic and Roman Catholic churches. This has led to clashes between the religious groups.

as one caused no deliberate offence to the divinities of others, one could worship what gods one pleased. Judaism, with its insistence on the exclusive worship of Yahweh, appeared foolishly arrogant. But at least Judaism could be associated with a particular people and land, and the potential of the Jews to revolt against Roman rule meant that Judaism was taken seriously. As the adherents of a marginal apocalyptic sect within Judaism, Christians could be dismissed as anti-social cranks. By the later 2nd century, however, pagan Romans such as Celsus were attacking Christianity in its own right.

The Antonine period (*c.* AD 118–235) was one of unprecedented stability in the Mediterranean under the *pax romana*. For the burgeoning Christian communities in the eastern Mediterranean cities, this was a period of rapid structural development, growing self-confidence of expression and thought – exemplified in the writings of Origen and Justin, and Clement of Alexandria – and material prosperity as seen by distinctive building and artistic decoration. The east Syrian town of Dura Europos boasts the earliest surviving purpose-built church (AD 240–1). For Palestine, however, the picture is more mixed. The first Jewish revolt had brought permanent legions to Palestine, and the campaigns against the Parthians waged by Trajan made Syria and Palestine strategically vital. Hadrian's decision to refound Jerusalem as a Hellenized city, Aelia Capitolina, with a temple to Jupiter where Solomon's Temple had stood, provoked the Bar Kokhba Revolt in AD 132–4. The consequence, once the revolt had been suppressed, was more far-reaching than Vespasian's reaction to the earlier revolt had been. Jewish communities in Palestine were systematically destroyed in an attempt to stamp out the practice of Judaism in its homeland, and Jews were forbidden to live in Jerusalem. Despite the severity of the reaction, Jewish groups returned to Galilee and Judea. The Temple was never rebuilt, but surviving mosaic floors and inscriptions attest to a return to prosperity for Jewish communities in Tiberias, Sepphoris, Gadara and elsewhere in Galilee by the 4th to 5th centuries.

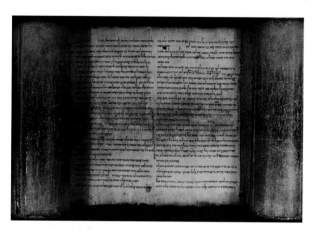

Section of the Great Isaiah Scroll found at the Essene settlement at Qumran in 1947. Alongside the Pharisees and Sadducees, the Essenes were one of three sects in 'Jewish philosophy' identified by the historian Josephus. All three groups had an influence on early Christianity. The Dead Sea scrolls include the oldest Hebrew manuscripts of the Bible dating to the 2nd century BC.

The acceptance of Christianity by Emperor Constantine in AD 312 opens a new chapter in the history and topography of Palestine. Although Constantine had hoped that Christianity would provide a force for unity in the Roman empire, by the later 4th century it was clear that there was little consensus about theological orthodoxy within the Church. This is hardly surprising given the rapid spread of the religion among far-flung urban centres across the Mediterranean. Different local churches developed their own customs of worship and procedure, and although local synods attempted to shape discipline and practice within the Church, there was no attempt to enforce a common orthodoxy before the first council of Nicaea in 325. Thus the Church before the 4th century enjoyed considerable latitude in theological belief.

## Christian Holy Sites

There is still considerable debate among historians and archaeologists over the extent of continuity between Jewish and Christian holy sites in Jerusalem. The current consensus distances the birth of the practice of veneration of holy sites and of pilgrimage in the 4th century from any pre-4th century Christian practices. Indeed, before the AD 320s, the place of primary importance in the early Church was not the site of Jesus' burial but the site identified as the birthplace of the Church itself – Mount Zion, where the Eucharist was established at the Last Supper and where the Apostles received the Holy Spirit at Pentecost. Early pilgrimage itineraries place Mount Zion at the centre of a complex liturgical drama involving processions between different shrines. It was not until the culture of the Church itself changed after the end of the Great Persecution (303), and the role of martyrdom took on new significance, that any attempt was made to venerate the site of the crucifixion or resurrection of Christ.

The identification of sites associated with the life of Christ began under Emperor Constantine in the AD 320s. It started, according to Christian tradition, after his mother Helena had a vision instructing her to dig under a rubbish heap where the remains of the cross and tomb would be found. The result was a huge church-building programme in the 4th century. Most prominent among these was the Anastasis Church (or Church of the Holy Sepulchre), built over the supposed site of the burial and resurrection of Jesus, which lay just outside the walls of the city in the 1st century, but within the rebuilt Hellenistic city of the 2nd century AD. The whole complex, comprising a martyrium, atrium and Calvary chapel as well as the domed Resurrection church, would be rebuilt following successive demolitions until reaching its present shape in the 12th century under the Crusaders. The presence of this shrine, as well as the church of Mount Zion (the earliest site of Christian worship in Jerusalem), the Church of the Nativity in Bethlehem, the Church of the Annunciation in Nazareth and other shrine churches in Galilee, assured a constant influx of pilgrims to Palestine from the mid-4th century onwards. This in turn gave the province a character quite distinct from other parts of the Christian Mediterranean. For one thing, it was more 'international', in the sense that Christians from all over the empire were drawn there, not only as pilgrims but also to settle in the religious life.

The Chapel of the Ascension at the Mount of Olives in Jerusalem marks the site where, according to Christian tradition, Jesus ascended into heaven. Although the Crusader church became a mosque in the 12th century AD, it has not been used by Muslims. Saladin had a second mosque built next to the chapel for Muslim worship.

## Monasticism in Palestine

Palestine became an early centre for a type of monasticism linked intimately to the holy places and to the service of pilgrims. The Judean desert monasteries, which flourished between the 4th and 7th centuries, were mostly within half a day's walk of Jerusalem, and maintained close links not only with each other but with the city itself. Although the earliest Palestinian monasteries are associated with Hilarion and Chariton in the 4th century, it was Sabas, in the late 5th to early 6th centuries, who brought Judean desert monasticism to its fulfilment. Sabas had been both a cenobitic (communal) monk and an anchorite (solitary) before founding his own 'laura' in the Kidron valley southeast of Bethlehem. The laura combined elements of solitary and communal monasticism, by encouraging monks to pray and meditate alone in individual cells during the week, and to gather for communal worship on Sundays and feast days. The result was a more moderate form of religious life than the extreme mortification characteristic of Syrian monasteries.

The monasteries also developed a theology more in tune with the centre of the Christian world than with the great eastern theological centres of Antioch and Alexandria. This explains why, when at the Council of Chalcedon in AD 451 the churches of those cities broke with the doctrinal orthodoxy of Rome and Constantinople, the Church of Jerusalem remained 'Chalcedonian' rather than following the logical development of the separated Churches of the Syrians and Copts. In recognition of its spiritual significance, the bishopric of Jerusalem became a patriarchate in 451. The 6th century AD saw an increasing dislocation of eastern provinces from the governmental centre in Constantinople. The Samaritan community was brought to a violent end following a revolt against the rule of Justinian in the mid-6th century. Political changes, however, did not affect the cultural and economic stability that Palestine enjoyed on the eve of the Persian and Islamic conquests.

# Palestine during Jesus' Lifetime

*During Jesus' lifetime, intense political turmoil threatened the independence of Judea. On Herod's death in 4 BC, his realm was split between three of his sons: Herod Archelaus received Samaria, Judea and Idumea; Philip inherited the Golan Heights; and Herod Antipas took control of Galilee and Perea, east of the River Jordan.*

A Samaritan sarcophagus from the 1st century AD. Samaria, once the capital of the Kingdom of Israel, was the chief town of the region of the same name controlled by Herod Archelaus. The city is linked with John the Baptist, who is thought to have been buried there.

*"Now at this time Caesar Augustus issued a decree for a census of the whole world to be taken. This census – the first – took place while Quirinius was governor of Syria, and everyone went to his own town to be registered."*

Luke 2.1–2

The coastal lands of Phoenicia and Decapolis to the east were part of the Roman province of Syria. Of the three Herodian brothers, Philip (r. 4 BC–AD 34) received the poorest inheritance, but enjoyed the most prosperous reign. He founded new cities and introduced many elements of Graeco-Roman culture into his realm.

Herod Antipas governed Galilee and Perea (r. 4 BC–AD 6) during the lifetime of Jesus Christ, which meant that he had to placate his Roman patrons and a population of exceptionally mixed ethnic backgrounds (some of whom were pro-Hellenization and some violently anti-Roman). He also had to deal with the growing popularity and potential threat of the followers of Jesus of Galilee. In 17 AD Herod Antipas founded Tiberias on the west coast of the Sea of Galilee; he built a grand Hellenistic city to serve as his capital. Unfortunately its location atop an ancient Jewish cemetery offended his Jewish subjects, generating little support and even less loyalty from them. Herod Antipas was responsible for the imprisonment and beheading of John the Baptist – largely through the machinations of his wife, Herodias – and he was also initially consulted following Jesus' arrest. In AD 37 the Nabateans invaded Perea. Having offended the king of Nabatea and the Roman emperor Caligula, Herod Antipas lost his lands in AD 39 to his nephew Herod Agrippa I (d. AD 44), a close friend of the emperors Caligula and Claudius. Agrippa had already been awarded the Golan Heights on the death of his uncle Philip. Herod Agrippa was the son of Aristobulus, another son of Herod the Great. The antagonistic relationship between Aristobulus and his own father had led the vengeful and unstable Herod to order his son's execution in AD 7. The fatherless Herod Agrippa, a Jewish prince, had been raised in Rome with children of the imperial family, and would receive lifelong support from his Roman friends.

## Herod Archelaus

It was Herod Archelaus (r. 4 BC–AD 6), Herod the Great's eldest surviving son, who had received the lion's share of his father's kingdom. The emperor Augustus granted him the title of ethnarch ('national leader') rather than that of 'king' as held by his father. Although his territories were larger than those of his brothers, the heavy concentration of Jews, many of whom regarded him as a foreign usurper of the Jewish kingdom – as they had his father before him – made his short rule a difficult one.

The evangelist Matthew hints at the poor state of affairs for Jews under Archelaus' rule when he claims that Jesus' parents fled Judea for Galilee prior to Jesus' birth. In the wake of great Jewish unrest and anger following the murders of two well-known Jewish scholars in the weeks before Herod's death, Archelaus travelled to Rome to be crowned, a journey which led to the outbreak of further unrest in his realm. Roman legions from Syria put down the rebellion, but Archelaus was soon after exiled to Gaul following accusations of misrule by his subjects. For the next 35 years (AD 6–41), Archelaus' territory was run by prefects who governed on behalf of Rome. Herod Agrippa had already been given the title King of Judea by Caligula in AD 37, but it was not until the accession of Claudius to the imperial throne in AD 41 that Judea, Samaria and Idumea were placed under Herod Agrippa's jurisdiction. Like his grandfather, Herod the Great, Herod Agrippa was now king of all of Palestine.

**N**

*Mediterranean Sea*

Sidon
Zarephath
▲ *Mount Hermon*
Paneas
Caesarea Philippi
**SYRIA**
Damascus
Tyre
**Phoenicia**
Acco
Capernaum
Gennesaret
Magdala
*Sea of Galilee*
**Gaulanitis**
**Batanaea**
**Trachonitis**
▲ *Mount Carmel*
**Galilee** Tiberias
Cana
Mount Tabor
Nazareth
Nain
Gadara
**Auranitis**
Caesarea
Beit-shean
Salim
Aenon
Samaria
Sychar
**Samaria**
**Decapolis**
*Jordan River*
Apollonia
Antipatris
Arimathaea
Joppa
Lydda
Ephraim
**Perea**
**Judea**
Emmaus
Nicopolis
Mount of Olives
Jericho
Julias
El Maghtas
Ashdod
Azotus
Jerusalem
Bethphage
Bethany
Ascalon
Bethlehem
**Philistia**
Gaza
**Idumea**
*Dead Sea*
Machaerus
Masada
Raphia
Beersheba
**NABATEAN KINGDOM**

c. 4 BC: Joseph and his family return from Egypt an settle in Nazareth (Matthew 2:19–23)

Jesus works in Nazareth as a carpenter (Luke 2:51)

John the Baptist baptizes many near Aenon

Jesus is taken as a baby to Jerusalem for presentation at the Temple (Luke 2:22)

c. AD 6: The 12-year-old Jesus visits Jerusalem with his family, and stays behind in the Temple (Luke 2:41–46)

Jesus is baptized in the River Jordan by John the Baptist (Matthew 3:13)

Before AD 5–6: John the Baptist is imprisoned in Machaerus by Herod Antipas and is beheaded there

c. 6 BC: Jesus born at Bethlehem (Luke 2:4–7)

c. 4 BC: Joseph and Mary take Jesus from Bethlehem to Egypt to escape the 'massacre of the innocents' by Herod the Great (Matthew 2:13–18)

35° · 36°E · 33°N · 32°

0 — 50 km
0 — 30 miles

## Palestine during Jesus' Lifetime

— boundary of Herod's kingdom in 20 BC

▨ Roman province of Syria

⊕ place associated with Jesus

● place associated with John the Baptist

— road

**Division of Herod's kingdom between his sons**

☐ Herod Archelaus (under Roman governors after AD 6)

☐ Herod Antipas

☐ Philip

# Jesus in Galilee

*The term 'Galilee' (meaning circuit or 'district' in Hebrew) was initially applied to several areas of Palestine. Under the Romans, it was the official name for the part of northern Palestine bounded by the River Jordan to the east and the Esdraelon valley to the south.*

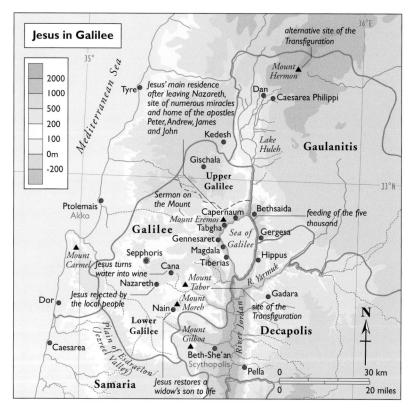

*"As he was walking by the Sea of Galilee he saw two brothers: Simon, who was called Peter, and his brother Andrew; they were making a cast in the lake with their net, for they were fishermen."*

Matthew 4.18–19

Galilee's northern and western borders are disputed, but most probably incorporated the lands immediately northeast of Lake Huleh, which was drained in the 1950s to provide fertile farmland, and possibly the coastal lands of Tyre between Acco (Ptolemais) and Mount Carmel. The region was divided into mountainous, sparsely settled Upper Galilee, and Lower Galilee, which was more heavily populated, urban and Hellenized.

## Hellenistic Influence

The strongly entrenched Canaanite presence in the Galilee region and its relative distance from the Jewish heartland around the city of Jerusalem has led most scholars to regard Galilee as more multicultural and possessing a larger and more influential Gentile (non-Jewish) population than Judea. Some scholars challenge this theory of a 'less Jewish' Galilee by claiming that most of the evidence of pagan practices in Galilee post-dates the Herodian era. Regardless of the relative influence of the Jewish population in Galilee during the lifetime of Jesus, it is known that Herod Antipas, a son of Herod the Great and a Jew himself although not of Hebrew ancestry, introduced many aspects of Hellenistic culture into Galilee. Also, the thriving Gentile cities that

Ancient ruins of the city of Capernaum (also known as Tell Hum). Capernaum was built along the edge of the Sea of Galilee and, according to Matthew's Gospel, Jesus lived there during his ministry.

surrounded Galilee, such as Tyre, Sidon and Scythopolis, may well have lent a more cosmopolitan flavour to the region.

The Romans saw Jerusalem and its environs as the centre of potential Jewish rebellion and so focused their attention on maintaining control over the Jewish leaders within that city, expecting that the wider Jewish population could be governed in this way. The Jewish population of Galilee, geographically removed from Jerusalem, was less involved in the religious debates that raged there. The division between the religiously conservative, pro-Roman Sadducees and more pragmatic, culturally exclusive Pharisees that was prevalent among Jews in southern Palestine was echoed in the north, but with much less intensity. This, combined with a much less obtrusive Roman presence, perhaps allowed a greater measure of religious freedom in Galilee.

## Miracles and Ministry

The following that grew up around Jesus Christ was not the first such 'radical' Jewish sect to have originated in Galilee, where relative tolerance created a more receptive environment for more 'individual' approaches. Although Jesus travelled many times down to Jerusalem (including for the dramatic events at the end of his life), it is significant that the majority of his miracles and much of his ministry took place in Galilee (and in Perea, another territory governed by Herod Antipas). His key disciples, the Apostles, came from Galilee (although there is a question about the origins of Judas Iscariot). Most of the locations where Jesus preached or performed miracles have been firmly identified, although the location of Cana, site of the famous wedding where Jesus turned water into wine, continues to be disputed. Neither Sepphoris nor Tiberias – the two most important cities in 1st-century Galilee – is specifically mentioned in discussions of the ministry of Jesus. Located less than 10 kilometres (6 miles) from Nazareth, Sepphoris would certainly have been familiar to Jesus. In fact it may even have been the birthplace of his mother, Mary. Tiberias, built by Herod Antipas to serve as his capital city, was erected on the site of a Jewish cemetery and was largely shunned by Jews during this period.

## Capernaum

The Bible states that Jesus left Nazareth and settled in the Galilean town of Capernaum, located on the northern coast of the Sea of Galilee; from Capernaum Jesus conducted much of his ministry. Capernaum was a thriving town – rather than a bustling city – and it was a station along the trading route between Beth-She'an and Damascus. Although evidence of a Roman garrison survives to the east of the settlement, Capernaum, in contrast with Tiberias or Sepphoris, would have enjoyed a relatively small Roman military presence, making it possible for Jesus to preach to those passing through without inciting too much Roman interest in his activities. Simon Peter, Andrew, James, John and Matthew, five of the twelve apostles, were residents of Capernaum and archaeological excavations have unearthed a large dwelling whose location corresponds to the biblical location of the house of Peter and his extended family; later graffiti certainly suggests that the building was viewed as important by Christians in the centuries immediately following Christ's death. The extant ruins of Capernaum's synagogue date from the 4th century AD, but they appear to stand on foundations erected early in the 1st century. This earlier structure may well be the site that was built through the benefices of the Roman legionary mentioned in the Gospel of St Luke (Luke 7:5) and from where Jesus preached and spread his message to local Jews and other visitors.

# Jesus in Judea and Jerusalem

*Jesus spent most of his life in Galilee, but Judea, and especially Jerusalem and its environs, played a very significant role in his life. The Bible states that Jesus was born in the village of Bethlehem just south of Jerusalem (probably between 6 and 4 BC).*

According to Luke's Gospel, Mary, his mother, had travelled with her husband Joseph from their home in Nazareth in Galilee to Judea to register Joseph (whose family came from there) for a Roman taxation census. The documented events from Jesus' early life all took place in Judea, and he was not taken back into Galilee until he and his parents returned from their journey into Egypt to escape Herod's plot to kill all Jewish male infants resident in Bethlehem.

Jesus grew up in Galilee and began his ministry there, attracting the attention of the public as well as the increasing concern of the pro-Roman government and the Jewish establishment. He had made occasional trips to Jerusalem in his youth, but it was not until he was well known as a charismatic religious figure that he left Galilee to travel south into Judea and Perea. Jerusalem was the final focus of his public ministry and it was there that he was

arrested, condemned and executed. During the years before Jesus died (*c.* AD 30), Judea was governed by Pontius Pilate, Roman prefect from AD 26 to 36. Pilate, a Gentile (non-Jew), governed from the coastal city of Caesarea and was eventually recalled to Rome, possibly to answer charges of harsh and unfair treatment of his subjects; little else is known about his life. Jews did not view him favourably as he regularly ignored their traditions and defiled their holy places with imperial and pagan imagery.

### The Jewish Establishment

Jerusalem itself, and to some extent the entire Jewish population, were directly ruled over by the High Priest. The office of High Priest began as a spiritual one, but encompassed increasing political powers from the 2nd century BC onwards. The High Priest during Jesus' final time in Jerusalem was Josephus Caiaphas. Caiaphas was appointed in AD 18 by the Roman prefect Valerius Gratius; he continued as High Priest during the reign of Pontius Pilate and was removed from office in AD 37 by Lucius Vitellius, Roman Governor of Syria. Caiaphas was supported by the wealthy, religiously conservative 'aristocracy' (the Sad-

The Cenacle on Mount Zion is believed to be the site of the Last Supper. The term 'cenacle' comes from the Latin word meaning dinner and is used to refer to the Upper Room where the Last Supper took place. The present building is, however, much later and was built on top of an older structure in the 14th century.

ducees), who no doubt influenced him in his role as chief judge of the Sanhedrin (the Jewish court system). Jesus and his teachings would have met with little support among this politically aware sector of Judaism. It was Caiaphas who sent Jesus before Pontius Pilate, the regional representaive of Rome. Although Caiaphas held the office of High Priest, day-to-day religious authority over the vast majority of Jews was held by the Pharisees, who controlled most synagogues and enjoyed great popularity within the Jewish population. The Pharisees were much less supportive of the Romans, and objected to Jesus and his ministry purely on a religious, non-political level. While the Pharisees exerted great influence over the Jewish masses, their domination was by no means unquestioned. It was from the Jewish inhabitants of Palestine that Jesus drew his many followers.

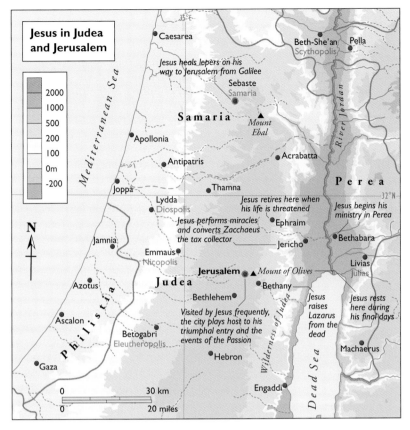

**Jesus in Judea and Jerusalem**

2000
1000
500
200
100
0m
-200

Mediterranean Sea

Caesarea

Beth-She'an
Scytholpolis
Pella

*Jesus heals lepers on his
way to Jerusalem from Galilee*

Sebaste
Samaria

**S a m a r i a**

▲ Mount
Ebal

River Jordan

Apollonia

Antipatris

Acrabatta

**P e r e a**

Joppa

Thamna

32°N

Lydda
Diospolis

*Jesus retires here when
his life is threatened*

*Jesus begins his
ministry in Perea*

*Jesus performs miracles
and converts Zacchaeus
the tax collector*

Ephraim

Bethabara

Jamnia

Jericho

Emmaus
Nicopolis

Livias
Julias

**Jerusalem** ◉ ▲ Mount of Olives

**J u d e a**

Bethany

Azotus

Bethlehem

*Jesus
raises
Lazarus
from the
dead*

*Jesus rests
here during
his final days*

Ascalon

*Visited by Jesus frequently,
the city plays host to his
triumphal entry and the
events of the Passion*

Betogabri
Eleutheropolis

Machaerus

Gaza

Hebron

Wilderness of Judea

Dead Sea

P h i l i s t i a

N

Engaddi

0    30 km
0    20 miles

Jersusalem was, of course, the major city in Judea; its religious and historical importance as well as its geographically central location and commercial successes ensured that it easily eclipsed Judea's other urban settlements. Smaller cities did exist, however, and a number of these served as regional seats of Roman power within Judea. In his book on the Jewish Wars, the 1st-century Jewish historian Josephus lists these cities, stating that Gophna was the province's second city. Gophna (modern Jifna) lies about 25 kilometres (15 miles) north of Jerusalem (on the West Bank) and is now primarily inhabited by Palestinian Christians. It was awarded an elevated administrative role following Judea's conquest by Rome in the 1st century BC. Little is known about the city before this period, and its importance appears to have diminished rather quickly following the Islamic conquest of the area.

The other cities mentioned by Josephus are Acrabatta (modern Aqrabeh), Thamna (modern Timnah), Lydda (modern Lod), Emmaus, Pella (now in Jordan), Idumea, Engaddi, Herodium and Jericho. Most of these cities are ancient settlements that played notable roles in the region's history before the arrival of the Romans. Others, like Herodium and Emmaus, appear to owe their newfound status directly to their Roman patrons. Several are mentioned in the Old Testament, however, the Bible connects only three with Jesus and his teachings. Jesus may have moved about while preaching in Judea, but, aside from Jerusalem, only Jericho is recorded as having hosted Jesus (Luke Chapters 18 and 19). After his death Jesus is stated as having appeared to two disciples as they returned to Emmaus following the crucifixion (Luke 24:13–35), and Chapter 9 of the Book of Acts tells of his apostle Peter performing miracles in Lydda.

*"The next day the crowds who had come up for the festival heard that Jesus was on his way to Jerusalem. They took branches of palm and went out to meet him, shouting, 'Hosanna! Blessings on the king of Israel, who comes in the name of the Lord'.*"

John 12.12–13

# Bethlehem

*The city of Bethlehem in Judea is best known as the birthplace of Jesus Christ. There is, however, no contemporary evidence for this and the relevant passages in the second chapters of the Gospels of Matthew and Luke, both written at least half a century after Jesus' death (and perhaps later than that), are the earliest written sources.*

The Church of the Nativity in Bethlehem is the oldest church in use in the Holy Land. It is jointly run by Roman Catholics, Greek Orthodox Christians and Armenian Apostolics.

Centuries of veneration of, and pilgrimage to, the site at Bethlehem indicate a very ancient association of this spot with the birth of Jesus Christ. There is, though, another village of Bethlehem in Galilee, only a few kilometres northwest of Nazareth. This village possesses archaeological remains that have been dated to the Herodian period, and a handful of scholars argue that this is a much more likely location for Christ's nativity. However, there is little popular support for this theory.

Judean Bethlehem, also referred to as Bethlehem Ephrathah, is an ancient settlement although little is known about its pre-Christian archaeological remains. The Bible is the principal documentary source of information about Bethlehem, although there is a possible reference to it in the Egyptian el-Amarna letters from the 14th century BC. Rachel, wife of Jacob and mother of Joseph

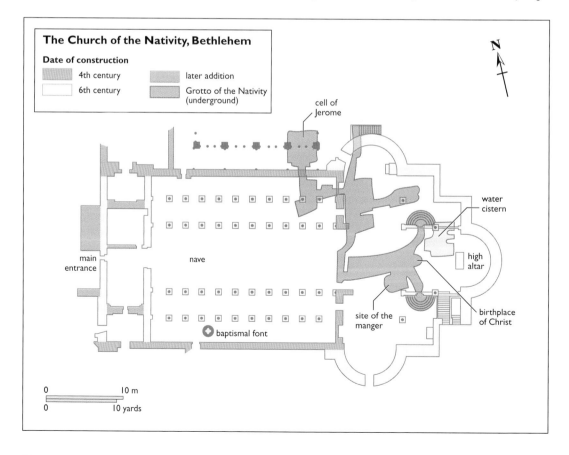

**The Church of the Nativity, Bethlehem**

**Date of construction**

| | |
|---|---|
| 4th century | later addition |
| 6th century | Grotto of the Nativity (underground) |

N

cell of Jerome

water cistern

main entrance

nave

high altar

site of the manger

birthplace of Christ

baptismal font

0      10 m

0      10 yards

and Benjamin, died in childbirth on the outskirts of Jerusalem (Genesis 35: 19); her tomb remains a Jewish pilgrimage site. The Old Testament Book of Ruth is largely set in Bethlehem, the hometown of Naomi and the site of Ruth's marriage to Boaz. David was a descendant of Ruth and he, too, was born in Bethlehem (as implied in Ruth Chapter 4). Jesus' birth in Bethlehem fulfilled a prophecy made by Micah that Bethlehem would provide God's chosen ruler of Israel (Micah 5:2). The Bible also suggests that, during the reign of David, Bethlehem was garrisoned by the Philistines (2 Samuel 23:14; 1 Chronicles 11:16) and that Rehoboam, the first king of Judah, rebuilt and fortified the city during the late 10th century BC (2 Chronicles 11:6).

## The Church of the Nativity

There has been a Christian shrine over the site believed to be Jesus' birthplace since the AD 320s when Helena, the mother of the emperor Constantine, had the first church built there. Helena's church was rebuilt by Emperor Justinian in the 6th century AD, and it is largely this structure that survives today, although the interior was extensively redecorated in the 1160s. In the late 4th century AD Bethlehem's importance as a pilgrimage destination increased with the founding of a monastery there by the Latin theologian Jerome. Two other sites in Bethlehem attracted pilgrims from the 5th century onwards: the 'Shepherds' Fields', two kilometres (1.2 miles) southeast of Bethlehem, supposedly the spot where the angels appeared to the shepherds to announce Jesus' birth; and the 'Milk Grotto', south of the Church of the Nativity, which according to early pilgrimage tradition commemorated the place where Mary stopped on the flight to Egypt to breastfeed the baby Jesus. The chalky stone of the cave gave rise to the popular belief that some of Mary's milk had fallen on the stone.

> *"Now when the angels had gone from them into heaven, the shepherds said to one another, 'Let us go to Bethlehem and see this thing that has happened which the Lord has made known to us.'"*
>
> Luke 2.15–16

Both this site and the Church of the Nativity were cult sites for Muslims as well as Christians during the Islamic period, which explains why Bethlehem remained relatively unaltered after the Arab conquests. The Church of the Nativity survived the persecution of Christians and attacks on churches by the caliph al-Hakim in AD 1009. According to one contemporary source, local Muslims who venerated the church refused to carry out orders to destroy it. In June 1099, Bethlehem was captured by a detachment of First Crusaders under Tancred. Despite its significance as a pilgrimage site, Bethlehem had never ranked higher in the Byzantine Church hierarchy than a parish. Under the Crusaders, however, it became the seat of a bishopric in the 12th century. In the nave and apse of the church, mosaics from the 1160s are testimony to the continuing presence of a Greek-speaking community at Bethlehem under Crusader rule. Even after the expulsion of the Crusaders, Bethlehem remained a key pilgrimage destination. Bethlehem continues to draw Christian pilgrims, although the site is also sacred to Jews and to Muslims, who view Jesus as an important prophet.

Grotto in the crypt of the Church of the Nativity in Bethlehem, where Jesus is believed to have been born. The site of Jesus' birth was identified as early as the 2nd century AD.

Modern Bethlehem has a population of just under 30,000 that includes a significant number of native Palestinian Christians. After centuries of Islamic rule, Bethlehem was part of the territory of the British Mandate (1920–48). The Jordanians governed it from 1950 until 1967, when, as part of the West Bank, Bethlehem came under Israeli control following the Six-Day War. Since 1995 Bethlehem has been governed by the Palestinians. It remains a major pilgrimage centre, and its economy, much as it always has, continues to rely heavily on tourism and agriculture.

# Qumran and the Dead Sea Scrolls

*In 1947 a Bedouin shepherd found some fragmentary scrolls in a cave near Khirbat Qumran on the northwest coast of the Dead Sea. From 1947 to 1956 over 850 documents were discovered in 11 caves. Further scrolls were uncovered at four other sites nearby.*

These texts, known as the Dead Sea Scrolls, have great religious and historical significance. Scientific testing, internal historical evidence and palaeographic and epigraphic comparisons suggest that the scrolls range in date from 250 BC to the years leading up to the destruction of the Second Temple by the Romans in AD

Khirbat Qumran, the Essene settlement close to the caves where the scrolls were found. Until the 1990s most scholars believed that the Essenes had produced the scrolls. Evidence for this theory includes the inkwells and tables that may have formed a scriptorium.

70. They are made of papyrus and treated animal skins, with one example made from sheets of copper. Most of the texts are written in Hebrew dialects, but there are examples in Aramaic and Greek. The scrolls consist of scripture, exegetical texts and commentaries, as well as prayers, regulations and treatises.

The numerous texts of acanonical scripture and the content of the non-scriptural scrolls suggest that they may represent the communal library of a minority sect within Judaism. Although some scholars dispute this theory, others believe

*"He shall guide them with knowledge and instruct them in the mysteries of wonder and truth in the midst of the members of the community, so that they shall behave decently with one another in all that has been revealed to them."*

Dead Sea Scrolls, Community Rule

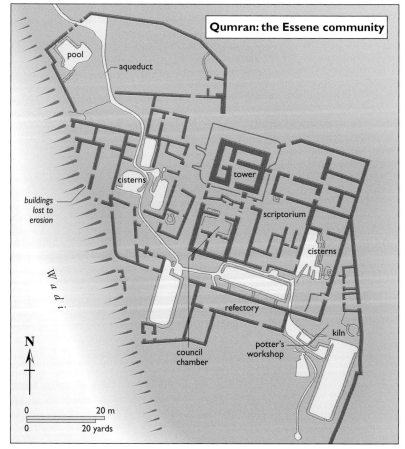

**Qumran: the Essene community**

pool
aqueduct
cisterns
tower
buildings lost to erosion
scriptorium
cisterns
Wadi
refectory
kiln
council chamber
potter's workshop
N

0     20 m
0     20 yards

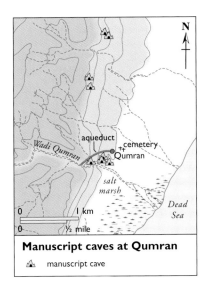

**Manuscript caves at Qumran**

⌂ manuscript cave

that the Dead Sea Scrolls are connected with the Essenes, a rigidly ascetical, apocalyptic sect. The Essenes, established in the 2nd century BC as a reaction against perceived corruption within the priesthood of the Temple in Jerusalem, were pacifists who practised celibacy, adopting sons in order to perpetuate their beliefs. It is also possible that the scrolls represent the personal library of a wealthy Jewish intellectual, or that they once formed part of a library associated with the Temple in Jerusalem. Regardless of their origin, it is likely that the Dead Sea Scrolls were hidden in the caves to protect them from discovery or damage by a hostile party. As the latest documents in the collection date from *c.* AD 68 – the date that Qumran fell to the Romans after the unsuccessful Jewish revolt of AD 66 – the case for the removal of the documents to caves near the Dead Sea at that time is a seductive one.

A French archaeologist, Roland de Vaux, excavated the ancient site of Qumran in the 1950s in an attempt to locate the community that had hidden the scrolls in the local caves. Believing that the scrolls were originally written and housed in the area in which they were found, he was quick to interpret his findings at Qumran as an Essene community, complete with scriptorium and a large bathing area (for ritual immersion). The settlement appears to have been founded around 150 BC and there is evidence that it sustained heavy damage from an earthquake during the reign of Herod the Great before it was destroyed by the Romans. Although de Vaux's theory has considerable support, there are many who question the connection between the Qumran community and the scrolls. The settlement excavated by the Frenchman may have been a privately owned villa, a community of a different sect or even a garrison of some type.

### Translating the Scrolls

The interpretation of the contents of the Dead Sea Scrolls presented a unique challenge to the academic world, as well as to the Judeo-Christian religious establishment. It was crucial that any transcriptions or translations be of the highest quality to minimize any confusion about the nature of the texts. A very small group of expert scholars was responsible for working through the scrolls and preparing each for publication. This approach increasingly came under criticism by other scholars concerned that it would be decades before a critical number would be available. Others also felt that it was not advantageous to keep scholarship concerning the scrolls under such tight control, thus preventing the academic community at large from examining them. The Israel Antiquities Authority enlarged the group of scholars, which led to the full publication of the Dead Sea Scrolls in 2001. Owing to their extremely fragile condition, the scrolls have been photographed only once; an international team based in Jerusalem is in the process of digitizing the scrolls for the Internet. Once this project is completed, probably by 2010, scholars, students and the public will be able to access high quality images of the scrolls without damaging these incredibly delicate objects.

One of the scroll caves at Qumran. A Bedouin shepherd is generally credited with discovering the first scrolls in 1947, after he went in search of a stray goat and came across a pottery jar containing the ancient scrolls wrapped in linen.

# New Testament Jerusalem

*By the 1st century AD, Jerusalem had grown into an impressive centre of commerce, religion and culture. This was largely due to the building campaigns of Herod the Great (r. 37–4 BC). Herod's most important project was the lavish reconstruction of Solomon's Temple, last rebuilt after its destruction by the Babylonians in 586 BC.*

By Herod's time, the Temple Mount and the City of David to its south had expanded to include two further areas: the Lower City and the Upper City. The Lower City occupied the area between the City of David and the Tyropoeon Valley that separated it from the Upper City to the north. The commercial hub of New Testament Jerusalem, the Lower City was packed with shops and markets and served as the residential area for Jerusalem's working classes. The Lower City also contained the Siloam Pool, which provided a source of fresh water to the hill-top city. Concealed tunnels built around 700 BC under the direction of King Hezekiah led from a natural spring outside the city walls and ensured Jerusalem's water supply in times of siege.

The Upper City overlooked the Lower City and the Temple Mount and was largely rebuilt under Herod's supervision. This section of Jerusalem was home to the wealthier merchant families, important religious officials and members of the royal household. This was the area of Jerusalem most influenced by the Hellenistic culture promoted by the Romans. The large palace complex built for Herod and his court occupied the northeastern corner of the Upper City, while numerous spacious private homes and official buildings lined its wide streets. Herod also erected a theatre here.

According to biblical accounts, the Upper City played an important role in the events leading up to Christ's crucifixion. The traditional site of the Upper Room where Jesus and the Apostles shared the Last Supper can be found in the Upper City, though the present structure dates only from the 14th century. The houses of the High Priests Annas and Caiaphas would have been located in the Upper City, and Herod's Palace, which was used by Roman prefects when they resided in Jerusalem, is probably the building where Jesus would have gone before Pilate. The Sanhedrin, or Jewish High Court, may well have met in the Upper City near to the Temple Mount, although the location of the Hall of Hewn Stones (in which the Sanhedrin traditionally sat) remains uncertain.

**The Via Dolorosa**

Austrian Hospice — Church of Sisters of Zion — Monastery of Flagellation

Polish chapel

Ethiopian patriarchate

El Khanqa mosque

Coptic patriarchate

Church of Holy Sepulchre — X–XIV

El Omarïye mosque

Armenian chapel

Franciscan Oratory

Church of St Veronica

Russian church

Greek Orthodox monastery

Church of the Redeemer

site of Antonia fortress

*Haram es-Sharif*

Dome of the Rock

N

•••••• Via Dolorosa
I–XIV Stations of the Cross

The Garden Tomb was identified by the British General Gordon as the real tomb of Jesus, rather than the Church of the Holy Sepulchre. His claim has not been widely accepted, but the Garden Tomb gives a better idea of how the tomb of Jesus probably looked.

A third area of Jerusalem, later known as Bezetha or the 'New City', remained outside the city walls during Jesus' lifetime. This area includes the ancient Pool of Bethesda (or Sheep Pool) north of the Temple Mount, where Jesus cured the paralytic (John 5:1-9). The logical area for expansion once the city had outgrown the limited space within the earlier settled sections of the city, the New City appears to have included Golgotha, the spot where Christ was crucified. The Church of the Holy Sepulchre now occupies the traditional site of Golgotha and the Garden Tomb, although alternative locations nearby have also been put forward.

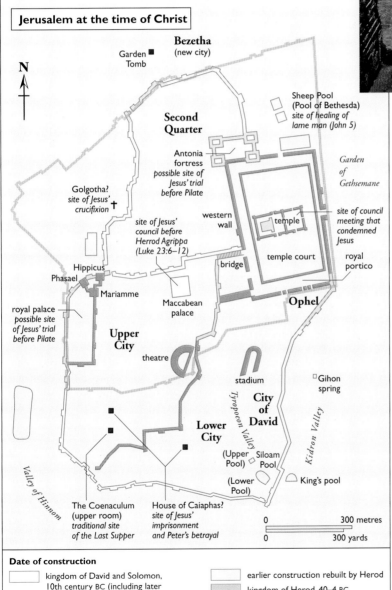

The Pool of Bethesda, now dry, was also known as the Sheep Pool because of its use for washing sheep before their sacrifice in the Temple. The pool acquired a reputation for sanctity by association, and was frequented by invalids in search of a cure.

## Jerusalem at the time of Christ

**Bezetha** (new city)

Garden Tomb

N

Sheep Pool (Pool of Bethesda) *site of healing of lame man (John 5)*

**Second Quarter**

Antonia fortress *possible site of Jesus' trial before Pilate*

*Garden of Gethsemane*

Golgotha? *site of Jesus' crucifixion*

*site of Jesus' council before Herrod Agrippa (Luke 23:6-12)*

western wall

temple

*site of council meeting that condemned Jesus*

Hippicus

Phasael

bridge

temple court

royal portico

Mariamme

Maccabean palace

**Ophel**

royal palace *possible site of Jesus' trial before Pilate*

**Upper City**

theatre

stadium

Gihon spring

*Tyropoeon Valley*

**City of David**

**Lower City**

*Kidron Valley*

(Upper Pool)

Siloam Pool

(Lower Pool)

King's pool

*Valley of Hinnom*

The Coenaculum (upper room) *traditional site of the Last Supper*

House of Caiaphas? *site of Jesus' imprisonment and Peter's betrayal*

0          300 metres
0          300 yards

### Date of construction

| | | |
|---|---|---|
| | kingdom of David and Solomon, 10th century BC (including later reconstruction by Nehemiah c. 440 BC) | earlier construction rebuilt by Herod |
| | Hasmonean kingdom 2nd century BC | kingdom of Herod, 40–4 BC |
| | | modern city wall |

*"Jerusalem, Jerusalem, you who kill the prophets and stone those who are sent to you!"*

Matthew 23.37

# St Paul's Missionary Journeys

Mosaic of St Paul from the Baptistery of the Arians in Ravenna, Italy. Paul was one of the most important early Christian missionaries. He had a vision of the resurrected Christ while travelling on the road to Damascus, which led him to spread the Gospel.

*St Paul, originally known as Saul, was born in Tarsus in Cilicia (modern Turkey) some time in the 1st decade AD. He came from a Jewish family but Roman citizenship was conferred upon him at birth. Paul received a traditional Jewish education in Jerusalem and became a Pharisee, a teacher who interpreted Jewish written and oral law and who generally oversaw local synagogues and the everyday lives of most Jews.*

The Pharisees set themselves firmly against Jesus, believing that he disregarded the importance of many Jewish non-scriptural teachings, and much of Paul's early career was spent persecuting his followers. Just after AD 30, Paul converted to Christianity (still a radical Jewish sect at this early date). From this point onwards Paul dedicated his life to converting both Jews and Gentiles (non-Jews) to the teachings of Christ.

Paul was not one of the original Twelve Apostles, although he did encounter at least some of these men during the course of his life. The incorporation of his biographical details within the Book of Acts and of some of his correspondence ('Epistles') to his disciples and to fledgling Christian communities makes him the second largest contributor to the content of the New Testament; only St Luke composed more of the text. The biblical sources written about Paul are the earliest to survive and the personal insights that fill his letters make him the most accessible and 'fleshed out' of the important figures of the early Church.

> *"Passing through Amphipolis and Apollonia, they eventually reached Thessalonika, where there was a Jewish synagogue. Paul as usual introduced himself and for three consecutive Sabbaths developed the arguments from scripture for them ... "*
>
> Acts 17.1–2

## Missionary Routes

Paul's missionary activity is generally divided into three distinct phases. After some initial preaching in synagogues in Damascus and Judea and three years preaching to the Nabateans to the south, Paul returned to his native Tarsus before travelling south to the Syrian city of Antioch to join a growing Christian community there. In AD 46 Paul and his friend Barnabas set out to preach in Cyprus and the Roman province of Galatia (in Asia Minor), founding communities of (both Jewish and Gentile) converts as they went. Following intense persecution, Paul sailed back to Antioch in 48 AD. In 49 AD he attended a council in Jerusalem where his views on the conversion of Gentiles were backed by other Church leaders. Known as the Council of Jerusalem, this meeting brought together important figures in the early Church and led to the beginning of the formation of Christianity as an independent religion. Paul's second mission (AD 50–52) took him to Macedonia and Achaia (modern Greece). Paul and Barnabas parted ways and Paul travelled with Silas and Timothy to establish churches in cities throughout the region, spending over a year with the Christian

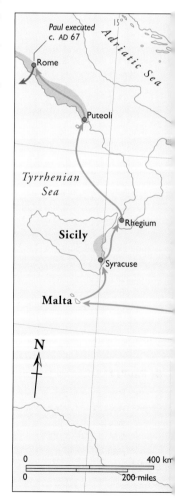

Paul executed c. AD 67

Rome

Puteoli

*Adriatic Sea*

*Tyrrhenian Sea*

Rhegium

**Sicily**

Syracuse

**Malta**

N

| 0 | 400 km |
| 0 | 200 miles |

community in Corinth. Again persecution, this time in the form of arrest and imprisonment, dogged their movements. Paul's third missionary journey centred on the city of Ephesus, although he also revisited the churches that he had established earlier in Galatia and the community in Antioch.

The final years of Paul's life were spent in direct conflict with the traditional Jewish community in Jerusalem and, ultimately, with Rome. In AD 57 Paul was attacked by furious Jews while worshipping on the Temple Mount. Roman authorities intervened and he was sent to Caesarea (the headquarters of the Roman prefect) and, after a wait of two years, to Rome to plead his case before the emperor Nero. A second two years spent under house arrest forced Paul to continue his missionary work by written correspondence. He was freed for two years (during which he may have travelled to Spain), before being arrested again and eventually beheaded at the command of Nero (c. AD 67).

The Pauline Epistles tell us relatively little about the earthly life of Jesus, but are mainly concerned with the concept of Christ's redemption of humankind through his crucifixion and resurrection. Paul's advice to newly converted Christians covers abstract issues of spirituality, but also offers practical help with issues like circumcision among non-Jewish converts and dietary and social constraints. St Paul continues to be viewed by many as the most important theologian of the early Church.

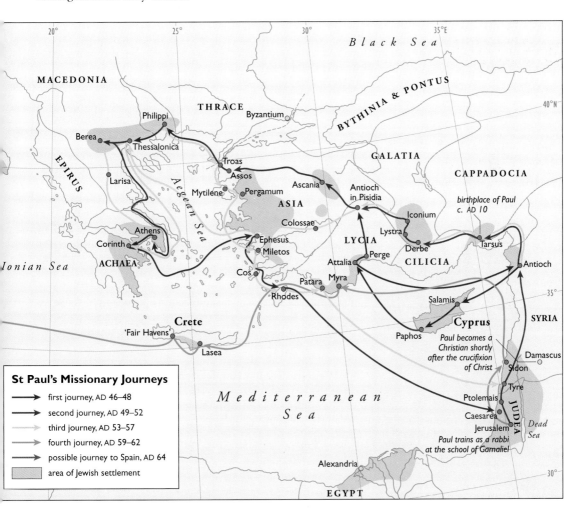

### St Paul's Missionary Journeys

→ first journey, AD 46–48
→ second journey, AD 49–52
→ third journey, AD 53–57
→ fourth journey, AD 59–62
→ possible journey to Spain, AD 64
▨ area of Jewish settlement

# The Apocalypse and Asia Minor

*Controversy surrounds nearly every aspect of the Book of Revelation, the sole apocalyptic text of the New Testament. The text consists of two main sections, the first containing letters to the Seven Churches of Asia and the second, longer portion containing prophetic visions of the end of the world and of the heavenly Jerusalem.*

*"Write down all that you see in a book, and send it to the seven churches of Ephesus, Smyrna, Pergamum, Thyatira, Sardis, Philadelphia and Laodicea."*

Revelation 1.11

A brief prologue to the Book of Revelation states that the author, John, received his vision directly from Jesus Christ, and the epilogue is a final warning from Jesus himself. The author claims that his apocalyptic visions came to him after he had preached about Jesus and while he was on Patmos, an island in the Dodecanese just off the west coast of Asia Minor.

Millenarian prophecies were popular among Jews during the Roman period, and the apocalyptic nature of John's text merely echoes a prevalent theme among mystical sects of the period. The text itself is problematic; it exhibits more than one literary style and syntactical usage, and it has been suggested that the Book of Revelation actually represents two (or more) separate prophecies reworked into a single narrative. The emphasis on the need for Christian communities to remain strong in their faith while the world around them collapses has led many scholars to suggest that the text(s) must have been written during a period of sustained and serious persecution of Christians. The years eading up to AD 100, during the reigns of Domitian or Trajan, and earlier under Nero just before the destruction of the Temple by the Romans (AD 70) would seem the most likely dates to consider. Although recently scholars have noted the paucity of evidence for Christian persecution during Domitian's reign, *c.* AD 95 remains the favoured date for the composition of John's prophetic text.

## Author of Revelation

That the island of Patmos was a frequent destination for those exiled by Rome adds further weight to the anti-Roman reading of the text. Its author remains unknown, although some scholars follow Christian tradition in identifying him with John the Evangelist. Although many scholars concur with Christian tradition in equating John of Patmos with the author of St John's Gospel as well as the Epistle of John, others believe that these three texts were in fact written by

A 13th-century fresco from Anagni Cathedral in Italy shows the Christ of the Apocalypse on his throne. With a sword in his mouth, he is holding seven stars and keys. Seven candles, seven angels and the seven churches of Asia Minor are also pictured. The number seven appears frequently as a symbol in the text of Revelation.

(at least) three separate people. In particular, the fluency and refined style of the Greek prose in St John's Gospel is at odds with the hesitancy and sloppiness often found in the Book of Revelation, although certain allegorical similarities are specific to both texts and may suggest some connection between the two. Several of these allegories, however, can be traced to passages from the Old Testament and thus need not indicate identical authorship for the fourth Gospel and the Book of Revelation.

The choice of the seven communities as recipients of John's warning messages has also drawn attention. These churches are those nearest to Patmos and would have served as local 'hubs' for the dissemination of John's prophetic warnings across Asia Minor. The relative distance of these communities from the Jewish heartlands and from Rome itself, and thus potentially from direct persecution, may have lent the seven churches a higher public profile than churches in Syria, Palestine or Rome. Allegorically the Seven Churches of Asia have been equated to seven ages of the Church, from its origins through history until the Apocalypse.

Although the churches of Asia Minor are indelibly linked with the missionary journeys of Paul and Barnabas, the establishment of Christianity in the region was more complex. The eastern Mediterranean in the 1st and 2nd centuries AD was also the scene of missionary activities by 'universalist' Jews, such as Philo of Alexandria and Trypho; Josephus likewise represents the same proselytizing strand within Judaism. To some extent, then, the missionary activities of Paul took place in competition with a vibrant and articulate Judaism. Moreover, Christian missions in Asia Minor spread far beyond the seven churches of the Apocalypse. Tours of inspection and preaching were instituted throughout urban centres with Jewish populations, and a Christian mission was established in c. 80 AD on the Black Sea coast in Bithynia and Pontus and subsequently in Cappadocia, in eastern Asia Minor. Of the Seven Churches of the Apocalypse, Ephesus and Laodicea were founded by Paul, but Smyrna, Pergamum, Philadelphia, Sardis and Thyatira date from the second generation of the mission, in other words to the last quarter of the 1st century. In the same period Christian missions were also active in other parts of southwest Asia Minor, such as Tralles (Caria), and Hierapolis and Magnesia (both in the Meander valley). The character of the Seven Churches was also far from homogenous.

The Monastery of St John on Patmos. The Greek Orthodox monastery was built in the 11th century AD by the monk Khristodoulos 'the Blessed'. Close to the monastery is the Cave of the Apocalypse where St John is believed to have received his revelations.

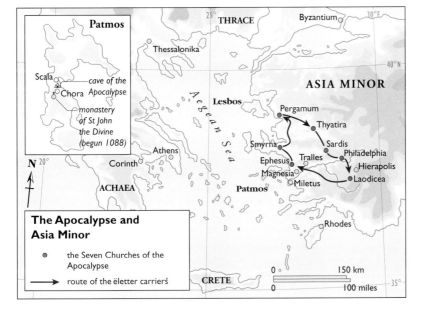

The Apocalypse and Asia Minor

- the Seven Churches of the Apocalypse
- → route of the letter carriers

Despite the address in the Apocalypse to the Seven Churches, Ephesus was clearly the leading centre of the Christians in Asia Minor. Its distinctively Palestinian character is borne out by the nature of the Apocalypse itself as a text. In the 4th century, the Christian historian Eusebius recalled that the author of the Apocalypse, John, wore the insignia of the Jewish High Priest as late as c. 90. At the same time, Ephesus attracted rival religious doctrines, for example that of the prominent Gnostic, Cerinthus. This may be one reason for the apparent stagnation of the Asia Minor missions during the first quarter of the 2nd century AD, and the sense of gloom suggested by the letters of Ignatius of Antioch.

# The Zealot Revolt

*Roman oppression of the Jews in Palestine heightened during the 1st century AD. The Romans appointed regional governors and seized control of the Jewish High Court.*

The Romans used the Hellenized Sadducees to control the Temple in Jerusalem. Many Jews resented Roman taxation and interference in their affairs. Those of

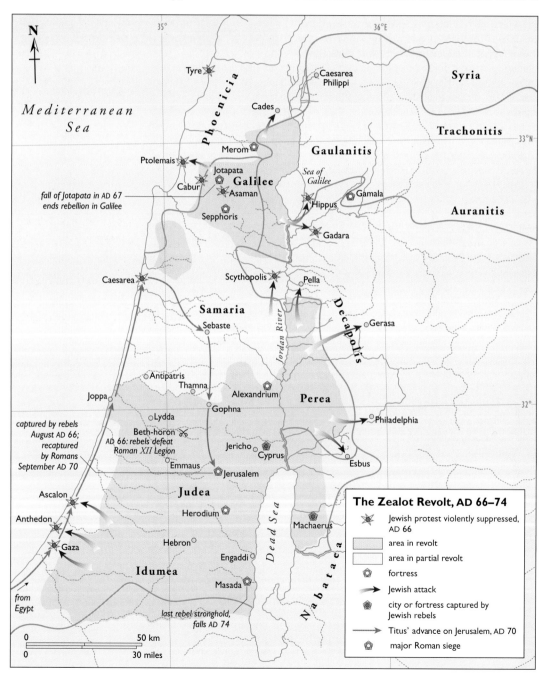

N

35°                                              36°E

*Mediterranean Sea*

Tyre

Caesarea Philippi

Syria

Cades

Trachonitis — 33°N

*Phoenicia*

Merom

Gaulanitis

Ptolemais

Jotapata

Galilee

*Sea of Galilee*

Cabur

Asaman

Gamala

*fall of Jotapata in AD 67 ends rebellion in Galilee*

Hippus

Auranitis

Sepphoris

Gadara

Caesarea

Scythopolis

Pella

*Decapolis*

Samaria

Gerasa

Sebaste

*Jordan River*

Antipatris

Thamna

Joppa

Alexandrium

Perea

— 32°

Gophna

Philadelphia

*captured by rebels August AD 66; recaptured by Romans September AD 70*

Lydda

Beth-horon
*AD 66: rebels defeat Roman XII Legion*

Jericho

Cyprus

Esbus

Emmaus

Jerusalem

*Judea*

Ascalon

Herodium

*Dead Sea*

Machaerus

Anthedon

*Nabataea*

Gaza

Hebron

Engaddi

*Idumea*

Masada

*from Egypt*

*last rebel stronghold, falls AD 74*

| | |
|---|---|
| 0 | 50 km |
| 0 | 30 miles |

**The Zealot Revolt, AD 66–74**

✳ Jewish protest violently suppressed, AD 66

▓ area in revolt

▢ area in partial revolt

⬡ fortress

➤ Jewish attack

⬡ city or fortress captured by Jewish rebels

→ Titus' advance on Jerusalem, AD 70

⬡ major Roman siege

a more radical nature regularly instigated riots against the government. The most violently anti-Roman Jews were a branch of the Pharisees called Zealots. The Assassins, or Sicarii, were Zealot extremists who often resorted to violence. Judas Iscariot, who betrayed Jesus to the Roman authorities, may have been a member of this group, and some scholars believe that Jesus was himself a Zealot. Zealots are often seen as the prime movers of the revolt, but it is unlikely that dissent on such a wide scale could have taken place without the support of the more moderate Pharisees.

Remains of the Roman siege ramp at Masada. The fortress was located on a steep, inaccessible plateau. To breach the walls, the Romans built a huge ramp of earth and stones against the western side of the cliff face.

In June AD 66, Jewish factions seized the Temple Mount. Cestius Gallus, the Roman governor of Syria, marched into Palestine to quash the rebellion, but was defeated by the Jewish militia at Beth-horon. A new government was set up in Jerusalem, but Jewish control was short-lived as the arrival of 60,000 Roman troops under Vespasian led to defeat. The Romans quelled the revolt in Galilee before taking Jerusalem in September AD 70. During the conflict factional infighting undermined unity among the rebels. Much of Jerusalem was destroyed and the Temple razed. At Masada, the final rebel stronghold, the defenders killed themselves rather than surrender in AD 73.

The most important contemporary source for the first Jewish revolt is the *Bellum Judaicum* (The War of the Jews) written by Josephus. A Jew who had himself fought in the revolt but then had retired to Rome, where he curried great favour, Josephus describes the war against the Romans in great detail. Anxious to appease his patrons, he made much of the might and brilliance of the Roman army.

*"The Romans, now masters of the walls, planted their standards on the towers, and with clapping of hands and jubilation raised a paean in honour of their victory."*

Josephus, *Jewish War* VI, 404–8

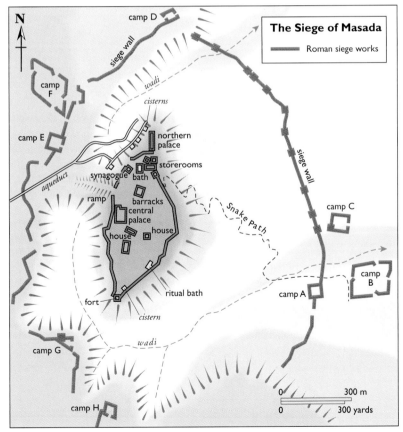

N

The Siege of Masada

——— Roman siege works

camp D
siege wall
camp F
wadi
cisterns
camp E
aqueduct
northern palace
storerooms
synagogue bath
ramp
barracks
central palace
house
house
fort
ritual bath
cistern
wadi
camp G
camp H
Snake Path
siege wall
camp C
camp A
camp B

0     300 m
0     300 yards

# The Bar Kokhba Revolt

*Life for Jews in Judea, Galilee and the surrounding territories was not easy after the First Jewish Revolt (AD 66–70). The region was now governed by a Roman Praetor (military governor) and for the first time Roman legions were permanently garrisoned in Judea.*

*"And thus, when the city had been emptied of the Jewish nation and had suffered the total destruction of its ancient inhabitants, it was colonized by a different race, and the Roman city which subsequently arose changed its name and was called Aelia ..."*

Eusebius,
*Eccles. Hist.* IV, vi, 4

A succession of Roman emperors offered the Jews little in the way of religious tolerance, at times prohibiting Jewish customs (such as circumcision) and always exacting high levels of taxation alongside other means of oppression. In AD 115 the Roman emperor Trajan founded three new eastern provinces – Armenia, Assyria and Mesopotamia – and returned to the West to discover a widespread rebellion among the citizens of many of the older, established provinces. Jewish communities in North Africa and on Cyprus as well as Jews living in Mesopotamia participated in this rebellion, destroying pagan temples and Roman towns. Trajan sent forces to Cyprus, Alexandria and Mesopotamia to quell the uprisings; many Jews were killed and harsh financial penalties were placed on the survivors. Jews in Syria, Judea and Galilee were also persecuted, perhaps to prevent them from joining in the rebellion.

Trajan died in AD 117 and he was succeeded by his nephew Hadrian (r. AD 118-138). Initially, and despite his prohibition of circumcision in AD 128, Hadrian appeared relatively well disposed towards the Jewish inhabitants of Judea and Galilee, even offering the possibility that the Temple in Jerusalem could be rebuilt. After visiting the province in 130, however, Hadrian had a change of heart and Jewish tempers flared when he refounded Jerusalem as Aelia Capitolina and erected a Temple to Jupiter Capitolinus on the Temple Mount. From the first years of Hadrian's reign, Jewish militias had secretly been preparing to rebel against Roman rule, staging small-scale raids and organizing an underground communication network.

### Rebellion in Judea

When Hadrian left Judea in AD 132, a large Jewish rebel force appeared as if from nowhere, taking the local Roman legion by surprise. Aelia Capitolina was retaken, and other towns throughout Palestine. In AD 134 Hadrian returned to the area, recalling one of his finest generals, Gaius Julius Severus, from his post in Britain to help subdue the rebels. After besieging numerous Jewish strongholds (and sustaining heavy losses), Roman soldiers ruthlessly destroyed towns and villages throughout the region, killing thousands of Jews and deporting any survivors. Jews were denied the right to worship and their cultural and religious traditions were forbidden. Jerusalem was rebuilt as a Roman city and Jews were admitted only once a year for a single day to mourn the loss of their Temple and its ancient traditions.

The initial strength of the Jewish forces and their superior knowledge of the terrain led the Romans to rely on siege warfare wherever possible. As the conflict progressed, however, the rebels were unable to avoid meeting the Roman forces in battle. It was during the last major battle of the revolt, at Bethar southwest of Jerusalem, that the Jewish rebel leader, Shimon bar Kokhba, was killed in AD 135. A ruthless military commander who some say claimed to be the Jewish Messiah, bar Kokhba had led the Jewish guerrilla forces throughout the three-year conflict. His name, translated as 'son of the star', was changed to 'bar Kosiba' ('son of the lie') by disillusioned Jews in the aftermath of the rebellion.

Bust of Roman emperor Hadrian. The Second Jewish Revolt was the only major military conflict of his reign. His anti-Jewish policies fuelled the uprising led by bar Kokhba.

The historical significance of the revolt lies partly in the way that it polarized views between Jews and Jewish Christians. Expecting their co-religionists to rally behind the messianic figure of bar Kokhba, the Jews were disappointed to find that most Christians refused to support the revolt. Christian messianism had waned as the view that Jesus had been the expected messiah took an increasingly firm hold. The revolt thus marks an important stage in the separation of Jewish and Christian traditions.

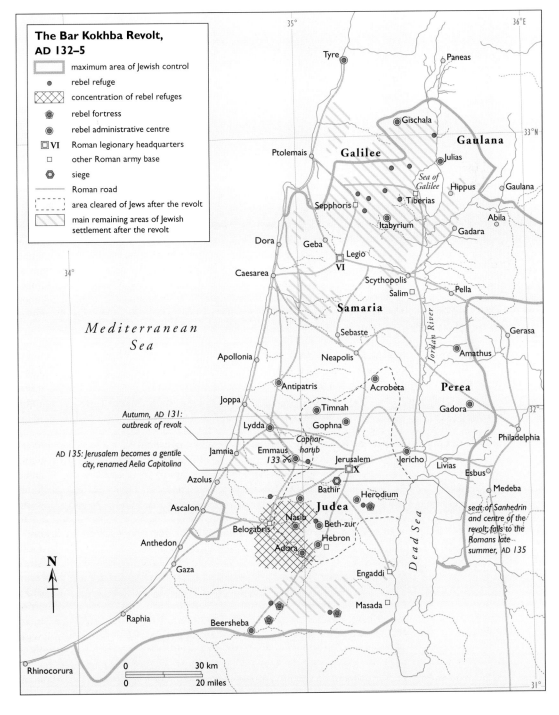

**The Bar Kokhba Revolt, AD 132–5**

- maximum area of Jewish control
- • rebel refuge
- concentration of rebel refuges
- ◉ rebel fortress
- ◉ rebel administrative centre
- ▣VI Roman legionary headquarters
- □ other Roman army base
- ◉ siege
- Roman road
- area cleared of Jews after the revolt
- main remaining areas of Jewish settlement after the revolt

Tyre · Paneas

Gischala

**Gaulana**

Ptolemais · **Galilee** · Julias

*Sea of Galilee* · Hippus · Gaulana

Sepphoris · Tiberias · Abila

Itabyrium · Gadara

Dora · Geba · Legio

Caesarea · **VI**

Scythopolis · Pella

Salim

**Samaria**

Gerasa

*Mediterranean Sea*

Sebaste

Apollonia · Neapolis · Amathus

Antipatris · Acrobeta · **Perea**

Joppa

*Autumn, AD 131: outbreak of revolt*

Timnah · Gadora

Philadelphia

Lydda · Gophna

Caphar-harub

Jamnia · Emmaus · Jerusalem · Jericho · Livias

*AD 135: Jerusalem becomes a gentile city, renamed Aelia Capitolina*

133 · **X** · Esbus

Azolus · Medeba

Bathir · Herodium

Ascalon · Nasib · **Judea**

*seat of Sanhedrin and centre of the revolt; falls to the Romans late summer, AD 135*

Belogabris · Beth-zur

Anthedon · Hebron

Adora · *Dead Sea*

Gaza · Engaddi

**N**

Masada

Raphia · Beersheba

Rhinocorura

0 _____ 30 km
0 _____ 20 miles

# The Beginning of the Diaspora

*The word 'diaspora' comes from Greek and means 'scattering of the seed'. It can be used in other contexts, but the term has long been associated with the dispersal of the Jewish people from Palestine. The Jewish diaspora is believed to begin with the exile of the Jews to Babylonia in the 6th century BC, although over a century earlier Jews from Samaria had been deported to the east by the Assyrians.*

*"For the emperor gave orders that [the Jews] should not even see from a distance the land of their fathers. "*

Eusebius,
*Eccl. Hist.* IV, vi, 3

Jewish colonies were subsequently founded in eastern Mesopotamia and in Syrian cities such as Damascus. Jewish refugees from Palestine also made their way into Egypt where they established thriving communities, notably at Alexandria, but also within the Egyptian interior. The arrival of the Romans in the 1st century BC led to Judaism spreading further. A number of successful, Hellenized Jews may have relocated for commercial or cultural reasons, but large numbers of Jews were forced to leave Palestine after the destruction of the Temple during the First Jewish Revolt (AD66–70) and the Bar Kokhba Revolt (AD 132–35). By the middle of the 1st century AD, Jews had been denied entry into – let alone sovereignty over – Jerusalem, the ancient cultic centre of their religion. The Jewish populations of Judea, Samaria and Galilee survived only in minor enclaves and Jewish rule over the ancient promised land of Canaan had become a thing of the past.

### The Spread of Religion

Judaism as a religion, however, continued to thrive in Jewish congregations across the Roman empire and beyond. Traditional rites of worship and scriptural study and exegesis flourished in North Africa, Syria, Asia Minor and even as far west as southern Gaul and the Iberian peninsula. Jewish communities adapted to their new surroundings in a variety of ways, depending on prevailing levels of religious tolerance. Some Jewish communities remained relatively aloof, mixing little with indigenous peoples and clinging to their use of the Hebrew language, which gradually incorporated words from local tongues to form hybrid dialects. However, many, especially those in more tolerant areas, opted for more overt Hellenization, living side by side with similarly Hellenized, native populations. That Greek culture and language did, indeed, play a major role in the development of Judaism during this period is shown by words such as 'diaspora' and 'synagogue' borrowed from Greek, the language used by many diasporic Jews for business ventures, study and everyday transactions.

### The Jewish Diaspora c. AD 300

- ☐ area of dense Jewish settlement
- ☐ area of scattered Jewish settlement
- ◉ citiy with major Jewish community
- ● other city with Jewish community
- —— trade route
- —— limit of Roman empire

Among the scattered Jews the observance and practice of traditional rites, customs and liturgical feasts, however rigidly or laxly followed, served to keep Judaism alive. This observance also allowed the Jewish religion to develop under the supervision of rabbis or teachers, even after the virtual demise of its spiritual and philosophical centre, which was based in the Temple in Jerusalem.

The intimate connection of Judaism to a specific geographical area that permeates Jewish scripture, history and culture – arguably uniquely among the major religions of the ancient and modern world – further bound the various Jewish communities together. Curiously, however, the extent to which Jewish control of Jerusalem and the surrounding region should mean literally under Jewish sovereignty has also long been a source of division as well. Many Hellenized Jews throughout the Roman empire, as well as their later counterparts in Europe and elsewhere, saw – and continue to see – their brand of 'transplanted Judaism' as a logical extension of the notion of the Promised Land.

Carving of a *menorah* from a Roman-period synagogue at Corinth, Greece. The seven-branched candelabrum was used in rituals at the Temple in Jerusalem until its destruction. It has become the traditional symbol of Judaism.

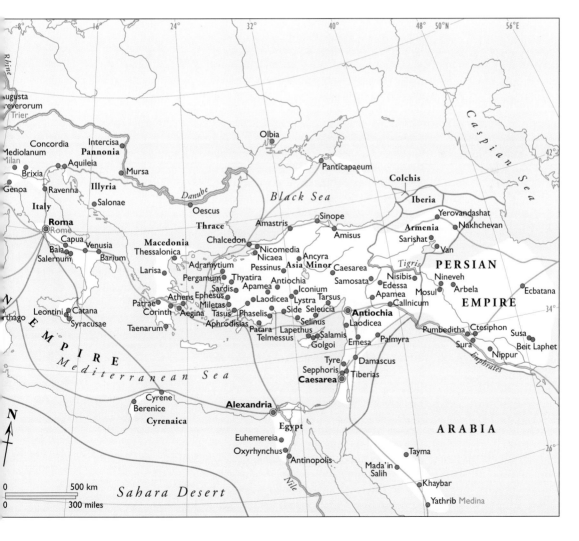

# Christianity in the Roman Empire

*According to Christian tradition, the Gospel was spread in all directions by Christ's disciples after his death. The well-documented journeys of Paul in the eastern Mediterranean and to Rome find more exotic parallels in the alleged missionary activities of Matthew and Philip in Africa and Thomas in India. As Christian Roman writers such as Augustine (AD 354–420) realized, the institutions of the Roman empire facilitated the spread of the new religion.*

*"Christus, from whom the name had its origin, suffered the extreme penalty during the reign of Tiberius at the hands of one of our procurators, Pontius Pilate, and a most mischievous superstition thus checked for the moment, again broke out not only in Judea, the first source of the evil, but even in Rome."*

Tacitus,
*Annals* XV, 44

Initially, Christianity flourished in the cities of the Jewish diaspora, and appeared to be a radical form of Judaism. However, polemical writings reveal persistent conflicts between Jews and Christians in Antioch and Alexandria, and by the 4th century anti-Semitism was a distinct feature of Christian doctrinal writing in the eastern Mediterranean.

Christianity took hold more quickly in the urban environment of the eastern Mediterranean than in the largely rural west. It first came to the attention of the Roman authorities in the late 1st century, but it was not until the mid-3rd century that any systematic attempt was made to stamp out the religion. The Christians' refusal to recognize the imperial divinity cult by public sacrifice was thought to undermine social cohesion and threaten the traditional pluralism of Roman religious practices. However, the 'Great Persecution' initiated by the Emperor Diocletian at a time of political and economic crisis, despite its brutality, ended in 303 without having succeeded in eradicating Christianity. In 312, Emperor Constantine claimed the help of the Christian God in overcoming his rival for mastery of the western empire, and a year later he issued the Edict of Milan, permitting all forms of religious worship. By this date about 10 per cent of the empire's inhabitants may have been Christian. By 324, Constantine, having become ruler of the whole empire, began moving his capital to a new city on the Bosporus. Constantinople was distinctive for the central position it gave to churches, and, in contrast to Rome, a new aristocratic and administrative elite developed in the city that was largely Christian. By 395 the tide had turned so far that Emperor Theodosius outlawed public performance of traditional pagan religion.

One reason for the success of Christianity was its syncretism. The Church identified with, rather than sought to overturn, the empire. Most bishops came from the land-owning elite in Roman society and believed, like Augustine, that the Christian

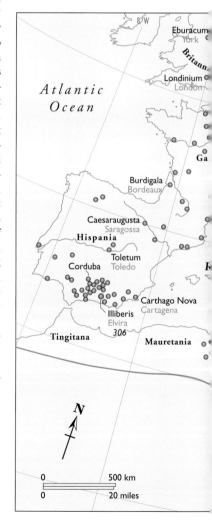

empire was the ideal form of government. Moreover, a hybrid form of Christian written and artistic culture developed, based on classical models. Another reason was the capacity of the Church to overlay traditional pagan cult sites with new forms of devotion based on the cult of saints and martyrs. Inevitably, the rapid spread of the religion also led to the growth of rival theologies, the less successful of which were declared heretical in a series of councils in the 3rd to 5th centuries.

St Catherine's Monastery at the foot of Mount Sinai. Built by Emperor Justinian between AD 527 and 565, it is one of the world's oldest functioning Christian monasteries. Allegedly located where Moses saw the burning bush, the monastery also houses the relics of St Catherine of Alexandria.

Early Christianity used the physical landscape of the eastern Mediterranean as a spiritual resource, through the practice of monasticism. From the late 3rd century onwards, men and women began withdrawing into uninhabited regions of Egypt, Palestine, Syria and Asia Minor, either alone (anchorites) or in communal settings (cenobites), to pursue lives dedicated to God and marked by ascetic practices. The most celebrated sites were in Egypt, especially in Nitria (Lower Egypt), but the Laura or Lavra monasteries of Palestine were instrumental in the development of Byzantine monasticism in the Middle Ages.

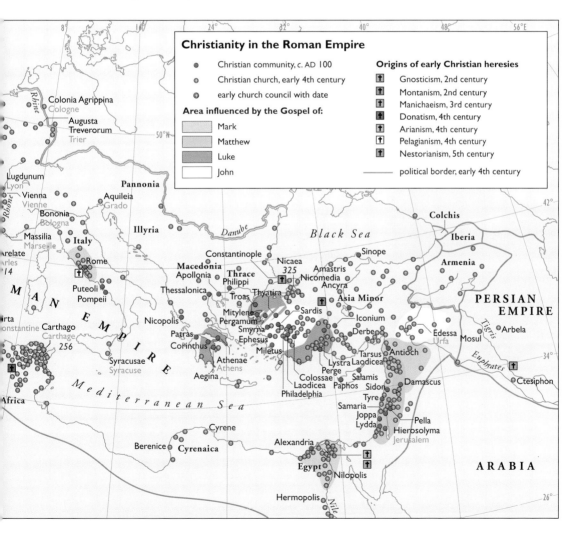

## Christianity in the Roman Empire

- ●   Christian community, c. AD 100
- ◉   Christian church, early 4th century
- ⊕   early church council with date

**Area influenced by the Gospel of:**

- Mark
- Matthew
- Luke
- John

**Origins of early Christian heresies**

- ✝   Gnosticism, 2nd century
- ✝   Montanism, 2nd century
- ✝   Manichaeism, 3rd century
- ✝   Donatism, 4th century
- ✝   Arianism, 4th century
- ✝   Pelagianism, 4th century
- ✝   Nestorianism, 5th century

————   political border, early 4th century

# Part IV: The Bible Lands After the Bible

*By the eve of the Arab conquest of the 7th century AD, Palestine had
a unique position in the Christian world as a focus for pilgrimage
and as the centre of a distinctive type of religious life. Symbolically,
it lay at the heart of the Christian Roman empire, although in
political, economic and social terms it remained a backwater.*

This paradox continued to be a feature of the Bible lands during the medieval
and Ottoman periods. Apart from the era of the Crusader States in the 12th and
13th centuries, only in the 20th century, with the establishment of the state of
Israel, would the region acquire autonomy from the greater powers that dominated the region. Palestine was still a thriving province, despite the economic
stagnation that gripped the Roman empire. Economically, it was dependent for
long-distance trade on coastal ports such as Tyre and Beirut, but Caesarea was
still active in local trade, including with Cyprus and Egypt, the main grain sup-
pliers. The agricultural economy was based on olive and grape cultivation. The
population was mixed: archaeological evidence attests to an important Jewish
presence in the Galilee towns, but the Samaritan communities of the central
hinterland around Nablus (Shechem) were destroyed as a result of a revolt in
the 6th century. Christians dominated in Judea and the southern coastline.

## Arab Control of Palestine

The 7th century AD marked a watershed in the history of Palestine. The Persian
invasion of 614, although devastating, especially to churches and the desert
monasteries, was politically ephemeral. Of far greater import was the Arab

invasion of the 630s. The results, although neither as immediate nor as
dramatically destructive as twenty years earlier, changed the region
forever. Most obviously, Palestine ceased to be part of the Roman
empire and became politically subjected to the Umayyad caliphate. It
is hard to assess the impact of this transfer of power in local terms.
There was no forced conversion of Jews and Christians to Islam,
although the clear advantages that Muslims enjoyed over non-Muslims
undoubtedly had an effect in changing religious allegiances. Christians
and Jews were seen as 'People of the Book', that is, people whose religious tradition was imperfect but recognizably related to Islam, and
therefore permitted in Islamic society. Certain professions and political
offices were initially prohibited to non-Muslims, who were also supposed to be identifiable by dress codes and the withholding of certain
social privileges. However, the extent to which such customs were
upheld by the authorities fluctuated. There seems to have been no
clear programme for the 'Islamicization' of the indigenous population
before the 9th century; until then, Palestine still enjoyed regular cultural contact with the centre of the Byzantine world, Constantinople.

The ruins of Avdat, a Nabatean
city in the Negev Desert.
Located on a mountain between
Petra and the Mediterranean,
Avdat was established as a road
station for caravans along the
Spice Route in the 3rd century
BC. It includes the remains of
two impressive Byzantine
churches and a wine press.

Indeed, up to the mid-8th century, the caliphate, based in the Hellenized city of Damascus, remained part of a distinctive late Roman world. The
transfer of power to the Abbasid dynasty and the move from Damascus to Baghdad in AD 750 represented an eastward shift in Islam's cultural centre of gravity.
It also rendered Palestine less important geopolitically than it had been at any
time since Constantine plucked Jerusalem from obscurity over 400 years earlier. This trend coincided with the growing introspection of Constantinople,
partly as a result of attack from the Arabs, and partly because of the iconoclas-
tic trend in Byzantine spirituality. Around the start of the 9th century a series of

conflicts over succession to the Abbasid caliphate devastated parts of Palestine. The Anastasis Church, the Laura of St Sabas in the Judean desert, and other surviving desert monasteries were raided. In the second quarter of the 9th century, a renegade warlord, Abu Harb, terrorized Samaria and Judea, rendering the Abbasid governor in Ramla powerless. The written evidence from this time onwards indicates that the indigenous population was becoming increasingly 'Arabicized': Arabic replaced the Palestinian form of Aramaic that had been the standard vernacular, and Christians and Muslims alike used Arabic personal names. This did not mean that Islam itself became more widespread in Palestine. Historians do not agree about the extent of conversion in the early Abbasid period, but recent arguments suggest that Christianity was still widespread at the turn of the 11th century, particularly in Judea and Galilee.

In AD 1009, however, the Church in Jerusalem reached its lowest ebb with the destruction of the Anastasis Church by al-Hakim. The Shi'ite Fatimid caliphate, which came to power in Egypt in 969, had wrested control of Palestine from the Abbasids, and al-Hakim's havoc was part of a more general persecution of Christians in his lands, in a ploy to bolster support from his Muslim subjects. The Church was rebuilt from the 1020s onwards, but this episode, followed in the middle of the century by the Seljuk conquest of the Middle East, gave further impetus to the Islamicization of Palestine.

Khan el-Umdan or Inn of the Columns at Acre. Built in a square around a central courtyard, the khan was used as a meeting place for traders and merchants. In 1229 Acre was placed under the control of the Knights Hospitaller, a religious-miliary order, and was the last capital of the Crusaders, falling in 1291. Originally a Canaanite and Phoenician city, Acre became part of the modern state of Israel in 1948.

## The Crusades

The demography of the region, however, was significantly altered by the Crusader conquest of Jerusalem in 1099 and the subsequent establishment of a Kingdom of Jerusalem, more or less corresponding territorially with the biblical kingdoms of Judah and Israel. The investment in military conquest reveals the symbolic power exercised over Western European Christendom by Jerusalem. The popularity of crusading had more to do with the mentalities of the lay knighthood and the growing capacity of the papacy to shape them than with conditions in the east. Crusading was not, until the mid-13th century at least, war against Islam as a rival religion, but rather for the recovery and maintenance of the 'Holy Land'. The conquest was followed by new settlement. If, in a long perspective, this settlement looks ephemeral, the 200 years of the kingdom of Jerusalem (1099–1291) achieved substantial changes in both the physical landscape and in the conditions under which the population lived. Muslims were resettled from the coastal towns where they had formed a majority of the population, and from Jerusalem itself, to the rural hinterlands of Samaria and upper Galilee. Although all non-Franks constituted 'second-class' citizens with fewer rights in law than the ruling elite, in practice indigenous Christians had greater access to land ownership and social privilege than Muslims. Many Muslims lived under conditions of slavery, although in some areas, such as the villages around Sidon, their standard of living was favourably compared by one contemporary Muslim observer, Ibn Jubayr, to that of peasants in Seljuk-controlled regions. Muslims were in general allowed to worship freely, and there was no attempt at forced conversion. All non-Franks paid taxes to the Frankish landowners, but there were very few instances of rebellion against Crusader rule.

Another important consequence of the Crusades for Palestine was the building of new churches and the restoration of neglected shrines to mark the sites associated with events in the Bible. Many of these had already been identified, but others, such as the supposed tombs of the patriarchs in Hebron, were included for the first time in pilgrimage itineraries. Western possession of the Holy Land brought unprecedented numbers of European pilgrims to Palestine to worship at the shrines. The Holy Land was, in the words of one contemporary, a 'garden of delights'. The kingdom of Jerusalem also influenced Western architecture, both ecclesiastical and military. The Holy Sepulchre came to enjoy a central place in monastic liturgy through the copies of the distinctive domed shrine built throughout Western Europe from the 11th to the 13th centuries. At the same time, castle-building techniques refined in the East were imported by returning Crusaders such as Richard I and Edward I of England. In material as well as spiritual ways, Westerners were impressed by what they found in the Crusader States. Access to Eastern markets allowed for a higher standard of living, at least for the ruling classes, than could be enjoyed almost anywhere in Western Europe, and a hybrid visual culture and style of living developed that made the Frankish baronage of the eastern Mediterranean the envy of their Western counterparts. This can still be seen from the production of deluxe manuscripts and icons for Frankish patrons by Eastern-trained craftsmen employing Byzantine models and styles. Even after the fall of the kingdom of Jerusalem in 1291, this cosmopolitan culture survived in Cyprus until the 16th century.

### Jerusalem

The city of Jerusalem became a Muslim-controlled city again in AD 1187, and remained so, save for a hiatus from 1229 to 1244, until 1917. The city was transformed under the Mamluks (1187–1516), for whom its spiritual importance was hardly less than for the Crusaders. From 1187, Saladin initiated a programme of re-Islamicizing the religious institutions of Jerusalem, including the restoration of the major mosques (principally the al-Aqsa) and the founding of a new hospital, madrasa (religious school) and *khanqah* (Sufi monastery). New civic buildings also date from this time, including a khan and various public fountains. Although Ottoman Jerusalem was, in geopolitical terms, more provincial than either the Crusader or Mamluk city, it benefited architecturally from the building programme initiated by Sultan Suleiman II ('the Magnificent') in the 1530s. Not only the impressive walls, but also the repair of canals and wells, and the redecoration of the Dome of the Rock, date from this period. *Waqfs* (charitable endowments) were created with revenues from nearby villages for the upkeep of a kitchen to feed the poor.

Mamluk fountain, Jerusalem. One of the finest examples of Mamluk architecture outside Egypt, this unique public drinking fountain on the Haram es-Sharif (Temple Mount) was commissioned by the sultan Qaitbay in 1482 as a charitable act pleasing to God.

### Pilgrimage

The Mamluks and Ottomans permitted Christian and Jewish pilgrimage to the holy sites, and although the number of Europeans prepared to risk the voyage and pay the tolls diminished, it never quite died out. Although pilgrimage became less popular in those parts of Europe that accepted the Reformation, the Franciscans continued their custody of the holy sites from 1336 with scarcely a break. That contact between the Holy Land and the West was not lost can be seen from surviving travel descriptions of the Holy Land from the 16th to the 19th centuries. During this period, the Bible lands lost the political significance they had enjoyed – or endured – during the early Islamic period under Crusader and Mamluk rule. The centres of political and military activity in the Ottoman empire were the northwest frontier, which was eventually settled in the Hungarian plain after the high-water mark of Vienna was reached in the 17th century, and the eastern frontier with the revived Persian empire. Jerusalem was one of ten *sanjaqs* (districts) that came under the rule of the provincial governor of Damascus, who tried as far as possible to work through tribal and clan chieftains. The title of 'commander of the pilgrimage' given to the principal Muslim family of the Jerusalem *sanjaq* indicates that the real significance of the region to the Ottomans was religious. Periodic rebellions against Ottoman taxation, however, brought more direct rule from janissaries appointed from central government, thereby marginalizing local clan leaders. Consequently, the 18th century saw a series of Arab uprisings against the Ottomans, the most serious of which was led by Muhammad al-Husaini, in protest against the harsh rule of the Ottoman governor Jurji Muhammad. In mid-century, Zahir al-'Umar's seizure of Acre during a Mamluk invasion from Egypt moved the political centre of gravity to Upper Galilee, but in 1775 Zahir was killed and Ottoman control returned.

Towards the end of the century, European powers began to become involved once more in the fate of the Holy Land. The brief occupation of Jaffa, Safed and Tiberias by Napoleon in 1799, and the attempt to capture Acre, as part of his effort to dominate the eastern Mediterranean and thereby deny it to the British, signalled the beginning of the end of Ottoman power. Napoleon's invasion of Egypt, which ended the Mamluk regime, also had the indirect effect of bringing to power a proto-nationalist movement under Muhammad Ali. Muhammad and his son, Ibrahim Pasha, who occupied Syria, were initially regarded as liberators from Ottoman tyranny. Despite reforms that opened up Syria and Palestine to Western influences and improved conditions for Christians there, Ibrahim's levy of the heavy *farda* tax proved his undoing. A series of revolts in Syria between 1834 and 1838, led eventually to the Ottoman reconquest of 1840.

## European Rediscovery of the Holy Land

By the middle of the 19th century, however, a combination of factors began to undermine the Ottoman hold on Palestine. First, the empire was suffering from the increasing effect of nationalist movements of separation. Although these had initial results in the Balkans and Greece, even those provinces that were unable to break free of Ottoman rule were nonetheless to some degree affected by the ideals articulated in those movements. Second, European interest in the region was becoming more profound. Travel in the Bible lands offered wealthy and intellectually curious Europeans a combination of the exotic and the historical. Artists such as Edward Lear and David Roberts, influenced by landscape romanticism, brought back a particular version of the 'picturesque exotic' to London. Writers such as Disraeli and Mark Twain, in very different ways, exploited the theme of

The Nimrod Fortress, situated in the Golan Heights, was built by a nephew of Saladin in around 1229. It was constructed to block a possible Christian advance on Damascus during the Sixth Crusade. It fell into disrepair at the end of the 13th century, with the collapse of Crusader rule. The Jews named it after the biblical figure Nimrod, who, according to tradition, had lived on the summit.

the Western rediscovery of the Holy Land. The scholar and bibliophile Robert Curzon, whose *A Visit to Monasteries in the Levant* combines adventurous encounters with local brigands and the learned discovery of precious manuscripts in Orthodox monasteries, found an equally compelling version of the exotic Near East. The French scholar René de Châteaubriand saw in his visit to the Holy Land the past glories of the Crusader age. A strong French nationalistic sentiment runs through the 'rediscovery' of the history of the Crusades in the writings of Michaud and Michelet, and even in the architectural descriptions of de Vogüé and Enlart.

International politics had a more profound effect. The alleged mistreatment of the Christian holy sites stirred the Russian government into war against the Ottoman empire in the Crimea (1853–6). Although the need to preserve the balance of power in the eastern Mediterranean persuaded France and Britain to defend the 'Sick Man of Europe' in a war that was fought far outside Palestine, the Russian intervention in the Holy Land exposed a very different situation in Jerusalem by the 1850s from that which had prevailed at the beginning of the 19th century. Ottoman participation in the Crimean War came at a heavy cost in the form of loans from European powers. By the 1870s the empire was already defaulting, and in 1881 the Ottoman Public Debt Administration, a consortium of mainly European creditors, was established. It is in this context that European Jewish settlement began in the last quarter of the 19th century. In 1874, the Palestine Exploration Fund estimated the number of Jews in Jerusalem at 22,000, out of a total population of 40,000. Significantly, 5–6,000 of these were living outside the city, the first sign of the expansion from its Ottoman walls and the development of the modern enlarged city. Alongside Jewish immigration came European representation in the form of consulates

and institutes. Between 1838 and 1857, Britain, Prussia, Italy, France, Austria-Hungary, Spain, the USA and Russia established consulates to represent the interests of their nationals and to oversee the founding of missions. Previously ruined churches were restored with European funding, such as the 12th-century church of St Anne, given to Napoleon III in 1856 and entrusted in 1878 to the missionary White Fathers. The British had already, in 1849, founded their own Anglican church, Christ Church, to the north of the old city. The Russian complex to the northwest of the old city comprised a hospital, guesthouse and pharmacy as well as a church to cater for the vast numbers of Russ-

A Zionist farmer ploughs the land at Kibbutz Amir near the Sea of Galilee in 1940. During the British Mandate Jewish immigration to Palestine was restricted by the White Paper of 1939, which limited immigration by Jews to 15,000 per year for five years. Some Jews still made it to Palestine illegally, however, escaping the devastation of the European Jewish communities under the genocidal policies of the Nazis.

ian pilgrims visiting the Holy Land. The financial significance of Russian pilgrim subsidies to the Orthodox Church in Jerusalem was only appreciated after 1917, when, after the Revolution, Russians stopped coming and the economy of the Orthodox Church collapsed.

## The First World War

Palestine became politically and militarily important again during the First World War. Britain, which had already established a protectorate over Egypt, had strategic reasons for wanting to secure the east flank of the Red Sea, so as to ensure free access through the Suez Canal to India. The Ottoman empire, which had been courted by Germany in the 1890s – Kaiser Wilhelm II visited Jerusalem in 1898 – entered the war on the side of Austria-Hungary and Germany, in an attempt to win back the Balkan possessions that had been lost to nationalists in the late 19th century. Thus the British strategy was to invade Palestine from Egypt and detach it from the Ottoman empire, alongside a similar French invasion of Syria. The imperatives of war, however, overshadowed the long-term planning for peace. The expectation of independent statehood for former Ottoman possessions in the Middle East was complicated by uncertainty over the geographical and cultural identity of any new state in the region. The increasing numbers of Jewish settlers during the first quarter of the 20th century, following the establishment of the World Zionist Council in 1898, meant that they could not be ignored when it came to determining the future shape of the region. On the other hand, the Arabs of Palestine had a history of resistance to Ottoman government going back to the 18th century; moreover the Arab Revolt led by Sharif Hussein during the war provided potential moral leadership for the creation of a new Arab state.

The contradictions between the Sykes-Picot Agreement of 1916 and the Balfour Declaration of 1917 exemplify the impossibility of meeting the demands of both of the major elements in the population. By the 1930s, it was clear that the Jewish settlers from Europe and the Americas were more articulate, urbanized and industrialized than their Arab neighbours, whose economy was largely agricultural and whose social structures were clan-based. Moreover, the British partition of its Mandate territory into Palestine and Transjordan, in order to secure an inheritance for the Hussein dynasty, swung the balance in favour of the Jews. The Arab revolts against Mandate rule in the 1920s and 1930s proved only to damage their own economic base by damaging internal markets. British retaliation, in the form of exiling the leaders, dismembered the Arab leadership in the long term. During the Second World War, the Zionist leadership was able to put pressure on the Mandate government through terrorist action. By the first Arab-Israeli War of 1948–9 there was clear disparity between the effective Zionist leadership and the absence of such leadership among Palestinian Arabs. Arguably, this absence of Palestinian leadership continued until the 1990s, with the emergence of an articulate leadership loyal to but critical of the leadership-in-exile provided by the Palestine Liberation Organization (PLO).

## Israeli-Palestinian Conflict

The continuing conflict between Israelis and Palestinians cannot be understood outside its historical context; equally, however, the unfolding of the conflict reflects the changing nature of both Israeli and Palestinian societies. Neither community has a monolithic identity. Israelis are divided ethnically between Ashkenazim and Sephardim, and within both groups there is considerable religious fragmentation and socio-economic differentials. These divisions have had significant political ramifications; the Sephardim, for instance, have largely voted for right-wing parties rather than the Ashkenazi-dominated Labour party that ruled Israel from 1948 to 1977. Divisions among Palestinians concern class, place of residence and religion: although Islam is the majority religion among them, many Palestinians are and have always been Christian (currently about 10–12 per cent). Palestinian identity has continued to change in response to socio-economic dynamics. Principal among these has been the weakening of the Palestinian middle class since 1967, largely as a result of Israeli land seizures and economic practices, which undermined the patronage of traditional landowning elites.

Arab and Jewish identities in Palestine before 1948 both developed as secular movements based on ideals of nationalism and social justice. Since the 1980s, however, both Israeli and Palestinian societies have become characterized by the emergence of sharper religious identities, often tending to extreme attitudes and actions based on scriptural justifications. This can be seen both in the West Bank settler movement, which, in contrast to the earliest generation of Zionist settlers, has attracted groups with strong religious identities rooted in the idea of returning to biblical lands, and, on the other hand, in the rise of Islamist groups such as Hamas in place of the secular nationalism of the PLO. One enduring characteristic in the relationship between Palestinians and Israelis is the demonization of the 'other' and, at the most extreme end of the spectrum, the refusal to admit its existence as a separate people. This series of developments has had a profound impact not only on the wider region, as seen for example in the Israeli invasions of Lebanon in 1982 and 2006, but in the deployment of the religious discourses of both sides in global politics. At the time of writing, the need for a solution to the problem of different peoples with strong links to the same small piece of land remains as pressing as ever.

A Palestinian boy rides his bicycle next to a security fence put up by the Israelis near the Jewish settlement of Har Homa (background). The controversial network of fences within the West Bank area is justified by the Israeli government as protection for civilians against Palestinian terrorism.

# The Islamic Conquests

*The Roman empire came to an end as a political and military force in the eastern Mediterranean in the 7th century AD. Ostensibly Roman control ended suddenly with the defeat of its forces at the hands of the newly Islamicized Arabs in 636.*

The Arab advance was made possible even before the rise of Islam by the dislocation of Roman power and influence in the region from the start of the 7th century. In 614 the Sassanid Persian empire invaded Palestine, bringing to an end a period of peace and prosperity for the Church of Jerusalem. Besides the city itself, the ascetic, desert monasteries of Judea were badly affected; some never recovered. Although the Persians were driven out in 628, Roman influence could not be restored before the Arab expansion began in 632.

The Arab advance began during the religious revival launched in the Arabian Peninsula by Muhammad (born 570), who was accepted by his followers as the authentic prophet of God. Muhammad's achievement was to use his revelation from God as a unifying principle for the disparate, polytheistic tribes of Arabia. The strong influences of Judaic and Christian monotheism in his revelation are testimony to the spread of Jews and Christians across the Middle East by the late 5th century. Muhammad, initially forced to flee from his home city of Mecca to

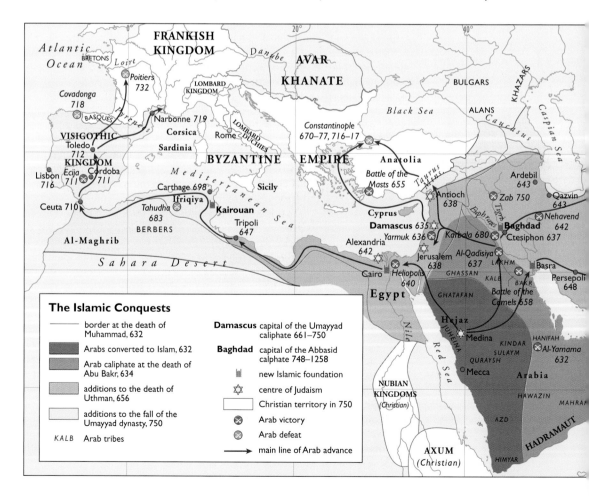

The Islamic Conquests

| | |
|---|---|
| ——— | border at the death of Muhammad, 632 |
| | Arabs converted to Islam, 632 |
| | Arab caliphate at the death of Abu Bakr, 634 |
| | additions to the death of Uthman, 656 |
| | additions to the fall of the Umayyad dynasty, 750 |
| KALB | Arab tribes |

| | |
|---|---|
| **Damascus** | capital of the Umayyad caliphate 661–750 |
| **Baghdad** | capital of the Abbasid calphate 748–1258 |
| | new Islamic foundation |
| | centre of Judaism |
| | Christian territory in 750 |
| | Arab victory |
| | Arab defeat |
| ——→ | main line of Arab advance |

Medina in 622, forged his dominance in the region at the battle of Badr (624), and in 630 made Mecca his base. After his death in 632, Caliph Abu Bakr made the first advance into Palestine, but it was his successor Omar (634–44) who defeated the Romans in Syria and Palestine, and later conquered Persia (642–3).

The impact of the Islamic conquest evolved gradually over the next centuries. There seems to have been no policy of forced conversion of Jews and Christians. Most historians agree that there was little Islamicization in Palestine at first, and the archaeological evidence suggests that most villages in the Christian south of the former Roman province and in Galilee continued to support Christian populations. The social and economic advantages of conversion, however, became clear as Jews and Christians were subject to certain restrictions, especially after the takeover of the Abbasid dynasty in Baghdad from the Umayyads in Damascus in the mid-8th century. Under the Umayyad dynasty, with its capital at Damascus, Islam's centre of gravity was the eastern Mediterranean. Palestine benefited from lavish new building programmes, such as the palace at Khirbet al-Mafjar, near Jericho. Umayyad syncretism, however, proved unsustainable, and the Abbasid conquest was accompanied by a cultural shift towards the east, exemplified by the removal of the dynasty's capital to Baghdad. Palestine became marginalized as a province of little importance and from the 9th century contact between the Church of Jerusalem and Constantinople dried up. Palestinian Christian hagiographical literature of this period testifies to the straitened circumstances of the Church as it came under increasing pressure from the Abbasid governors. Palestine suffered from the wars of succession to the caliphate in the early 9th century; as during the Persian invasion 200 years earlier, monasteries and churches were attacked in a period of general anarchy.

Two events further affected Palestine. In 969 a Shi'ite dynasty from North Africa, the Fatimids, took control of Egypt, founding a rival caliphate to the Abbasids. Profiting from Abbasid weakness in the west, the Fatimids extended their influence over Palestine. At the same time, the Byzantine reconquest of Antioch and northern Syria signalled the revival of imperial interests in the region. In 1009 the Fatimid caliph al-Hakim, to quell suspicions that he had Christian sympathies, ordered the destruction of the Church of the Holy Sepulchre and began a period of persecution of Christians in the Holy Land. By the mid-11th century the Fatimids and Byzantines had reached an understanding over the fate of Palestine, but it was overturned by further Islamic conquests by the Seljuk Turks, who swept westwards from Central Asia from the 1040s. By c. 1080 the Seljuks had effective control of the entire Abbasid caliphate and had driven the Fatimids out of Palestine.

Decorated interior of the Dome of the Chain, a small dome next to the Dome of the Rock on Temple Mount in Jerusalem. The purpose of the smaller dome remains unclear. One theory is that it was a treasury built during the Umayyad era or perhaps prior to Islamic rule in Jerusalem.

*"When Allah caused the unbelievers to be defeated and granted victory to the Muslims, they opened the gates of their cities and sent out a festive welcome with music, and they paid the tribute."*

al-Baladhuri, *Futuh al-Buldan*

# The Crusader States

*The First Crusade (1095–99) was triggered by the Byzantine desire to recover territory in Asia Minor lost to the Seljuk Turks – a recently Islamicized Central Asian people – after the defeat at Manzikert in 1071. An appeal for military aid from the West by Emperor Alexios Komnenos was fashioned into a demand for a holy war through the skilful rhetoric of Pope Urban II (r. 1088–99).*

*"And when these words had begun to be rumoured abroad through all the duchies and counties of the Frankish lands, the Franks, hearing them, straightaway began to sew the cross on the right shoulders of their garments, saying that they would with one accord follow in the footsteps of Christ."*

*Gesta Francorum* I, i

Together with Byzantine forces, the five separate armies of the First Crusade recaptured the Seljuk capital of Nicea (1097), and recovered Tarsus and Adana in southeastern Asia Minor. The capture of Antioch in 1098, however, led to a split between Byzantines and Crusaders that would have repercussions long after the establishment of the Crusader States. The capture of Jerusalem from the Fatimids, in July 1099, marked the victorious end of the campaign, the success of which was in part due to the political disunity of the Muslim lands following the death of the Seljuk sultan Malik Shah in 1092.

## The Battle for the Holy Land

Until the rise of Zengi (r. 1128-46) and his son Nur ad-Din (r. 1146-74), the four Crusader states – the Kingdom of Jerusalem, the County of Tripoli, the Principality of Antioch and the County of Edessa – continued to profit from divisions in the Islamic world. Edessa fell to Zengi in 1144, however, and the Second Crusade (1147-48) squandered an opportunity to strengthen the northern flank of the Crusader states by a fruitless attack on Damascus. In the 1170s and 1180s, the Kingdom of Jerusalem, weakened by the accession to the throne of the leper Baldwin IV, came under increasing threat from the first Ayyubid sultan, Saladin (r. 1174-93), who, by reinvigorating the *jihad* tradition, brought Syria and Egypt under his control. In July 1187, the kingdom was lost at the battle of Hattin. Jerusalem itself fell in October, and most of the kingdom was overrun by Saladin's forces.

The Third Crusade (1189-92), under the leadership of Richard I of England (r. 1189-99), succeeded in recovering Acre and much of the coastline, and over the next 30 years the Kingdom of Jerusalem was gradually restored. Jerusalem itself was even regained in 1229 through the diplomacy of the Holy Roman Emperor Frederick II (1194-1250), only to be lost again in 1244. Without firm leadership for most of the 13th century, however, the Crusader states became increasingly unstable.

The Crusades of the 13th century were of two basic types: large-scale expeditions against Egypt – the heartland of the Ayyubids - and smaller campaigns to shore up the Kingdom's defences. None succeeded in doing more than delaying the eventual Mamluk conquest of the Crusader states begun by the Baybars in the 1260s. Antioch fell in 1268, Tripoli in 1289 and, after a dramatic siege, Acre, the last stronghold of the Crusaders, in 1291. Despite repeated attempts, no crusade was launched from the West

A remnant of the old Crusader walls in Acre's Pisan harbour. Captured by Richard the Lionheart in 1191, the ancient port city became a stronghold of the Crusaders in the Holy Land. They fortified the city with a double defensive sea wall, and redesigned the harbour, creating an inner and outer harbour.

after 1270. The Frankish Kingdom of Cyprus, however, which had been conquered during the Third Crusade, grew in prosperity throughout the period until its final conquest by the Ottomans in the 15th century.

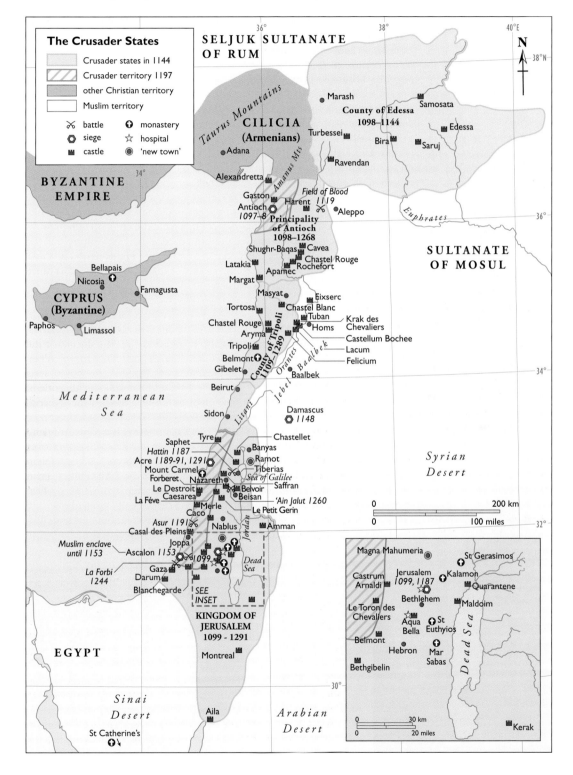

# The Ottoman Empire

*The Ottoman conquest of Jerusalem from the Mamluks in 1516 returned the region to a geopolitical position that it had not occupied since Roman times. For the Mamluks, as for the Crusaders, Jerusalem had been at the heart of a Levantine territorial presence, its centrality to the regime cemented by its symbolic value in the ongoing holy war against the infidels.*

*"Our Lord the great Sultan and brilliant governor, Sultan of the strangers, Arabs and Persians, has commanded the construction of this blessed wall ... Suleiman the son of Selim Khan, may Allah preserve his reign and his kingdom."*

Inscription over the Damascus Gate, Jerusalem

In contrast, when the Ottoman sultan Selim I (r. 1512–20) conquered the Levant, the immediate political and military priorities of the Ottoman world lay far to the northwest, in the Balkans, and to the east, with the attempted conquest of Iran. Although Palestine was a backwater in an empire that stretched, by the mid-17th century, from Egypt in the south to the Danube in the northwest and to Iran in the east, the Ottoman sultans took seriously their role as guardians of the holy places of Islam. Jerusalem, as well as Mecca and Medina, was therefore subjected to a prolonged building campaign under Suleiman II (the Magnificent, r. 1520–66). The most visible signs of this were the erection of new walls around the city, which had remained unfortified since the 13th century, and the exterior tiling of the Dome of the Rock. The population in this period was estimated by a Western visitor at only around 4,000, of whom 1,000 were Christians, 500 Jews and the rest Muslims.

## Governing Palestine

The Ottomans divided Palestine into separate administrative units within the province of Damascus, but pragmatically recognized the influence of local chieftains through the office 'commander of the pilgrimage'. The Ottomans preferred to rule Palestine through prominent local families, to whom they delegated the responsibilities for tax collection and for keeping the peace. Implicit in this policy was the manipulation of authority in the provinces by creating a balance of power between rival families and clans. This system worked well until the late 17th century, when the office came under the control of Janissaries (slave soldiers) appointed from the Ottoman capital of Istanbul. The failure of a revolt against the Ottoman governor in 1707 resulted in even firmer central control from Istanbul in the 18th century. Zahir al-'Umar (c. 1730–75), an Ottoman tax farmer, fortified Acre as the seat of an autonomous Arab region in defiance of Ottoman rule, and even succeeded in occupying Damascus in 1771, but he was defeated in 1775. In 1799 Upper Galilee briefly featured in European politics when Napoleon besieged Acre and occupied Jaffa and Gaza. A tax revolt against Ottoman exactions in 1825–6 by the Arab inhabitants of Palestine, supported by local Bedouin, prefigured the Egyptian invasion of Syria in 1831 by Muhammad Ali. However, under Muhammad's son Ibrahim Pasha, the Egyptians increasingly came to be seen as oppressors rather than liberators of the local population, chiefly through the imposition of fresh taxes. A revolt against Ibrahim's rule (1834–8) gave the Ottomans the opportunity to regain control and reconquer Jerusalem in 1840.

From the mid-19th century onwards, Jerusalem became subject to European influence through the opening of consulates to oversee the increasing numbers of Western travellers and pilgrims. Russians in particular visited the Holy Land in vast numbers annually. By 1874 the Palestine Exploration Fund estimated the

Jezzar Pasha mosque at Acre. With its distinctive green dome and minaret it is a fine example of Ottoman architecture. It is named after its builder, the Ottoman governor of Acre.

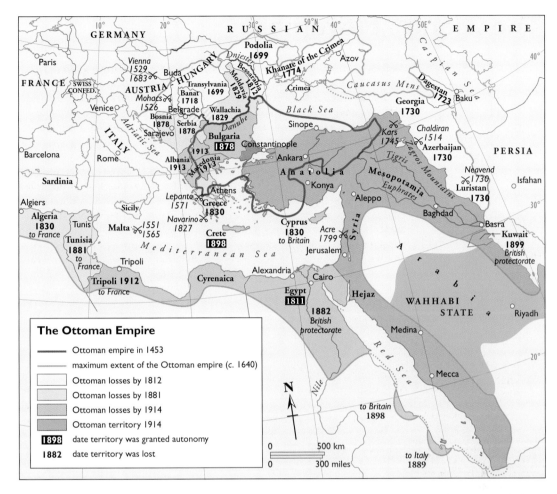

The Ottoman Empire

— Ottoman empire in 1453
— maximum extent of the Ottoman empire (c. 1640)
□ Ottoman losses by 1812
□ Ottoman losses by 1881
▨ Ottoman losses by 1914
▨ Ottoman territory 1914
**1898** date territory was granted autonomy
**1882** date territory was lost

population of Jerusalem at 40,000, with the combined Christian and Jewish population having overtaken the Muslims.

By the mid-19th century, Ottoman military impotence enabled the European powers to interfere in the empire's affairs in the interests of trade. The ending of imperial monopolies and the regulation of customs had by the 1850s created a situation in which European merchants operating in the empire were effectively beyond the reach of the Ottoman authorities. European powers took special interest in the Christian subjects of the empire, and therefore in Jerusalem. French and English support for the Ottomans against Russia in the Crimean War (1853–6) arose from rivalry between France and Russia over the guardianship of the holy places. In 1852, Sultan Abd al-Malik granted to France rights of protection and purchase over churches that were also demanded by Russia; the Ottoman refusal to grant similar rights to Russia resulted in the Russian invasion of Ottoman possessions in the Balkans. The latter part of the 19th century saw concerted attempts by European powers, notably France, Britain and Germany, to restore churches and found religious societies in Jerusalem. St Anne by the Pool of Bethesda was restored by Napoleon III in 1856, while in 1898 Kaiser Wilhelm II laid the foundation stone for the Lutheran Church of the Redeemer on the site of the 11th-century Benedictine monastery of St Mary Latin.

Damascus Gate in the Old City of Jerusalem. Suleiman built the modern gate in 1542 on the site of a Roman one that gave it its Arabic name Bab el-Amud.

# The Zionist Movement

*"The aim of Zionism is to create for the Jewish people a home in Palestine secured by public law."*

Basle Declaration
(August 1897)

***Jewish settlement in Palestine, mostly from Europe, increased in the second half of the 19th century. The Prussian consul estimated in 1858 that almost half of Jerusalem's population of 15,400 were Jews, and this was to grow throughout the century. By 1874, the Palestine Exploration Fund estimated that 22,000 out of 40,000 were Jewish.***

These figures differ greatly from those produced by the Ottoman census of 1893, according to which the percentage of Jewish settlers in the *qada* of Jerusalem was only 8.76 per cent. This huge discrepancy in itself explains the context in which Jewish settlement took place, for the Ottoman census did not take into account illegal immigration, which accounted for most new settlement. Despite this, however, Jewish agencies in Europe and the United States had established schools, hospitals and old peoples' homes in Palestine by the 1890s. One reason for the success of Jewish immigration was that Jews buying

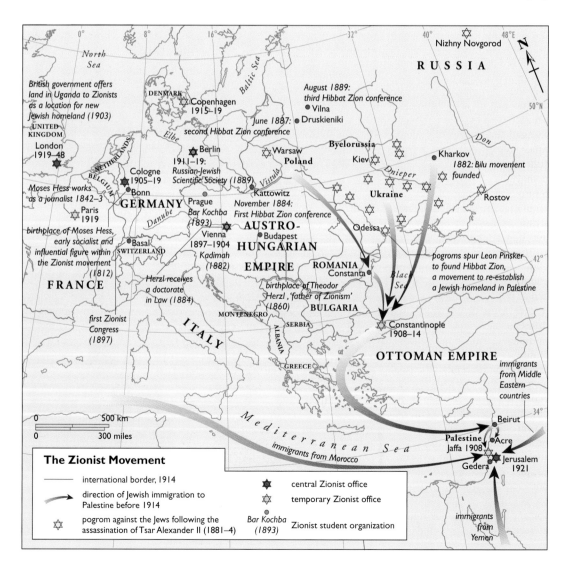

**The Zionist Movement**

| | |
|---|---|
| —— | international border, 1914 |
| → | direction of Jewish immigration to Palestine before 1914 |
| ✡ | pogrom against the Jews following the assassination of Tsar Alexander II (1881–4) |
| ✡ | central Zionist office |
| ✡ | temporary Zionist office |
| *Bar Kochba (1893)* | Zionist student organization |

property were classed in Ottoman records not by religion but by nationality. Since 1867 citizens of the Austro–Hungarian empire and other European countries had been allowed to buy property in the Ottoman empire, but many of the new settlers were Russians. Between 1882 and 1903, 20–30,000 Russian Jews settled in the *Aliya* (Ascent to Zion) movement; 25,000 more arrived after the failure of the 1905 revolution. It was from this wave of largely peasant immigrants that the future leaders of the state of Israel would emerge. By the 1920s there were about 84,000 official Jewish settlers in Palestine; by 1939 the total Jewish population was around 445,000, amounting to 30 per cent of the total. Whereas the earliest settlers were agriculturalists, subsequent immigration brought the mercantile expertise and industrial labour that would make the state infrastructure after 1948 possible.

## Jewish Homeland

The Ottomans officially opposed mass Jewish immigration to Palestine, but were unable to prevent it. European Jewry, influential in banking, offered to write off the huge Ottoman debt to European banks in return for the establishment of a Jewish homeland in Palestine. Although this offer was declined, Theodor Herzl (1860–1904) convened the first Zionist Conference in Basle in 1897 to propose just such a state. From the start of the Zionist movement, the idea that the Jews constituted a distinct people went hand-in-hand with the identification of Palestine as their 'natural' homeland. Neither principle was obvious even to Jews at the time. Herzl himself was an assimilationist until the anti-Semitism revealed by the Dreyfus Affair convinced him that Jewish self-determination was necessary. Moreover, although the belief in *Eretz Israel* (the biblical Jewish lands) as the Jewish homeland can be identified in Jewish writing from the Middle Ages onwards, return there was thought to be possible only with the coming of the Messiah. From the 17th century onwards, disparate groups of European Jews, often apocalyptic in character, had settled in Palestine under the leadership of their rabbis, but they lacked both unity and financial backing.

There was no systematic attempt to create Jewish settlement until the early 19th century, when Lithuanian Jews attempted to found an agricultural community. Subsequent 19th-century efforts at purchasing land for Jewish settlement in Palestine were made by rich assimilated Jews like Moses Montefiore (1839–40). Modern Zionism therefore arose in a particular political and economic context that combined the decline of Ottoman power, the philanthropy of prominent European Jews such as the Rothschilds, coupled with the poverty of numerous others for whom immigration was attractive, and the perceived collapse of cultural assimilation.

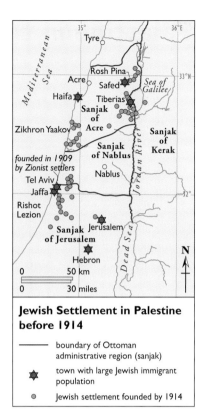

## Jewish Settlement in Palestine before 1914

| | |
|---|---|
| —— | boundary of Ottoman administrative region (sanjak) |
| ✡ | town with large Jewish immigrant population |
| ⦾ | Jewish settlement founded by 1914 |

Theodor Herzl giving an inaugural address to the 6th Congress of Zionists in Basle, Switzerland, in 1903. Herzl, an Austrian journalist, was the founder of modern political Zionism. Despite being Jewish, he was an avowed atheist.

# Palestine in the First World War

*By the outbreak of hostilities in 1914, the Ottoman empire was moribund. Its European territories had shrunk to a small area of Thrace, including Istanbul and its environs. Not only had the 19th-century nationalist movement inspired Arabs as well as Europeans with ideals of independent statehood, but the great powers of Europe had also become critically involved in the Middle East, not least through massive money loans to the Ottoman state.*

*"The Arabs, led by Lawrence, have been doing pretty well; but they are an unstable lot. "*

General Allenby, letter dated 23 February 1918 (*Allenby in Palestine*, ed. Matthew Hughes, Army Records Society, 2004)

Some factors, however, made Palestine unique among Ottoman provinces. One was the growing European cultural and religious interest in the historical Bible lands, and consequently the presence of large numbers of European visitors. Another was the increasing settlement of Jews from Europe and North Africa.

In 1914 the Ottoman empire entered the war on the side of Germany and Austria-Hungary, doubtless in the hope of regaining territory from the newly independent Balkan countries. Anglo-French military strategy in the Middle East centred on defeating Turkish power in the region; the French concentrated on Syria, where they had expectations of territorial oversight, whereas the British focused on Palestine and Iraq.

### Defeating the Ottomans

The Egyptian Expeditionary Force, however, made little headway against entrenched Turkish garrisons in Palestine before 1917, when the newly appointed General Sir Edmund Allenby (1861-1936) mounted an offensive. Allenby's surprise attack on Beersheba secured victory in the battle of Gaza (31 October-7 November 1917). This was followed by an advance towards Jerusalem, which fell on 9 December. For the first time since 1244, Jerusalem was controlled by a European army. However, the British push eastwards to Amman was blocked, and Allenby lost many of his forces to the Western Front and had to wait until fresh troops could be raised from Australia and New Zealand before he could advance further. The battle of Megiddo (19-21 September 1918) opened up the way for a cavalry advance to Damascus, which fell on 1 October, and by the end of that month the Ottoman empire surrendered.

The Arab Revolt led by Hussein, Grand Sharif of Mecca (1908-24), and his sons, should be seen as the last of a series of nationalist uprisings against the Ottomans going back to the 18th century. It was supported by Britain as a means of undermining the Turkish presence in Palestine and Syria. It was in the theatre of desert guerrilla operations against Turkish railway communications and possessions that T. E. Lawrence came to prominence as the military adviser to Hussein's son, Emir Faisal. The revolt would not by itself have brought Ottoman rule to an end, but heroic and unpredictable actions such as the Arab seizure of Aqaba in 1917 and their swift advance to Damascus in 1918 demoralized the Turks and diverted their energies from the Palestinian front. The seizure of Aqaba by a mobile land force against superior defences convinced Allenby to collaborate with and subsidize the revolt, although it was Allenby's military muscle that effectively secured victory in Palestine.

General Sir Edmund Allenby on his journey to Jerusalem in December 1917, after defeating the Ottomans at Gaza. Allenby entered the city, via the Jaffa Gate, on foot, apparently out of respect for the holiness of the city.

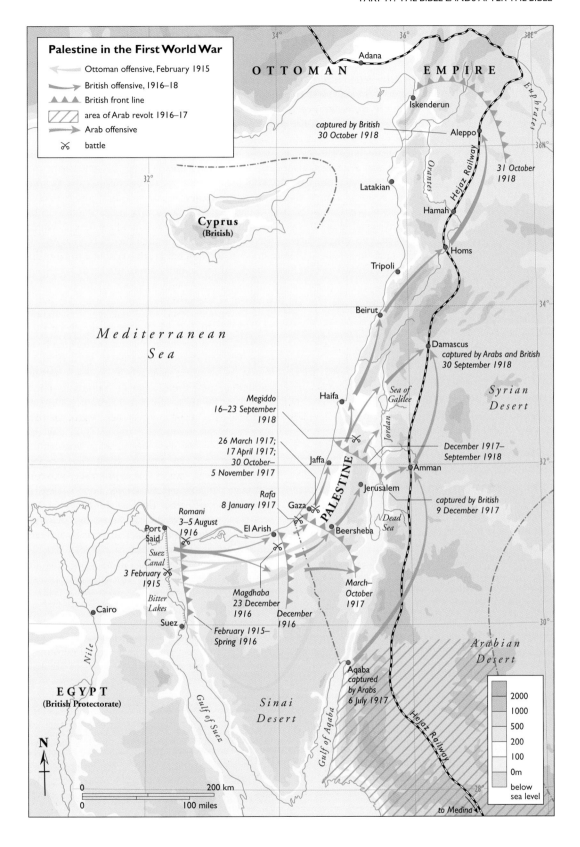

**Palestine in the First World War**

← Ottoman offensive, February 1915
→ British offensive, 1916–18
▲▲▲ British front line
▨ area of Arab revolt 1916–17
→ Arab offensive
✗ battle

OTTOMAN    EMPIRE

Adana

Iskenderun

captured by British
30 October 1918

Aleppo

31 October
1918

Latakian

Hamah

Orontes

Hejaz Railway

Cyprus
(British)

Homs

Tripoli

Beirut

Mediterranean
Sea

Damascus
captured by Arabs and British
30 September 1918

Syrian
Desert

Haifa

Sea of
Galilee

Megiddo
16–23 September
1918

Jordan

December 1917–
September 1918

26 March 1917;
17 April 1917;
30 October–
5 November 1917

Jaffa

PALESTINE

Amman

Rafa
8 January 1917

Jerusalem

captured by British
9 December 1917

Gaza

Dead
Sea

Romani
3–5 August
1916

El Arish

Beersheba

Port
Said

Suez
Canal

3 February
1915

Magdhaba
23 December
1916

March–
October
1917

Bitter
Lakes

December
1916

Cairo

Suez

February 1915–
Spring 1916

Arabian
Desert

Nile

Aqaba
captured
by Arabs
6 July 1917

EGYPT
(British Protectorate)

Gulf of Suez

Sinai
Desert

Gulf of Aqaba

Hejaz Railway

| | |
|---|---|
| | 2000 |
| | 1000 |
| | 500 |
| | 200 |
| | 100 |
| | 0m |
| | below sea level |

N

0          200 km
0          100 miles

to Medina

# Palestine in the Mandate Period

*"We cannot ... both concede the Arab claim to self-government and secure the establishment of the Jewish National Home."*

Royal Commission White Paper (1937)

**In May 1916, while the war in Palestine was still in stalemate, the Anglo-French Sykes-Picot Agreement, named for the diplomats who drew it up, determined how the political map of the Middle East would be drawn in the event of an Allied victory.**

Ottoman territories in the Middle East were to be partitioned into spheres of influence, with Britain directly controlling or exercising influence over the Transjordan region and Iraq, which were vital for its interests in the Persian Gulf, whereas France was to enjoy the same control over Syria and Lebanon. Palestine was to be declared an International Zone with the exception of an enclave around the Bay of Haifa, including the towns of Haifa and Acre, which was to come under direct British control. At the same time, in recognition of the Arab Revolt, an Arab state or confederation under Arab rule was to be established. This agreement, however, never came into force in this form.

## Balfour Declaration

In November 1917 the Balfour Declaration appeared to undermine the international status of Palestine by proposing a 'national homeland' for Jews. The San Remo conference in April 1920, in which the Ottoman empire was dismembered by committee, and the League of Nations in 1922, subjected Palestine and other former Ottoman territories to 'mandatory' status as a transition between imperial rule and full independence in the future. In the case of Palestine, mandatory status, assigned to Britain as the occupying military power, was a compromise between European imperialist ambitions and Wilsonian ideals of self-determination, in the absence of a firm view as to what shape a future independent state in Palestine might take. The Zionists and Jewish settlers already resident in Palestine largely welcomed British control on the basis of the Balfour Declaration; on the other hand, the Arab communities in Palestine had hoped for a

The Prison Citadel in the old city of Acre. In 1947 the militant Zionist group Irgun broke into the prison and liberated several of their imprisoned comrades.

## The Sykes-Picot Agreement

- British sovereignty
- British sphere of influence
- French sovereignty
- French sphere of influence
- International control

form of statehood more directly based on local and historical habitation.

The territory of Mandatory Palestine was reduced from the original League of Nations

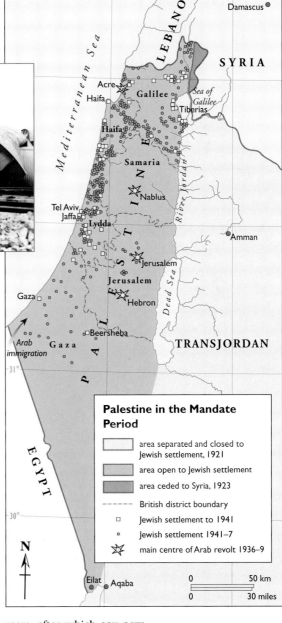

A wrecked train during the British Mandate in Palestine. Jewish underground militias used terrorist tactics to try and drive the British out of the region.

Mandate by the British creation of Transjordan to 26,000 square kilometres (10,038 square miles). Within this area, some regions, such as the Negev Desert, were declared special zones closed to new settlement. Riots in 1920-1 and 1929, which demonstrated Arab fears of being marginalized by increased Jewish immigration, led to the formation of Haganah, a Jewish defence league. While the Colonial Office acknowledged that the riots had been incited by the Palestinian Arabs, they also recognized that the principal cause of tension between the populations was the rise and increasing effectiveness of Zionism. The 1929 riots, which centred on rights of worship at shared holy sites, were particularly violent in Jerusalem and Hebron. Further rioting and an Arab general strike took place in 1939. After the St James Conference of that year had failed to bring about agreement between Jewish and Arab representatives, British policy set a limit on Jewish immigration to 75,000 over five years, after which any new numbers would be subject to further negotiation, and declared that there was no intention for Palestine to become a Jewish homeland. This policy, which appeared to renege on the Balfour Declaration, set Haganah against the Mandate, and during the 1940s acts of terrorism, such as the assassination of Lord Moyne in 1944 and the bombing of the King David Hotel in 1946, undermined British authority at a time when military resources were stretched by the war effort. In 1947 the Attlee government declared the Mandate unworkable, and the newly formed United Nations established a Special Committee on Palestine, which recommended an end to the Mandate and the partitioning of the region.

**Palestine in the Mandate Period**

- area separated and closed to Jewish settlement, 1921
- area open to Jewish settlement
- area ceded to Syria, 1923
- - - - - British district boundary
- □ Jewish settlement to 1941
- ○ Jewish settlement 1941–7
- ✡ main centre of Arab revolt 1936–9

# The Establishment of the State of Israel

*"This right is the natural right of the Jewish people to be masters of their own fate..."*

Israeli Declaration of Independence (1948)

**The British Mandate in Palestine had proved unworkable by the 1940s, as Britain sought unsuccessfully to maintain a provisional government that fulfilled the aspirations of neither Jews nor Arabs. Zionist resistance to the Mandate became increasingly violent and organized after the end of the Second World War.**

Revelations of the events of the Holocaust had inevitably swung Western opinion towards the plight of the displaced survivors of European Jewry. The United Nations solution, adopted in November 1947, was to create two separate states in Palestine. However, after the withdrawal of the Mandate government and the proclamation of the state of Israel on 14 May 1948, Arab armies from other nations in the region immediately invaded the new state. In fact, Jewish forces had already entered Jerusalem, which the UN partition had intended to become an international zone, even before the British withdrawal. The city became the scene of fierce fighting between Jews and the Arab Legion, the force created in the 1920s in Mandatory Transjordan which was to become the backbone of the Jordanian army. The Arab Legion managed to hold on to east Jerusalem for the duration of the war, eventually leading to the partition of the city in 1949.

## Palestinian Exodus

By the time the war ended early in 1949, the Arab state in Palestine, which lacked both an infrastructure and recognition as a separate state by other Arab states in the region, had disappeared. Israel itself made territorial gains amounting to an extra 21 per cent above what had been allotted to the Jewish state in the partition plan of 1947. But, although the whole coastline as far north as Lebanon and much of the hinterland were secured, Israel failed to capture Jerusalem, which became a partitioned city, half in Israel and half in Jordan. Perhaps as significant as the territorial re-drawing of the map brought about by the war was the creation of 750,000 displaced Arabs, whose homes had now become part of a new state in which they had no claim. The social problems caused by the crowding of these refugees into the Gaza Strip and the West Bank further exacerbated the political crisis created by the war.

The new state of Israel had to establish the institutions of government under wartime conditions. Haganah, the militia defence force of the 1920s, became the Israel Defence Force, which by mid-1948 also comprised an air force and navy, and comprised about 100,00 personnel. In the process, the extreme militias such as Irgun, a radical Zionist group responsible for the bombing

### The UN Partition Plan of November 1947

- boundary of the British Palestine Mandate
- proposed Arab state
- proposed Jewish state
- international zone
- ✱ main centre of violence between Jews and Arabs, January–April 1948

*Map labels: Mediterranean Sea; LEBANON (independent 1946); Kfar Sold; January 10 1948 Invasion by Arab Liberation Army repulsed by British forces; Safad; Acre; Galilee; Haifa; Tiberias; Sea of Galilee; Nazareth; SYRIA (independent 1946); Jezreel Valley; Hula Valley; Beth-She'an; Tel Aviv–Jerusalem Road: frequent clashes between Arabs and Jews, November 1947–May 1948; Jenin; Plain of Sharon; Nablus; Samaria; Tel Aviv; Jaffa; Ramallah; Jericho; Amman; River Jordan; Deir Yassin; Jerusalem; Judea; Bethlehem; July 22 1946: British military HQ at the King David Hotel blown up by Irgun; Gaza; Hebron; Kfar Etsion; Dead Sea; Khan Yunis; Beersheba; TRANSJORDAN (independent 1946); Negev Desert; 0 50 km; 0 30 miles; EGYPT; Arabah Valley; Aqaba*

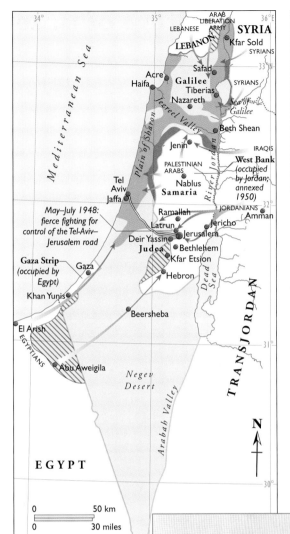

## The Israeli War of Independence, 1948–9

area under Jewish control at the declaration of Israel's independence, May 14 1948

area conquered by Israel in the War of Independence, May 1948–January 1949

1949 armistice line ('Green Line')

area added to Israel under the armistice agreement

area relinquished by Israel under the armistice agreement

former frontier of the Palestine Mandate

Arab attack, May–June 1948

Tel-Aviv–Jerusalem road

of the King David Hotel in 1946 – the deadliest attack against the British during the Mandate era – were forcibly disbanded. The first elected prime minister of Israel was David Ben-Gurion (1949–53 and 1955–63), the former head of the Jewish Agency, while Chaim Weitzmann, head of the World Zionist Organization, who had been influential in drafting the Balfour Declaration in 1917, became president. The executive assembly, the 120-seat Knesset, developed from the Assembly of Representatives established by the Jewish community during the British Mandate. One of the first priorities was to lift all restrictions on immigration for Jews, with the consequence that between 1948 and 1951, 687,000 new settlers arrived from the global Jewish diaspora. The diaspora itself, along with reparation payments imposed on Germany after 1945, was essential in providing an economic foundation for the new state through loans and contributions.

Jubilant Jewish immigrants arrive in Haifa, Israel. With the founding of the new state on 14 May 1948, all restrictions on immigration were lifted. Many of the new arrivals were to take up arms against Arab forces during the first Arab-Israeli war that year.

# The Arab-Israeli Wars

*"Peace requires respect for the sovereignty, territorial integrity and political independence of every state in the area and their right to live in peace within secure and recognized boundaries free from threats or acts of force."*

Framework for Peace in the Middle East at Camp David (1978)

***The ceasefire marking the end of the 1949 war brought an end to the conflict but did nothing to address the underlying causes behind it. The re-drawing of the UN partition created huge populations of displaced Arabs whose homes and lands were lost during the war.***

The population of the West Bank of Jordan, for example, almost doubled from 425,000 before 1948 to 785,000 afterwards; that of Gaza more than tripled from 80,000 to 280,000. The resulting overcrowding of Arabs into areas already poor in economic resources was in contrast with the growing prosperity of Israel, which was backed by foreign investment and loans as well as an industrial base. Moreover, the dispersal of Arabs also hindered the emergence of a new leadership to replace that disbanded by the British in 1939.

In the absence of such leadership, Palestinian Arabs tried to destabilize Israel from bases in neighbouring Arab states. Incursions from Palestinian Fedayeen (militia fighters) in 1956 sparked Israel's invasion of Egypt on 29 October, and the occupation of the Sinai Peninsula and Gaza Strip. In fact, the invasion was masked by the Anglo-French invasion at the same time to secure the Suez Canal. Although Gamal Abdel Nasser, Egypt's leader (1954–70), claimed the Suez conflict as a diplomatic victory because the UN brokered the withdrawal of all external forces from Egypt, the 1956 war revealed the military might of Israel.

### The Six-Day and Yom Kippur Wars

The same imbalance was shown in the Six-Day War of June 1967. By 1966 Fedayeen attacks were resulting in Israeli retaliation on all its borders, despite the attempts of the newly formed Palestine Liberation Organization (PLO) to control them. A new military regime sympathetic to the PLO came to power in Syria in 1966. Bellicose statements from Nasser, who needed to improve his own standing in the Arab world after a disastrous intervention in Yemen, resulted in pre-emptive action from Israel, whose prime minister, Levi Eshkol, was under domestic pressure. On 5 June 1967, the Israeli air force destroyed the Egyptian air force on the ground; in the next two days Egyptian forces in Gaza and the Sinai were overrun. On 7 June, once again after securing command of the skies, Israel routed Jordanian forces in the West Bank and took control of Jerusalem. Two days later the attack on the Golan Heights in Syria began. Syria had agreed to a UN ceasefire, but Israeli forces only ended hostilities on 11 June. The Six-Day War was, from a military perspective, stunning. Its psychological effect on the balance of power in the region was decisive. Israel had humiliated its Arab neighbours, taken important border territories and captured the spiritual heartland of Jerusalem.

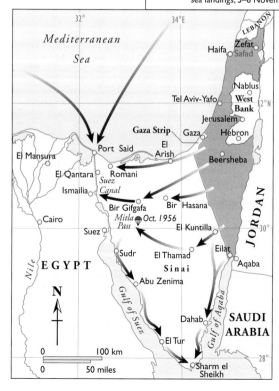

**The 1956 War**

- Israel, 1948–9
- Israeli airborne attack, 1956
- Israeli campaign, 1956
- Anglo-French airborne and sea landings, 5–6 November 1956

**The Six-Day and Yom Kippur Wars**

- Israel, 1967
- Israeli offensive
- Israeli air strike on Arab airfield
- occupied by Israel in the Six-Day War
- PLO stronghold
- Arab attack (Yom Kippur War, October 1973)

Mediterranean Sea

Beirut
Sidon
Dumeir
Damascus
Mount Hermon
Kuneitra
Golan Heights
Haifa
SYRIA
ISRAEL
Jordan
Mafraq
32°N
Tel Aviv-Yafo
West Bank
Jerusalem
Amman
Hebron
Dead Sea
Gaza
Karak
Gaza Strip
Port Said
El Arish
El Mansura
Suez Canal
Inchas
Jebel Libni
JORDAN
Deversoir
Abu Sueir
Bir Gifgafa
Fayid
Kabrit
Cairo
Bir Thamada
Suez
30°
EGYPT
Sudr
Battle of Chinese Farm, October 16–18 1973
Eilat
Aqaba
Sinai (restored to Egypt 1979–82)
Beni Sueif
Gulf of Suez
Abu Rudeis
SAUDI ARABIA
Nile
Gulf of Aqaba
El Minya

N

0    100 km
0    50 miles

Sharm el Sheikh

Red Sea

32°    34°

One result of the war was growing Palestinian resistance. As Israel began a programme of new Jewish settlement in conquered territories, a fresh wave of Palestinian refugees waged border war from Jordan and then, after 1970, from Lebanon, under the aegis of the PLO. By 1973 Nasser's successor in Egypt, Anwar Sadat, needed a military victory in order to bolster his political authority. On 6 October, during the Islamic holy season of Ramadan and the Jewish Yom Kippur holiday, Egypt and Syria co-ordinated attacks on the Golan Heights and the Sinai. After initial success, the rushed airlift of tanks, aircraft and equipment from US bases enabled an Israeli counter-attack. By 23 October, when Israel agreed to a UN ceasefire, military parity had been restored. Although no tangible results occurred in the form of conquered territory, the 1973 war showed that Israel was militarily vulnerable, but also that neither the United States nor the UN would tolerate its defeat at the hands of its Arab neighbours.

A disabled Israeli tank and an abandoned bunker on Mount Hermonit in the Golan Heights. This was the scene of one of the fiercest tank battles of the 1973 Yom Kippur War.

# Israel and Palestine

*The most immediate beneficiary of the 1973 Yom Kippur War was, surprisingly, the Palestine Liberation Organization (PLO), which in 1974 was recognized by the Arab League as the sole representative of the Palestinians. This effectively sidelined the Arab states that had lost territory in the Six-Day War, particularly Jordan. One consequence of military victory was that the refugee Palestinian population was now a subject element in the Israeli state.*

*"The government of the State of Israel and the PLO team ... agree that it is time to put an end to decades of confrontation and conflict, recognize their mutual and legitimate rights, and strive to live in peaceful coexistence and mutual dignity and security ... "*

Israeli-PLO Declaration of Principles (1993)

The status of the Palestinians has become the most pressing problem in the Middle East over the last generation, lying at the heart of continuing conflicts either directly or as a cause to be espoused by Israel's strategic rivals. From the mid-1970s, attitudes to the Palestinian problem began to polarize among the Israeli public. Jewish settlements in the West Bank, Gaza and Sinai increased, demanding new military commitments to their defence.

## Resistance and the *intifada*

By the late 1980s, Palestinians had begun a policy of internal resistance rather than reliance on Arab neighbouring states to promote their cause. Only 41 per cent of Palestinians live in Israel or the territories it acquired since 1948, and of the 29 per cent resident in the latter, about 66 per cent live in refugee camps. Palestinian identity, which developed in circumstances of deprivation and uncertainty, had by the 1990s produced a counter-elite to the PLO leadership and to the refugees in Jordan and elsewhere. This made possible not only the co-ordinated *intifada* (literally 'shaking off') of 1987–93, but also the negotiations for the Oslo Accords of 1993, as a result of which the Palestinian National Authority (PNA) was established. Responsibility for the internal governance of the West Bank and Gaza was handed over to representative governments elected by Palestinians in those regions. Since 1993, however, the PNA, deprived of a secure economic base and without powers to formulate an external policy, has struggled to impose its authority on Palestinians. A further attempt to resolve conflict at the Camp David II summit in July 2000 stalled, largely on the issue of the status of Jerusalem, which – as a site of great religious and historical significance for both Jews and Muslims – epitomizes the general problem of two peoples competing for a single land.

The 'al-Aqsa' *intifada*, which started in September 2000, has identified the weakness of the initial agreement accepted on behalf of the Palestinians at Oslo. Although Yasser Arafat (1929–2004), leading the Palestinian negotiators, secured personal power through a new security force, control over territory, transport arteries and overall security was retained by Israel. A new rubric proposed by the United States in 2003 – the 'road map' – has itself been overtaken both by events in the wider Middle East and by the developing dynamics within Palestinian identity. In response to the inability of the PNA to curb suicide bombings by Palestinians against Israeli citizens, the government of Ariel Sharon began in 2002 the erection of a 'security fence' to give concrete shape not only to Palestinian separation from Israel but also to the continued presence of Israeli settlements in the West Bank. At the time of writing, the likelihood of any resolution to the Israeli-Palestinian problem looks bleak, not least because of violent struggles for the leadership of the Palestinian people between the Islamist Hamas party, which secured victory in internal elections in 2006, and Fatah, the largest faction of the PLO.

Poster commemorating a Hamas 'martyrdom'. Hamas emerged in 1987, at the start of the first *intifada*, and has made suicide attacks on Israeli civilians.

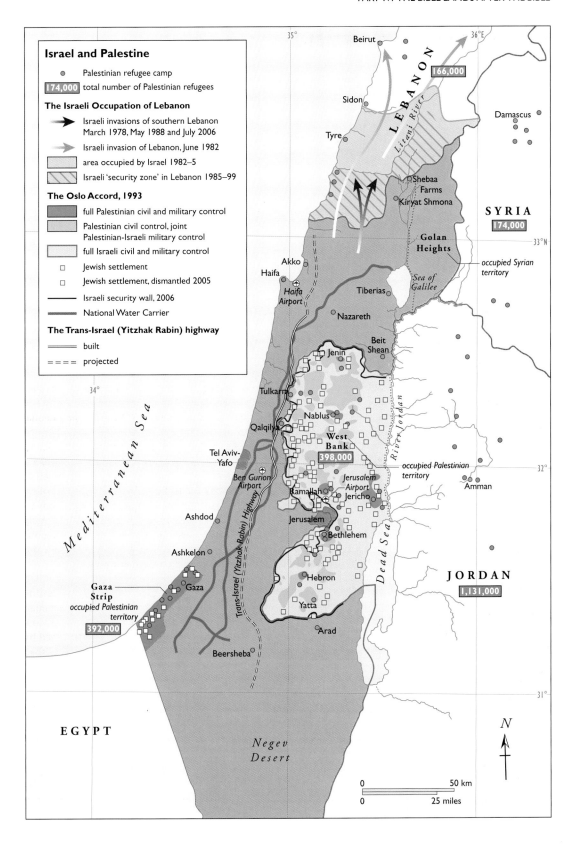

## Israel and Palestine

- ● Palestinian refugee camp
- 174,000 total number of Palestinian refugees

### The Israeli Occupation of Lebanon

- → Israeli invasions of southern Lebanon March 1978, May 1988 and July 2006
- → Israeli invasion of Lebanon, June 1982
- area occupied by Israel 1982–5
- Israeli 'security zone' in Lebanon 1985–99

### The Oslo Accord, 1993

- full Palestinian civil and military control
- Palestinian civil control, joint Palestinian-Israeli military control
- full Israeli civil and military control
- □ Jewish settlement
- □ Jewish settlement, dismantled 2005
- —— Israeli security wall, 2006
- ═══ National Water Carrier

### The Trans-Israel (Yitzhak Rabin) highway

- ═══ built
- ==== projected

Beirut

*LEBANON*

166,000

Sidon

*Litani River*

Tyre

Damascus

Shebaa Farms
Kiryat Shmona

**SYRIA**

174,000

occupied Syrian territory

**Golan Heights**

Akko
Haifa

*Sea of Galilee*

Haifa Airport

Tiberias

Nazareth

Beit Shean

Jenin

*River Jordan*

Tulkarm

Nablus

Qalqilya

**West Bank**

398,000

Tel Aviv-Yafo

Ben Gurion Airport

occupied Palestinian territory

Jerusalem Airport
Jericho

Amman

Ramallah

Jerusalem

*Mediterranean Sea*

Bethlehem

*Dead Sea*

Ashdod

**JORDAN**

1,131,000

Ashkelon

Hebron

**Gaza Strip**
*occupied Palestinian territory*

392,000

Gaza

*Trans-Israel (Yitzhak Rabin) Highway*

Yatta

Arad

Beersheba

**EGYPT**

*Negev Desert*

N

0 ____ 50 km
0 ____ 25 miles

35°
36°E
33°N
34°
32°
31°

# Modern Jerusalem

***Since 1949, and even after the conquest of 1967 removed its international border between Israel and Jordan, Jerusalem has effectively remained two cities. East Jerusalem, which includes the Old City, is largely Palestinian in character and population, whereas West Jerusalem, up to a notional line roughly parallel with the Western Wall of the Old City, is largely Israeli and Jewish.***

*“There is a feeling in Jerusalem, sometimes, of stepping, like Alice, through a looking glass.”*

Amos Elon, *Jerusalem, City of Mirrors* (Little Brown, 1989)

Both sides of the city spill over into suburbs, which to the west resemble those of other modern eastern Mediterranean cities, whereas to the east and south the landscape gives way, by sharp contrast, to Arab villages such as Bethany. Settlement in West Jerusalem began during the first *Aliya* (immigration of Jews to Israel) towards the end of the 19th century, to the south of the Old City at Mishkenot Sha'ananim. At the same time, the Russian Compound grew up to the northwest of the Old City to cater for the large numbers of Russian pilgrims. From the British Mandate period onwards, the 'new city' has expanded westwards from these two points.

**The Old City**

- Muslim quarter
- Christian quarter
- Armenian quarter
- Jewish quarter
- □ property taken over by Jewish settlers
- —— Via Dolorosa

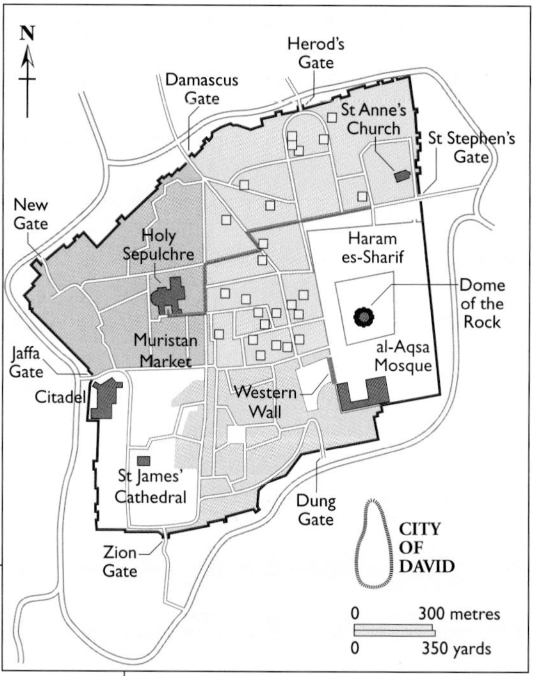

## Settlements

Since the 1980s, however, the Israeli policy of road construction and new settlement has increasingly encircled East Jerusalem, cutting it off from the West Bank to the north, east and south. By 2002, around 200,000 Israelis lived in those parts of Jerusalem and its environs acquired in 1967, although only 52,000 lived in Greater Jerusalem itself, in Gush Etzion, Ma'aleh Adumim, Givat Zeev, Betar Ilit, Efrat Har-Adar, and about fifteen other settlements. Some of this land, particularly when the initial settlements were built, was unoccupied, while other settlements, such as Gush Etzion, were on land already owned by Jews before 1948. However, other land has been legally requisitioned under laws requiring Palestinian landowners to re-register title deeds, which is often impossible because pre-1948 deeds no longer exist.

The status of Jerusalem is one of the most difficult sticking-points in the ongoing conflict. As a holy centre for Jews, Christians and Muslims, it is the focus of religious and cultural claims to identity by both Israelis and Palestinians, of whom about 5 per cent are Christian. The central religious sites are located in the Old City, which has changed very little since the construction

of the walls in the 1530s. The primary Islamic holy sites are the al-Aqsa Mosque and the Qubbat as-Sakra (Dome of the Rock), both of which date from the 7th-century Arab conquest, and are situated on the Temple Mount. Christian worship centres on the Church of the Holy Sepulchre, built by Constantine in the 4th century but largely rebuilt in the 12th century. Jews worship at the Western Wall of the Temple Mount and at other sites, such as the Tomb of Rachel, south of Jerusalem. The total population of the Old City is about 33,500, out of a total of 701,512 for the municipality as a whole. Of these, around 3,800 are Jewish, 6,570 Christian and the rest Muslim. Whereas Muslim and Jewish populations have increased, the numbers of Christians has declined, from 29.5 per cent of the total in 1967 to 20.3 per cent in 1995. This decline reflects the overall picture of increasing Christian Palestinian emigration and a decline in birthrates.

Jerusalem continues to be a focus of world attention in the 21st century, as it has been repeatedly in its long history. The UN currently accepts neither Israeli nor Palestinian claims to the city as a national capital, and it retains its emotional role as the disputed heart of three of the world's great religions.

Aerial view of the Knesset building in Jerusalem. Located on a hilltop in Givat Ram, in the western part of the city, the building was built as a gift to the state of Israel by James A. de Rothschild, British politician and philanthropist. The Knesset is the legislative branch of the Israeli government.

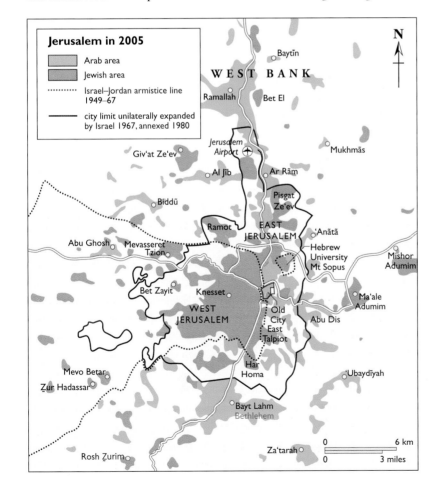

**Jerusalem in 2005**

- Arab area
- Jewish area
- ·········· Israel–Jordan armistice line 1949–67
- —— city limit unilaterally expanded by Israel 1967, annexed 1980

N

Baytīn
WEST BANK
Ramallah    Bet El
Jerusalem Airport ✈    Mukhmās
Giv'at Ze'ev    Al Jīb    Ar Rām
Biddū    Pisgat Ze'ev
Ramot    EAST JERUSALEM    'Anātā
Abu Ghosh    Mevasseret Tzion    Hebrew University Mt Sopus    Mishor Adumim
Bet Zayit    Knesset    Old City    Ma'ale Adumim
WEST JERUSALEM    Abu Dis
East Talpiot
Mevo Betar    Har Homa    'Ubaydīyah
Ẓur Hadassar
Bayt Lahm
Bethlehem
Za'tarah    0    6 km
Rosh Ẓurim    0    3 miles

# King Lists

## United Monarchy of Israel

Saul    *c.* 1020–*c.* 1002 BC
David    *c.* 1002–*c.* 962 BC
Solomon    *c.* 962–922 BC

## Kings of Israel

Rehoboam
    King of united Israel    922–928 BC;
    King of Israel    928–911 BC
Abijah    911–908 BC
Asa    908–867 BC
Jehoshaphat    867–851 BC
Jehoram    851–843 BC
Ahaziah    843–842 BC
Athaliah    842–836 BC
Joash    836–/99 BC
Amaziah    799–786 BC
Uzziah    786–758 BC
Jotham    758–742 BC
Ahaz    742–726 BC
Hezekiah    726–697 BC
Manasseh    697–642 BC
Amon    642–640 BC
Josiah    640–609 BC
Jehoahaz    609–608 BC
Jehoiakim    608–597 BC
Jehoiachin    597 BC
Zedekiah    597–586 BC

## Kings of Judah

Jeroboam I    928–907 BC
Nadab    907–906 BC
Baasha    906–883 BC
Elah    883–882 BC
Zimri    882 BC
Omri    882–871 BC
Ahab    871–851 BC
Ahaziah    851–850 BC
Joram    850–842 BC
Jehu    842–814 BC
Jehoahaz    814–800 BC
Joash    800–785 BC
Jeroboam II    785–749 BC
Zechariah    749 BC
Shallum    748 BC
Menahem    748–737 BC
Pekahiah    737–735 BC
Pekah    735–731 BC
Hoshea    731–722 BC

## Hasmonean Dynasty

Mattathias ben Johanen    167–165 BC
Judah Maccabeus    165–160 BC
Jonathan Apphus    162–141 BC
Simon Maccabeus (Thassi)    142–135 BC
Johanan Hyrcanus    135–104 BC
Aristobulus I    104–103 BC
Alexander Jannaeus    103–76 BC
Salome Alexandra    76–67 BC
Aristobulus II    66–63 BC
Hyrcanus II    64–40 BC
Antigonus    40–37 BC

## Herodian Kings

Herod (the Great)    37–4 BC
Herod Archelacus (Ethnarch of Samaria,
    Judea and Idomea)    4 BC–AD 6
Herod Philip (Tetrarch of Iturea
    and Trachonitis)    4 BC–AD 34
Herod Antipas (Tetrarch of Galilee
    and Perea)    4 BC–AD 39
[Roman prefects (Rulers of Judea    6–37;
Rulers of Samaria and Idumea    6–41)]
Herod Agrippa I
    (ruler of Golan Heights    34–44;
    King of Judea    37–44;
    Ruler of Galilee and Perea    39–44)
[Roman prefects (rulers of Golan Heights,
    Galilee and Perea    44–52)]
Herod Agrippa II    52–93
    [in conjunction with Roman governors]

## Crusader Kings of Jerusalem (1099–1291)

Godfrey    1099–1100
    not king but *Advocatus sancti sepulcri*
    ('Advocate of the Holy Sepulchre')
Baldwin I    1100–18
Baldwin II    1118–31
Melisende    1131–53
    with Fulk    1131–43
Baldwin III    1143–62
Amalric I    1162–74
Baldwin IV    1174–85
Baldwin V    1185–6
Guy    1186–92
    and Sibylla    1186–90
Isabella I    1192–1205
Conrad I    1192
    not usually considered
Henry I    1192–7

Amalric II    1198–1205
Maria    1205–12
    with John I    1210–25
Isabella II (Yolande)    1212–28
    with Frederick    1225–8
Conrad IV (Hohenstaufen)    1228–54
Conradin    1254–68
Hugh of Antioch    1268–84
    opposed by
    Charles of Anjou    1277–85
    and John II    1284–5
Henry II    1285–91

## MODERN ISRAEL

### Presidents of Israel

Chaim Weizmann    1949–52
Itzhak Ben-Zvi    1952–63
Zalman Shazar    1963–73
Ephraim Katzir    1973–8
Yitzhak Navon    1978–83
Chaim Herzog    1983–93
Ezer Weizman    1993–2000
Moshe Katsav    2000–7
Shimon Peres    2007–

### Prime Ministers of Israel

David Ben-Gurion    1948–53
Moshe Sharett    1953–5
David Ben-Gurion    1955–63
Levi Eshkol    1963–9
Golda Meir    1969–74
Yitzhak Rabin    1974–7
Menachem Begin    1977–83
Yitzhak Shamir    1983–4
Shimon Peres    1984–6
Yitzhak Shamir    1986–92
Yitzhak Rabin    1992–5
Shimon Peres    1995–6
Binyamin Netanyahu    1996–9
Ehud Barak    1999–2001
Ariel Sharon    2001–6
Ehud Olmert    2006–

# Books of the Bible

The Christian Bible is a library of over 70 books encompassing writings of many different types including creation stories, law, handbooks for priests, history, songs and poetry, proverbs, prophecy and letters. The Bible (from Greek *biblia* meaning 'books') is divided into two parts: the Old Testament, comprising the sacred and historical writings of the Jewish people, and the New Testament, which recounts the life of Jesus and the beginnings of the Christian religion. The Old Testament was written originally in Hebrew, except for a few parts written in Aramaic: the New Testament was written in Greek. Although the New Testament begins with the Gospels, many of the Letters were written earlier. The Bible has since been translated into over 1500 different languages. The diagram below shows the books of the Bible as they are arranged in the Latin Vulgate edition.

## THE OLD TESTAMENT

| | | | |
|---|---|---|---|
| Genesis | 2 Chronicles | Isaiah | Zephaniah |
| Exodus | Ezra | Jeremiah | Haggai |
| Leviticus | Nehemiah | Lamentations | Zechariah |
| Numbers | Tobit* | Baruch* | Malachi |
| Deuteronomy | Judith* | Ezekiel | |
| | Esther | Daniel | |
| Joshua | | Hosea | 1 Maccabees* |
| Judges | Job | Joel | 2 Maccabees* |
| Ruth | Psalms | Amos | |
| 1 Samuel | Proverbs | Obadiah | |
| 2 Samuel | Ecclesiastes | Jonah | *These books are |
| 1 Kings | Song of Solomon | Micah | sometimes omitted |
| 2 Kings | Wisdom* | Nahum | from Protestant editions of the Bible and are not |
| 1 Chronicles | Ecclesiasticus (Sirach)* | Habakkuk | accepted as part of the Hebrew Bible. |

## THE NEW TESTAMENT

| | | |
|---|---|---|
| Matthew | Philippians | 1 John |
| Mark | Colossians | 2 John |
| Luke | 1 Thessalonians | 3 John |
| John | 2 Thessalonians | Jude |
| | 1 Timothy | |
| Acts | 2 Timothy | Revelation |
| | Titus | |
| Romans | Philemon | |
| 1 Corinthians | Hebrews | |
| 2 Corinthians | James | |
| Galatians | 1 Peter | |
| Ephesians | 2 Peter | |

**Key**

- The Pentateuch – The Torah (The Law) in the Hebrew Bible
- Historical Books
- Poetical or Wisdom Books
- Prophetical Books
- The Gospels
- Letters

# Further Reading

## I. BIBLICAL ARCHAEOLOGY AND HISTORY

Albright, W. F., *Archaeology and the Religion of Israel* (Louisville, KY, 2006)

Albright, W. F., *The Amarna Letters from Palestine* (Cambridge, 1966)

Avi-Yonah, *Encyclopedia of Archaeological Excavations in the Holy Land*. 4 vols. (Oxford, 1975–8)

Coogan, Michael D. (ed.), *The Oxford History of the Biblical World* (Oxford and New York, 1998)

Davis, Thomas, *Shifting Sands: The Rise and Fall of Biblical Archaeology* (Oxford, 2004)

Finkelstein, Israel, and Silberman, Neil Asher, *The Bible Unearthed: Archaeology's New Vision of Ancient Israel* (New York, 2002)

Hanson, K. C., and Oakman, Douglas E., *Palestine in the Time of Jesus* (Minneapolis, MN, 1998)

Keller, Werner, *The Bible as History* (New York, 1980)

Kenyon, Kathleen, *Digging up Jerusalem* (London, 1974)

Levy, Thomas (ed.), *The Archaeology of Society in the Holy Land* (London, 1995)

Masalha, Nur, *The Bible and Zionism: Invented Traditions, Archaeology and Post-Colonialism in Palestine-Israel* (London, 2007)

Murphy-O'Connor, Jerome, *The Holy Land: An Archaeological Guide from Earliest Times to 1700*, 2nd edn. (Oxford: 1986)

Negev, Avraham, *Archaeological Encyclopedia of the Holy Land* (London, 1972)

Rogerson, John, *Atlas of the Bible* (Oxford, 1989)

Sterm, Ephraim, et al, *The New Encyclopedia of Archaeological Excavations in the Holy Land* (Jerusalem, 1993)

Tubb, Jonathan M., *The Canaanites* (London, 2002)

## 2. ROME TO THE OTTOMANS

Frend, W. H. C., *The Rise of Christianity* (Philadelphia, PA, 1984)

Gil, Moshe, *A History of Palestine 634–1099* (Cambridge, 1992)

Goodman, Martin, *State and Society in Roman Galilee AD 132–212* (London, 2000)

Hillenbrand, Robert, and Auld, Sylvia (eds.), *Ottoman Jerusalem 1517–1917* (London, 2000)

Hourani, Albert, *History of the Arab Peoples* (Cambridge, MA, 2002)

Jotischky, Andrew, *Crusading and the Crusader States* (Harlow, 2004)

Kennedy, Hugh (ed.), *Historical Atlas of Islam* (Leiden, 2002)

Richard, J., *The Latin Kingdom of Jerusalem* (Amsterdam, 1979)

Schick, Robert, *The Christian Communities of Palestine from Byzantine to Arab Rule* (Princeton, NJ, 1995)

Sicker, Martin, *Between Rome and Jerusalem: 300 Years of Roman-Judaean Relations* (Westport, CT, 2001)

Taylor, Joan, *Christians and the Holy Places: The Myth of Jewish-Christian Origins* (Oxford, 1993)

## 3. MODERN PALESTINE AND ISRAEL

Cohen, M. J., *Palestine and the Great Powers 1945–1948*, (Princeton, NJ, 1982)

Fraser, T. G., *The Arab-Israeli Conflict* (Basingstoke, 2008)

Hirst, David, *The Gun and the Olive Branch: The Roots of Violence in the Middle East* (London, 2003)

Kedourie, Elie, and Haim, Sylvia G. (eds.), *Palestine and Israel in the 19th and 20th Centuries* (London, 1982)

Kedourie, Elie, *England and the Middle East: The Destruction of the Ottoman Empire, 1914–1921* (London, 1956)

Ovendale, Ritchie, *Britain, the United States and the End of the Palestine Mandate, 1942–48* (London, 1989)

Robertson, Ritchie, *Theodor Herzl and the Origins of Zionism* (Edinburgh, 1997)

Robinson, Glen, *Building a Palestinian State: The Incomplete Revolution* (Bloomington, IN, 1997)

# Index

# Acknowledgements

## PICTURE CREDITS

Pages: 8 Scala, Florence; 12 Corbis; 14 akg-images; 15 The Art Archive; 16 The Bridgeman Art Library, London; 17 British Museum; 18 John Haywood; 21 *t* Scala, Florence; *b* Corbis; 22 John Haywood; 24 akg-images; 25 The Bridgeman Art Library, London; 26-8 John Haywood; 29 Werner Forman Archives; 30-2 Corbis; 33 The Bridgeman Art Library, London; 34 Scala, Florence; 36-8 Corbis; 40 akg-images; 42 The Bridgeman Art Library, London; 43 Corbis; 44 Alamy; 45 akg-images; 46 Corbis; 48, 50 John Haywood; 52 The Art Archive; 54-60 Corbis; 62-4 John Haywood; 66 Corbis; 67 Werner Forman Archives; 68 akg-images; 69 British Museum; 70 John Haywood; 73 Corbis; 74 John Haywood; 76 The Art Archive; 78 akg-images; 80 John Haywood; 82 Sonia Halliday Photographs; 83 The Art Archive; 85 Sonia Halliday Photographs; 86 Corbis; 87 Sonia Halliday Photographs; 88-91 John Haywood; 92 Sonia Halliday Photographs; 94-9 John Haywood; 100 Scala, Florence; 102 The Art Archive; 103 Andrew Jotischky; 105 John Haywood; 106 Scala, Florence; 109 John Haywood; 111 Sonia Halliday Photographs; 112-15 John Haywood; 116 Getty Images; 117 Corbis; 119-23 John Haywood; 125 6 Gctty Images; 128-9 John Haywood; 131 Getty Images; 133-4 John Haywood; 137 Corbis

Conceived and produced by John Haywood and Simon Hall
Designed by Darren Bennett
Edited by Fiona Plowman
Picture research by Veneta Bullen
Cartography by Tim Aspden
Index prepared by Gerard M.-F. Hill

... a Haywood & Hall production for Penguin Books